THE
MASTER
BLADESMITH

THE
MASTER
BLADESMITH

ADVANCED
STUDIES IN STEEL

JIM HRISOULAS

PALADIN PRESS
BOULDER, COLORADO

Also by Jim Hrisoulas:

The Complete Bladesmith: Forging Your Way to Perfection

Forging Damascus: How to Create Pattern-Welded Blades (video)

The Pattern-Welded Blade: Artistry in Iron

The Master Bladesmith:
Advanced Studies in Steel
by Jim Hrisoulas

Copyright © 1991 by Jim Hrisoulas

ISBN 0-87364-612-6
Printed in the United States of America

Library of Congress Catalog Number: 90-53683

Published by Paladin Press, a division of
Paladin Enterprises, Inc., P.O. Box 1307,
Boulder, Colorado 80306, USA.
(303) 443-7250

Direct inquires and/or orders to the above address.

Illustrations by Joyce Morris
Jacket photos by Stephen Jacobson

CONTENTS

Chapter One
Setting Up the Workshop   1

Chapter Two
Steels & Alloys   25

Chapter Three
Advanced Forging Techniques   43

Chapter Four
The Power Hammer   73

Chapter Five
Grinding   93

Chapter Six
Heat Treating and Tempering   101

Chapter Seven
Hilts   107

Chapter Eight
Metal and Wood Finishing   127

Chapter Nine
Leather Working & Scabbard Making   143

Chapter Ten
Swordmaking: The Romance of the Sword   161

Chapter Eleven
The Spear: The Ancient Weapon of Choice 181

Chapter Twelve
Axes 205

Chapter Thirteen
Japanese Nonferrous Alloys and Their Coloration 221

Chapter Fourteen
Damascus Steel: The Pattern-Welded Blade 233

Chapter Fifteen
Compounds and Formulas 269

Chapter Sixteen
Weights and Measures 277

Bibliography 285

ACKNOWLEDGMENTS

I would like to thank the following people, who have been of great help in my completing this volume.

Bob Engnath, who is a great friend and a good listener.

Alex Bellanger, a friend in need.

Jan Ake Lundstrom, for help in researching Viking swords.

Last but not least, my dear, beloved Trudi, who was there in the darkest time of my life, and to whom I owe, literally, my life. I have to thank her for the ability and the will to write this book.

The study of bladesmithing can be rewarding and somewhat frustrating. Most of the information available today is meant for the novice knifemaker. Little has been written for the more experienced craftsman. To answer this need, I have written this book for the more advanced student of the custom blade.

Numerous techniques and materials available to today's artisans were once revealed only to the chosen few who were within the inner circles of this craft. This secretive tendency, while more or less still in effect, is the last bastion of the old medieval guilds. There is no need for this secrecy. The free exchange of information and techniques enriches rather than lessens the craft.

Sharing knowledge and technique improves the teacher as well as the student. All of us should strive for perfection and learn our chosen craft as fully as we possibly can. That is the intention of this book, to share knowledge—and a few secrets as well.

I leave you with this quote:

"There is no deed greater than the passing of knowledge from one to another, for without it, we would all be lost in ignorance."

—Atar Bakhtar

Only you, my reader, will know if I have succeeded in this endeavour. *Illegitimati non carburundum.*

Jim Hrisoulas
1991

SETTING UP
THE WORKSHOP

Beginning bladesmiths may have difficulty understanding some of the terms and techniques in this book. As I stated in my preface, this book was written for experienced blacksmiths, so I assumed a certain level of knowledge on the part of readers. If you have any trouble with any of the terms or concepts, my first book, *The Complete Bladesmith*, should help prepare you for this text.

Now, let's get down to basics. First, you need a place to work, and your work area must meet certain requirements, including adequate space, proper ventilation, and good lighting.

SPACE

If you are starting out from scratch, you should lay out the shop according to your needs and the space to which you have access. If you are already set up for blade work, then you may need additional space for the kilns, caster, extra hammers, tools, materials, and supplies. A large-enough work space is a must. Although most work can be done in a confined area, there is no sense in trying to work over and around crowded equipment. This situation is at best a nuisance and at worst a hazard. So shop layout is important.

VENTILATION

Forges need a lot of air because they produce carbon monoxide gas at an alarming rate. This gas is highly toxic and can be fatal in enclosed areas. So your workshop must get rid of fumes quickly and effectively, as well as provide a free-flowing fresh-air supply. This is especially important for a gas-fired forge because the fumes produced are colorless and, for the most part, odorless as well.

LIGHTING

Once you have met your space and ventilation requirements, adequate lighting is next. Proper lighting makes your work a lot easier. The forge area should be dim (but not dark) to allow for proper judgment of metal color, while the rest of the shop, especially the grinding and fitting areas, should be well-lit so you can see what you're doing. The best lighting is natural background light, but this is not always available. The next best source is overhead fluorescent light. Any lighting that allows you to see clearly without eyestrain is acceptable.

The shop layout below is one that I recommend.

TOOLING

In addition to space, ventilation, and lighting, you also need tooling. Most of the tooling used in general bladesmithing can be used for making swords, daggers, axes, spears, and other advanced projects. Aside from specialized dies and a few other specialty tools, there is little difference

WORKSHOP LAYOUT

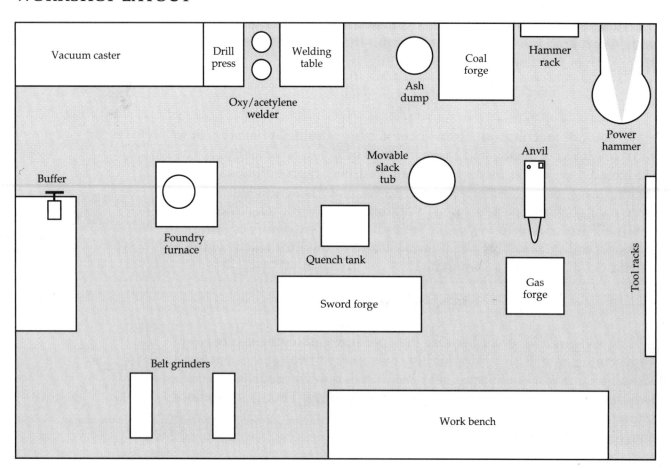

between a beginner's shop and that of an advanced smith's.

The first tool we'll discuss is the forge. A forge provides a means of heating steel to the desired temperature to shape it. The two most common types of forges used by blacksmiths are coal-fired and gas-fired. Of course, there are electric furnaces and oil-fired forges, but these are far too complicated and costly for the average individual, so I will not discuss them.

Coal Forge

This is the classic forge that everyone imagines when the term blacksmith is mentioned. Coal-fired forges were the first ones made, and a lot of quality work has been done in them. They are easily fabricated, and, while I will not go into great detail about their construction or use, I have included a set of plans for you to study. I built mine out of a truck brake drum, and I have used it for years without complaint. These plans are for the fire pot only, as this allows you to modify the height and position to meet your needs.

Of course, commercial coal-fired forges are available, and some are very good. If you would rather purchase a coal forge, these are the points that you should consider before doing so.

• *Fire box shape and size.* The box should be rectangular and deep enough to allow for an even heat in the fire. Its depth should be at least 5 inches, with 7 inches being even better. The hearth should be large enough to hold enough coal for sustained operation and to accommodate the heating of larger pieces.

• *Clinker breaker.* This handy little item lets you clean the fire of clinkers without disturbing it. There are numerous types of clinker breakers to choose from, but the most common is the rotating ball design that not only breaks up the clinker but also directs the air blast. It can give a blast to the right, left, or center of the fire pot, depending on where the ball is placed in the tuyere.

• *Ash dump.* The ash dump should be deep yet easy to access and open. These are usually of the lever-open/gravity-close type.

• *Air supply.* You can use either an electric blower/fan or a manual blower/fan. The electric fan should have a positive speed/air blast control, either a rheostat for fan speed or a "butterfly" valve/sliding gate in the airway to regulate air flow. I used an electric blower for many years, and I must say that they are effective. Recently, I went back to a hand crank, which gives me better heat and more control.

As for the hand blower, the primary consideration is ease of operation. The crank should move smoothly and evenly without any free play. The volume of air is far more important than the amount of air pressure that comes up through the tuyere. The air volume moved by the blower should be more than you would ever expect to use. A low-

BRAKE DRUM FORGE

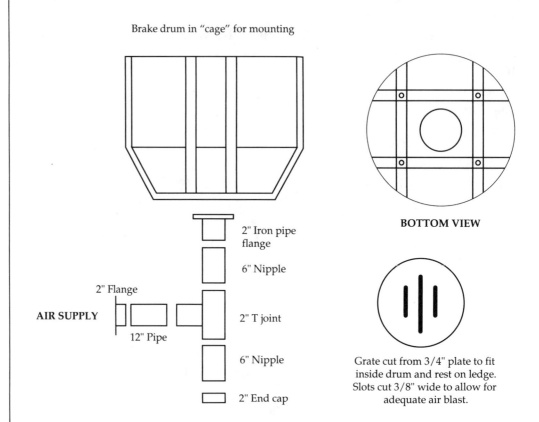

Brake drum in "cage" for mounting

BOTTOM VIEW

2" Iron pipe flange

6" Nipple

2" Flange

AIR SUPPLY

12" Pipe

2" T joint

6" Nipple

2" End cap

Grate cut from 3/4" plate to fit inside drum and rest on ledge. Slots cut 3/8" wide to allow for adequate air blast.

pressure, large-volume movement of air produces a better fire than a high-pressure, small-volume blast.

Regardless of the type of air supply you use, coal forges do have one big drawback: smoke. They are dirty and sooty and can be quite an attention-getter when first fired up. At that time, they need a stack vent to deal with the billowing clouds. But once they are going, the amount of smoke diminishes to no more than a fireplace produces, and, if you build an efficient fire, then there is hardly any smoke at all. Included are plans for a retractable hood/stack arrangement that has worked very well for me over the years.

Coal forges give you a lot of control, and in spite of the problems with smoke, fire tending, and clinkers, they should be considered. After all, coal-fired forges of one type or another have been used since the dawn of ironworking. They are the traditional forges of the bladesmith.

Gas Forge

If you are in a space that makes a coal-fired forge out of the question, what heat source do you use? The answer could lie in a gas forge.

Gas forges are a bit more complicated in their construction than coal-fired ones, but they do offer simpler operation, no billowing clouds of smoke, and no clinkers, ash, or dust with which to cope. However, they must be vented to ensure that there is no buildup of carbon monoxide gas. This gas, as I said before, is very hazardous and can be fatal. A poorly vented forge can kill you. So be certain that the air flow and ventilation are more than adequate for your needs.

Many of the gas-fired forges on the market can use liquefied petroleum gas (LPG, or propane) or natural gas. They burn cleanly and work quite nicely for most forging operations.

STACK/HOOD

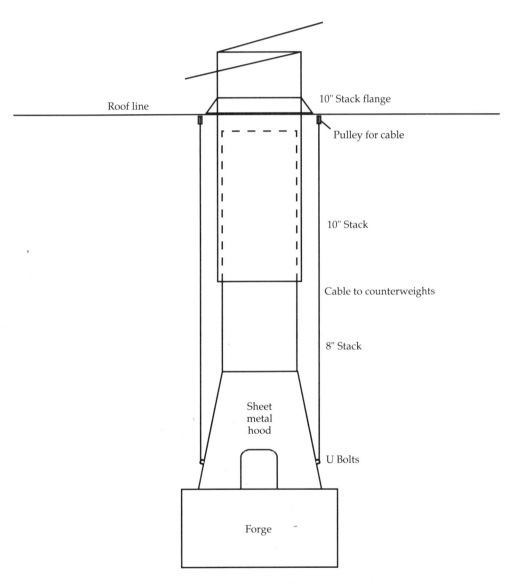

Stack/hood telescopes into the larger stack
that goes through the roof and must extend
at least 2 feet into the stack pipe when hood is down.

Other significant factors in their favor are speed of operation and lack of fire care. A gas forge can be up to heat from a cold start in 5 to 10 minutes. A coal-fired forge takes considerably longer to get ready when coking and fire building are considered. Also, gas forges take no time away from work (as do coal forges) to add fuel, coke it down, or remove clinkers, ashes, or culls.

A gas forge can save time and energy during production work, especially when it comes to heat-treating or forging long pieces. It is easy to get and maintain an even heat on bigger pieces, and a gas forge can be built to suit almost any size or shape of work to be done.

Gas forges have their drawbacks as well. A gas fire tends to oxidize steel a bit more when the steel is first removed, and this can adversely affect the welding. Also, because gas forges produce an even heat, a localized heat is difficult to get. I find it easier and more effective to weld in a coal forge than a gas-fired one, but this is just a personal preference.

The gas itself presents some problems. Although economical to run, you are still dealing with compressed, highly flammable gas. You can easily damage the forge or seriously injure or kill yourself if you don't follow the proper safety precautions to the letter.

LPG storage tanks are highly pressurized and must be stored in accordance with local laws and fire regulations. So check with your fire department for tank placement and operation guidelines.

Even with the hazards, gas forges operate safely and effectively every day without any accidents or injuries. Common-sense safety practices recommended by firemen or veteran smithies are easy to follow and soon become habit, part of your everyday work schedule.

Another drawback to gas is that the volume needed is usually greater than a standard household natural gas or LPG line can provide. I urge you to use bottled LPG for firing instead of natural gas. This setup is far more agreeable to your pocketbook than to have your local gas company run a larger line from its main.

There are also semiportable tanks available that hold from 20 to 50 gallons. I operate a rather large custom forge with a 6 x 6 x 36 inch inside dimension on twin 25-gallon tanks with a coupling. That 50-gallon capacity can run my beast for almost a week of 6-hour-a-day operation.

Commercial gas forges are readily available, but they are often expensive and too small to sustain lengthy work, such as swordmaking. You can build your own at a much lower cost to fit your particular needs.

How to Build a Gas Forge

The basic building materials for a gas forge are refractory materials. These are available from ceramic suppliers that cater to the ceramic industry, rather than the hobbiest. Several types of refractories can be used, including fire brick, pourable refractory clays, mineral wools, and refractory boards. Developed for use in ceramic kilns and industrial burn-out ovens, they can also be used for gas forges. The following are some of the things you should look for in refractories.

• *Fire brick*. These are available in the standard brick size of 8 1/2 x 4 x 2 1/4 inches, as well as in special sizes and shapes. They are also rated for temperature ranges from 2000 degrees to 3000 degrees Fahrenheit (F). They come hard or soft, with the softer ones usually being the most temperature-resistant in the higher ranges. Masonry cutting blades that fit on a hand-held circular saw cut these bricks like crazy and are available from hardware/builder's supply stores.

As always, when you cut anything—but fire bricks especially—use eye protection and wear a respirator at all times. The ultrafine dust not only causes you to sneeze, it can get in your lungs and play holy hell with your health.

• *Fire brick mortar*. This is what it says: the mortar used between fire bricks. Although fine to use as is, I have found that if you add about 40 percent of ground fire brick and about 5 percent fire clay, it is even better. Fire bricks and mortar should be the basic building materials of the forge body, floor, and sides. The bricks are easy to lay and give many years of service.

• *Pourable refractories*. This is a type of fire clay formulated to withstand high temperatures without cracking, expanding, or shrinking, and forms a hard, durable surface. The big advantage to using this material is that you are not limited to shape and size as with with fire bricks. The drawbacks are that the material must be poured and used immediately, and proper curing procedures must be followed to the letter or problems may arise.

• *Rammable plastic refractories*. These are similar to pourable ones, but instead of being castable, they require physical placement and packing. Rammed into forms, they fill all open spaces and are efficient insulators and heat reflectors.

• *Mineral wools*. Perhaps the most efficient insulating material, mineral wool is also delicate and expensive. But a little of it goes a long way. A layer of 3/4-inch thick wool can be more effective than fire brick. Use it to seal between sections of a forge, such as between the removable top and the forge body, or as sides of the fire box. It works safely and efficiently as long as no work touches or bumps into the insulation.

Also, when cutting and handling this material, wear a respirator, eye protection, and gloves. The minute fibers are as abrasive as fiberglass, causing irritations and severe itching.

• *Fire clays*. Almost everyone in this business is familiar with this type of refractory. It should be used only for "mortaring" between bricks and making "patching grout" for furnace repair.

Repairing Refractories

You can replace or repair a section of a poured refractory. A quick, effective, and serviceable repair can be made by using the following materials:

1 part fire clay
2 parts fire-brick mortar
4 parts finely ground fire brick

Mix well with enough water to form the consistency of a heavy cake frosting. *Slightly* moisten the area to be patched and apply the mixture. Let set overnight or until dry to the touch before firing.

• *Kiln shelves.* These are available in various thicknesses, lengths, and widths. Before doing any welding in a gas forge, I strongly suggest that you place a section of kiln shelf on the bottom of the forge to prevent any welding fluxes from coming into contact with the refractory. The

BURNERS
(USE ONLY FOR LPG)

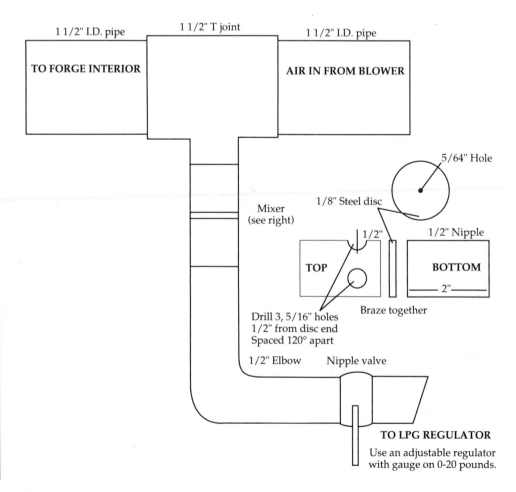

GAS FORGE PLANS #1

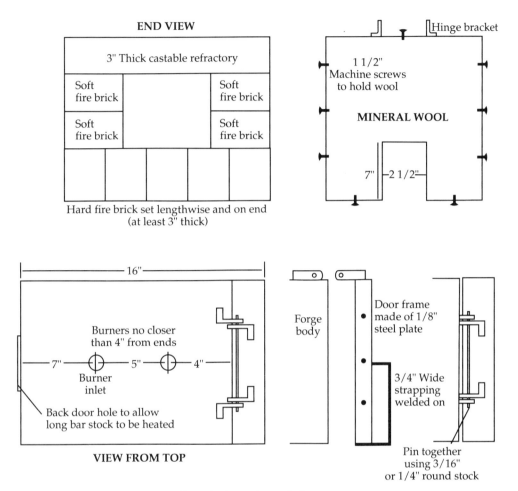

END VIEW

3" Thick castable refractory	
Soft fire brick	Soft fire brick
Soft fire brick	Soft fire brick

Hard fire brick set lengthwise and on end
(at least 3" thick)

Hinge bracket

1 1/2"
Machine screws
to hold wool

MINERAL WOOL

7" 2 1/2"

16"

Burners no closer
than 4" from ends

7" 5" 4"

Burner
inlet

Back door hole to allow
long bar stock to be heated

VIEW FROM TOP

Forge
body

Door frame
made of 1/8"
steel plate

3/4" Wide
strapping
welded on

Pin together
using 3/16"
or 1/4" round stock

Forge body can be made from
12-gauge sheet.
Do not use galvanized material.

corrosive fluxes used in welding eat their way through refractories at an alarming rate. A kiln shelf stops the fluxes from reaching the refractory, and you can replace the shelf as needed to save the forge's refractory lining. (These shelves can be cut with the same masonry blade that you used for fire brick.)

These are all of the special materials you need to build a gas forge by the following plan. It can be changed to meet your particular needs. The the only component that I recommend *not* changing is the burner assembly. Of course, that can be changed if you wish, but I have found that burners made in this fashion are more efficient than other designs.

When properly designed, the forge can reach temperatures high enough to do most work, including forge brazing and welding.

IMPROVED FORGE DESIGN
(Exact measurements are up to individual requirements of smith.)

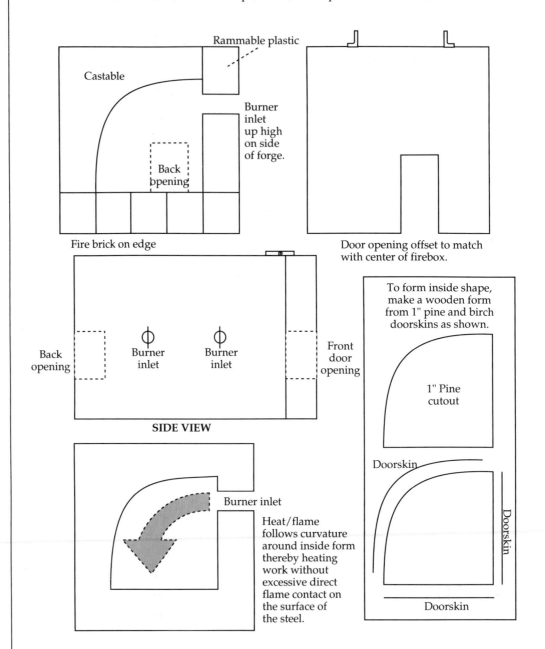

Rammable plastic

Castable

Burner inlet up high on side of forge.

Back opening

Fire brick on edge

Door opening offset to match with center of firebox.

Back opening

Burner inlet

Burner inlet

Front door opening

SIDE VIEW

To form inside shape, make a wooden form from 1" pine and birch doorskins as shown.

1" Pine cutout

Doorskin

Doorskin

Doorskin

Burner inlet

Heat/flame follows curvature around inside form thereby heating work without excessive direct flame contact on the surface of the steel.

Gas Forge Safety

The most important safety precaution: when lighting the forge, put a piece of burning paper inside the forge, turn on the blast, and *then* turn on the gas. *If you don't remember to turn the air on before the gas, you very likely will blow yourself up.*

When shutting down the forge, turn the gas off first, then the air. This prevents gas from building, which could be hazardous.

Once you have your most important piece of tooling, a forge, you should look at some others. The following tools are ones you can fabricate, and while they may not be required, they will save you a great deal of time. They especially come in handy when forging heavy sections and specialized blades.

Top and Bottom Tools

These useful tools allow a smith working alone to forge a variety of shapes, cross sections, and designs. They are placed into the the anvil's hardy hole and secured by a bracket that extends over both edges of the anvil, preventing any movement. With slight modification, they can be used with a power hammer. (See Chapter 4 for more information about the power hammer.) The most useful tools are the top and bottom fuller and the tenon tool.

Top and Bottom Fuller
This tool can be used to forge or groove blades. It also simplifies tang drawing and other processes that require a heavy change in cross section.

Tenon Tool
This is the opposite of a fullering tool. Depending on the dies, it can make a variety of shapes, but the most common ones are round and square. By using this tool, you can easily form tenons and—if used in the early forging—center ribs as well. It can also be used for rounding the ends of tangs prior to threading or for squaring-up tang sections (with a square-die cavity) before attaching the pommel.

These tools can be fashioned from any medium-carbon steel of 45 to 60 points. The springs should be made of 60-point steel at a full spring temper. Its working surfaces should be tempered dark brown to blue, while the remaining sections should be annealed to prevent chipping and damage to the sledgehammer's face. As illustrated on page 13, these dies can be made to interchange in a single framework.

Tongs

Tongs are the extension of one's hand and are used to hold items too hot for bare hands. They come in a wide variety of types and sizes. For gas-forge work, I recommend using ones with handles of at least 30 inches to prevent flash burns (and to save the hair on your arms as well). Tongs should fit the work and be sized according to the piece to be held. I have more than a dozen different-size tongs for my pattern-welding work alone.

TOP AND BOTTOM FULLER TOOLING

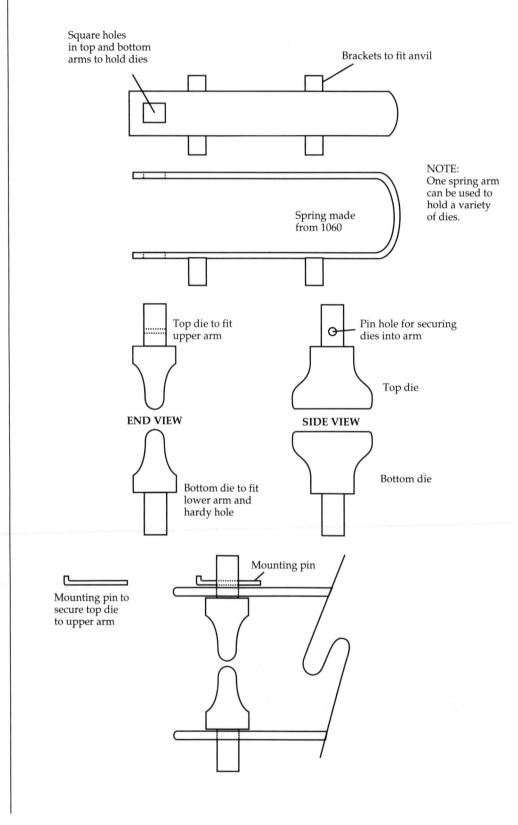

Square holes
in top and bottom
arms to hold dies

Brackets to fit anvil

Spring made
from 1060

NOTE:
One spring arm
can be used to
hold a variety
of dies.

Top die to fit
upper arm

Pin hole for securing
dies into arm

Top die

END VIEW

SIDE VIEW

Bottom die to fit
lower arm and
hardy hole

Bottom die

Mounting pin

Mounting pin to
secure top die
to upper arm

TENON DIES

These dies can be made to interchange with the fuller dies in the same frame.

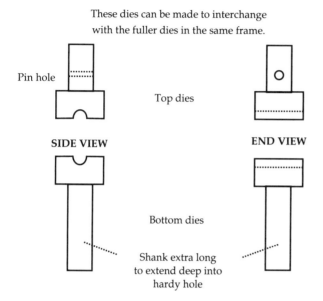

Pin hole

SIDE VIEW

Top dies

END VIEW

Bottom dies

Shank extra long to extend deep into hardy hole

Hot Chisels

This tool enables you to make fast, accurate cuts on hot metal. It has a handle and looks like a cross between a hammer and a hatchet. Its edge is finer than a cold chisel's because hot metal is considerably softer than cold. While using, you should cool the chisel blade every three to four hits to prevent the edge from annealing. The blade absorbs heat from the hot metal. Hot chisels come in different weights. One in the 3- to 5-pound range should suffice for most work. Using a hot chisel, I have made 16-inch splits in 3/8-inch steel in no time at all.

Cold Chisels

Cold chisels are used to cut cold metals, and their edges are considerably stouter than those on hot chisels. They can have handles, or they can be plain bars of steel edged on one end and flat on the other.

As with any tool struck with a hammer, users must regularly inspect the condition of the cold chisel to make certain that its ends have not mushroomed. If allowed to mushroom, fragments of the tool could fracture when struck, causing serious injuries. And, of course, when striking anything, always wear eye protection.

Hammers

Except for a few specialized designs, any bladesmithing hammers used for basic smithing can be used for advanced work—as long as they are properly crowned with no square-shouldered edges. Square-shouldered edges leave hammer marks in the steel surface that are difficult to remove.

If you use top and bottom tools without a power hammer, you need at least a 6-pound sledge hammer, and an 8- or 10-pound one would be even better. However, a 10-pound hammer is too heavy for anvils under 250 to 300 pounds. A good rule to follow is for every 1

CROWNED AND UNCROWNED HAMMER FACES

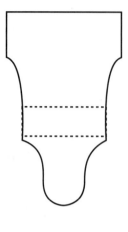

Square corners
leave surface-marring
hammer marks.

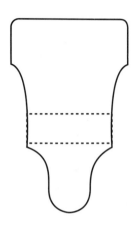

Rounded edges do not
mar the surface.

pound of sledgehammer weight, the anvil should weigh at least 25 to 30 pounds.

Anvils

If your present anvil was fashioned out of a railroad tie, now is the time to step up to a heavier anvil. For forging most big pieces that entail heavy impact upon the anvil—such as swords and top and bottom die work—use an anvil weighing at least 300 pounds. You do not have to use the classical anvil with horn and heel. Smiths can now choose from several specialized anvils that feature square or rectangular blocks, including the sawmaker's anvil or platemaker's block. These anvils work nicely, but they do lack the horn and hardy/pritchel holes that come in handy in bladesmithing. Dies can be made to fit specialized or irregular anvils by adding an integral bracket to the bottom arm. This bracket fits over the top of the anvil to hold the dies stationary.

Belt Grinder

You don't *have* to have a belt grinder. You can get by using draw filing and a stone-grinding wheel, but this severely limits your capabilities and wastes a lot of time. Belt grinders have a major advantage over other grinders because their wheel size remains constant, while the abrasive belts that fit onto the wheel come in various grades of grit sizes from very, very coarse to ultrafine. If the wheels change in size, the size of the radii on the edge bevels also changes, which looks terrible, is difficult to correct, and makes them extremely hard to control. This allows for rough grinding, fine grinding, and final polishing with the same radius as on the edge bevels and at surprising speeds when compared to doing it all by hand. There are several different makes and models of belt grinders on the market. Most of them are expensive, but considering the amount of time saved and the versatility of the machines, the costs are reasonable. There are a few important features you should look for in a belt grinder.

The motor is the most important feature to consider. It should be at least 1 horsepower (HP), and 1 1/2 is even better. These motors come in 110 or 220 voltages, and the 220 model gives smoother, more powerful operation. Most motors run at 1725 rounds per minute (rpm), but some of the faster motors turn 3450 rpm. The faster motors remove more material, but you get better control at slower speeds. Variable-speed models are available, and this feature comes in handy for very fine polishing and on some materials such as ivory, bone horn, and most man-made materials.

Belts come in many different types and in all price ranges. Usually the cheaper belts don't last as long as the more expensive ones, but this is not always the case. Below are what you should look for in a grinding belt.

1. *Grit materials.* This is usually aluminium oxide (corundum), a very hard, durable material. In the more expensive belts, silicon carbide provides the grit. Either one works well for this type of work. Do not use belts that have garnet or flint abrasive grit because they are nothing more than sandpaper. These materials simply aren't hard enough to do anything to steel or iron except scratch it up a bit.

2. *Belt-backing.* For our purposes, this should be heavyweight cloth for the heavier grits (120 or less) and lighter-weight fabric for the finer belts. Some of the superfine 600-grit-plus belts and micron-fine-polishing belts use Mylar or Kevlar, which makes a very durable belt for these applications. Paper-backed belts simply won't hold up under the severe strains that they are subjected to in most grinding operations.

3. *Adhesive.* If you use a standard grinder without a water- or mist-cooling system, this item is of little concern to you. If, however, you use a wet grinder, the adhesive used on the belts has to be moisture-proof, or the abrasive will simply fling off into the air while the belt disintegrates.

4. *Joint type.* Two different joints can be used to form the belt into a circle. The first is a lap joint, where both ends simply lap over each other and are glued in place. You do not want this type. The overlapped area bumps against the piece on which you are working and causes the work to jump all over. You want a butt joint, where both ends abut edgewise, and a very thin piece of Kevlar holds them together. Also, the joint should be angular, not straight across. The angular joint lasts longer and doesn't come apart as easily.

Belt size is also a consideration. Belts wider than 2 inches can be a bit of a problem when shaping certain pieces. As for belt length, 60 inches should be a minimum. Actually, it seems that a 2- x 72-inch belt has become standard in the custom-blade industry.

Positive belt tracking is another important feature on a belt grinder. There is nothing more annoying than having a belt run all over the contact wheel while you are trying to grind. Most grinders offer positive tracking as a standard feature, but make certain that the grinder you are looking at has it.

Cone-Loc Wheels

Some blacksmiths use Cone-Loc wheels instead of belt grinders. These contact wheels function much like a stone grinding wheel—on an arbor attached to a motor. This is where all similarity ends. These wheels, usually made from aluminum, have "tires" made of a heavy-duty synthetic material. They are designed to open up along the radius, allowing an abrasive strip to be inserted. The wheel then locks securely together and works like a contact wheel. The abrasive strips can be quickly and easily replaced.

Although not as efficient as belt grinders, these wheels cost less (as do the abrasive strips when compared to belts) and are almost as versatile in terms of grit sizes and uses. The wheels come in different sizes and should be looked into as an alternative to a costly belt grinder.

Bandsaw

Bandsaws come in two basic types: wood- and metal-cutting. Metal-cutting saws are themselves divided into two types: wet- or dry-cutting. Although a wood-cutting bandsaw is useful to have around for slabbing out grip materials, I will concentrate on metal-cutting saws in this section.

Advanced students of steel should have a metal-cutting bandsaw. It cuts a greater variety of sizes and materials than a hacksaw. It also saves a great deal of time—not to mention saving your arm from a sling. There are too many types and makes of bandsaws to evaluate each individually, so I'll stick with important features.

Of course, the most important consideration in any tool is the quality of construction. A bandsaw should be sturdy and made of top-quality materials. Other factors:

1. *Type of saw.* Is it a dry-cutting saw, or does it use a coolant stream/spray? Dry saws are usually vertical saws with a work table around the blade. This saw allows you to cut materials freehand. You really cannot do much heavy cutting of iron or steel thicker than 1/2 inch or so without some degree of difficulty. Vertical saws are nice to have when bandsawing guards, slotting, freehand profiling, or salvaging

materials from sheet steel. Horizontal bandsaws are usually wet-cutting and are primarily a cut-off saw designed to cut thicker materials. While there are some saws that function as both vertical and horizontal saws, I have found that they don't work very well in either capacity.

All in all, either design is acceptable, depending on what you are planning on doing. I have a wet-cutting horizontal cut-off saw because my work calls for that type of cutting.

2. *Blades*. Metal-cutting bandsaws use two different types of blades: all-tool steel and bimetal. The standard is all-tool steel. This versatile blade comes in most widths and tooth sizes. Although not the greatest blades in the world, they do get the job done. Bimetal blades are far superior for cut-off operations because they stay sharper longer and are more durable. Bimetal blades are also more expensive, but they usually outlast the others two to one.

Another factor in blade selection is ease in replacing blades. You should be able to change blades quickly and easily.

3. *Blade size*. For heavy cutting, a blade should be at least 3/4-inch wide, and the longer, the better. I would not recommend a blade length of less than 5 feet (60 inches) because they tend to wear out quicker than the longer ones.

4. *Variable speeds*. This is important. Although you probably will run the saw at full speed when cutting iron or steel, there are times when you need a slower speed on the blade.

Making an Abrasive Cut-Off Saw

An abrasive cut-off saw is useful if you are planning on doing a lot of blades, and you can easily make one. Begin by making a table with a slot in it, as illustrated on the next page. Then attach the motor and blade mounts. This enables you to cut off steel and iron bars quickly and easily.

Make the framework from 1- x 1/8-inch angle iron, with the blade arbor mounted above the motor. Mount the motor below the blade on a hinge mount to make changing belts easier when using a variable-diameter drive wheel for different speeds.

The whole arbor/motor mount assembly attaches to the table on one side of the blade slot. The mounts are hinged, and the two "tabs" on the front side of the mounts are slotted to accommodate wing nuts, which raise and lower the blade. Be sure to countersink the holes on the table top so the mounting bolts for the blade/motor assembly are flush with the table surface.

This type of cut-off saw can also be used with the blade set just above the table to cut the rung grooves in a piece of Damascus bar stock when making a ladder-pattern piece. The uses for this tool are limited only by your imagination.

ABRASIVE CUT-OFF TABLE SAW
with adjustable blade height

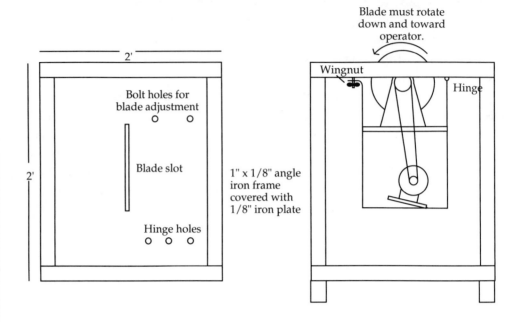

Blade must rotate down and toward operator.

2'

Bolt holes for blade adjustment

Blade slot

2'

1" x 1/8" angle iron frame covered with 1/8" iron plate

Hinge holes

Wingnut

Hinge

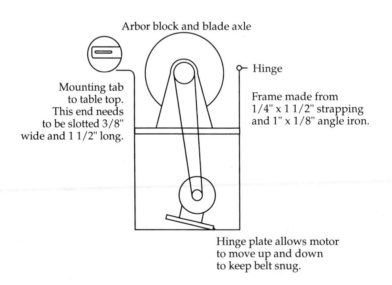

Arbor block and blade axle

Mounting tab to table top. This end needs to be slotted 3/8" wide and 1 1/2" long.

Hinge

Frame made from 1/4" x 1 1/2" strapping and 1" x 1/8" angle iron.

Hinge plate allows motor to move up and down to keep belt snug.

Bench Shears

Also called Beverley shears and a lot of other things, these tools are used to cut sheet metal manually. The top blade of these shears can be raised and lowered with a great deal of force and shearing power. They are available in several sizes, with the larger ones able to cut a 1/4-inch-thick (5mm) plate in low-carbon steels and slightly less in stainless- and high-carbon (tool) steels. I suggest getting the biggest one available. You can always cut thinner metals than the machine is designed for, but you can't cut heavier ones.

These shears are a great aid in cutting plate steel used for axes, spears, or mounting sockets. They can be used for cutting rectangular bar stock, but I do not recommend it, as this can notch or otherwise damage the blades.

Power Hammer

Although not required for the advanced student, power hammers are labor-saving devices second to none. The only designs currently in production are air-operated and *very* expensive. The older ones are still useful, and—although it may take some hunting around to find one that fits your needs—there are still some out there.

Power hammers have been used by almost all of the bigger blacksmith shops at one time or another. They are versatile, can save your arms from endless pounding, and enable you to do heavier forge work by yourself. One reason power hammers are so versatile is because the top and bottom dies are removable, and different dies can be fabricated and used for different work. The list of die types is endless, but the most common dies are drawing dies (these look like the peen end of a cross-peen hammer) and planishing dies (these resemble flat hammer faces).

Power hammers come in a variety of sizes and styles, with the most popular being the "Little Giant" family of hammers. This type of hammer has been around for many years, but it is no longer in production. They were made in 25-, 50-, 100-, 250-, and 500-pound sizes with two types of clutches. The 25-pound hammer, while still useful, is limited in what it can do. I suggest this as a starter hammer. I have a 25- and 50-pound Little Giant, and I cannot begin to estimate the work they have saved me. A 50-pound hammer is a good choice for most advanced shops.

As with all used machinery, the condition of the machine varies. Most of them are heavily used, but they may be salvageable. Babbit bearings, while not a joy to work with, are replaceable and are easy to cast into sheets, form, and scrape to fit the individual machine.

Power hammers were first designed to run from overhead jack lines with power delivered by wide leather belts. Later on, they were redesigned with electric motors. Both versions are usable, but to make the overhead-drive hammer serviceable, you will have to fabricate a motor mount and attach it to the machine.

What to look for in a used power hammer:

1. *Bearings.* These are located in the top of the machine where the axle runs through the frame (through the journal boxes). If there is no play or movement up and down or in or out of the journals, then the bearings are probably OK. If needed, they can be replaced.

The bearings were made of babbit, a soft, leadlike material that wears

POWER HAMMER

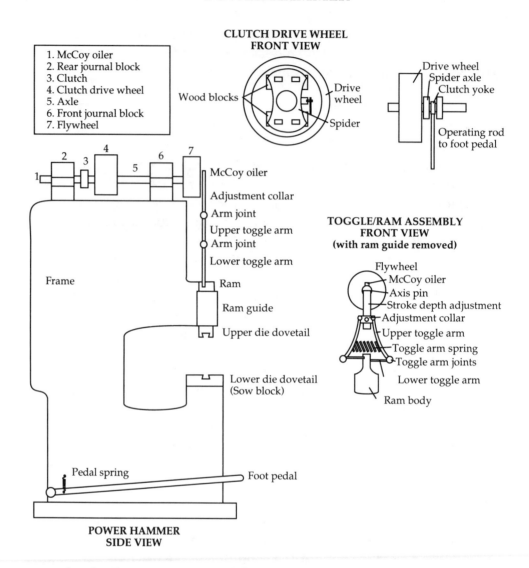

1. McCoy oiler
2. Rear journal block
3. Clutch
4. Clutch drive wheel
5. Axle
6. Front journal block
7. Flywheel

**CLUTCH DRIVE WHEEL
FRONT VIEW**

Wood blocks — Drive wheel — Spider

Drive wheel
Spider axle
Clutch yoke
Operating rod to foot pedal

McCoy oiler
Adjustment collar
Arm joint
Upper toggle arm
Arm joint
Lower toggle arm
Ram
Ram guide
Upper die dovetail
Lower die dovetail (Sow block)

Frame

**TOGGLE/RAM ASSEMBLY
FRONT VIEW
(with ram guide removed)**

Flywheel
McCoy oiler
Axis pin
Stroke depth adjustment
Adjustment collar
Upper toggle arm
Toggle arm spring
Toggle arm joints
Lower toggle arm
Ram body

Pedal spring — Foot pedal

**POWER HAMMER
SIDE VIEW**

very slowly. It was once used for bearings because, when properly lubricated, it doesn't produce a lot of heat. Phosphor or bearing bronze has replaced babbit for bearings in modern machinery, but babbit is still available in sheet and wool form from most of the larger industrial machinery supply firms.

To replace babbit bearings, remove the bolts that hold the axle assembly to the top of the machine, and then remove the tops of the journals. Next, disconnect the clutch assembly as well as the ram from the flywheel and carefully lift the axle and clutch assembly off of the machine. These are *very heavy*, so you should have a helper.

Removing the the axle gives you access to the bearings. Remove and replace these with a sheet of babbit in the proper size. Usually they are 1/8 inch in thickness, but thicker babbit is available. If you need thicker babbit and you have none, you can melt what you have and pour it, following the manufacturer's instructions.

NOTE: There is a spacer between the top and bottom journals that keeps them from being overtightened and thereby affecting the rotation of the axle shaft. These are usually babbit, but they can also be made from heavy leather if you have no babbit.

There is a hole in the top of each bearing to allow oil to enter from the well on the top of the journal block, so be certain to drill these holes out using a 3/16-inch drill. When they are fitted, replace the axle and the clutch, bolt down the journals, and reconnect the ram to the flywheel.

Replacing babbit bearings entails a good bit of work, but it is not impossible to do.

2. *Ram movement.* There should be a slight bit of play in the movement from side to side, but it should not exceed 1/32 inch. If it does, then major repairs may be required.

3. *Overall condition of the machine.* If the machine looks trashed, then more than likely it is. Don't even consider buying it. If the general condition looks good, then examine it further. Regardless of the condition of the machine, it will probably need a good cleaning. So take the major components apart and clean off all of the old grease, oil, and other crud that have accumulated over the years. I would also repaint the machine with two coats of rust preventative paint, let it dry, then reassemble and oil the parts. Make certain that the grease cups are cleaned and refilled with a top-quality lithium grease.

4. *Clutch.* Power hammers have one of two types of clutch designs to activate the ram. The first one has two maple blocks in the spider (the part inside the rotating drive ring), which are adjustable for wear and engagement. These blocks are easily replaced with new hardwood (hardrock maple is best). You simply use the old blocks as a guide for hole placement and trim the replacement blocks to fit. I prefer this clutch type because it is so easily repaired.

The second clutch type uses a composition belt arrangement on a cone-shaped spider to engage the outer ring, hence transferring the power to the axle. Replacing the belt on these can be a bit of a problem. You can rubber-cement heavy leather into place, but this doesn't last long.

Whichever type of clutch type your power hammer has, it should operate freely, engaging and disengaging when the foot lever is depressed and released.

5. *Frame.* The frame should be inspected for cracks, fractures, and other signs of fatigue. If all looks in good shape, the price is right, and you have a place for it, by all means buy it. But remember, the machine must be properly mounted and secured by bolts to a solid reinforced concrete slab for safe operation. (Hammers weighing less than 25 pounds can be mounted on a bed made of 6 x 6 lumber and placed onto the slab with little, if any, movement. But hammers larger than this have to be mounted properly on a slab base at least 24-inches thick and 4-feet

square—and even larger and thicker for the *really* big hammers.)

6. *Isolation pads.* Some industrial structures now have foundations called "isolation pads." These massive slabs were designed with heavy, impact-prone machinery in mind. They are specially reinforced and poured separately from the surrounding slab. Usually joined to the adjacent concrete with a special synthetic material, these pads prevent the vibration and impact from machinery from being conducted throughout the foundation slab. This prevents vibrational damage to the foundation slab and makes it easier on you and your neighbors as well.

The designing and pouring of special pads are beyond the scope of this work. If you are interested in installing one, contact a building contractor who specializes in this sort of work. They know the special requirements for your area, including building codes, foundation and mounting hardware for various types and sizes of machines, and other specifics.

7. *Safety.* Another major factor to consider is the inherent danger of the power hammer itself. Many bladesmiths have been injured or maimed for life by careless acts around these hammers. Since they were designed before the turn of the century, when there was no Occupational Safety and Health Administration (OSHA), there are no guards or shields on most of these hammers. The ram assembly, with all of its moving parts, is totally exposed to the operator, and you can easily run afoul of the moving machinery. There should be a shield enclosing the belt drive to prevent anything from being caught in the belt and forcibly being run around the pulley, and another one protecting the operator from the ram and the spring. You must design and make a shield that encloses the ram while also allowing access to it for adjustments. These shields can be made of expanded metal sheet or a caging of sorts.

Most Little Giants have a rather heavy coil spring that holds the top toggle arms apart when the machine is idle but allows them to come together during operation. This spring is at the operator's head level while the machine is running, and if that spring were to let go all of a sudden . . . well, it could get rather grisly. Sure, you say, it could happen, but how often does it *actually* happen? Often enough that a lot of the older hammers already have some sort of caging installed on them. So if your hammer doesn't have shields, *put some on it* for your own safety. A little inconvenience now can save you from a trip to the doctor—or worse. Why take the chance?

I built my shield on a framework that attaches directly on the hammer frame. It also has a separate shield that fits into holes in the fabricated frame, so it is removable to allow access to the machine for adjustments and lubrication.

A point to remember about power hammers and other power devices is this: hand tools injure, power tools maim. Always wear face/eye protection no matter what you are doing. Even the smallest bit of scale, grit, or filing can severely damage your sight.

◆ ◆ ◆

These are just some of the tools that you might find useful in your advanced forging. Get the highest quality tooling that you can afford, as a good craftsman suffers from a poor tool. At first you may complain about the price of a top-quality tool, but you will forget it as time passes. A poorly made, cheaper tool will be cause of complaint for a long time to come. Learn to use all tools as they were designed to be used, and you will find that your abilities have grown. But also remember: there is no tool that can replace good craftsmanship. This has to be learned firsthand.

STEELS & ALLOYS

The selection of the steel from which the blade is forged is perhaps the most important factor (other than how it is worked) in the making of any blade.

Before the invention of the Bessemer converter in 1926, bladesmiths had a great deal of difficulty obtaining quality iron and steel. Most of the steel had to be made by the bladesmiths themselves, and the process involved at the time was haphazard at best.

Fortunately, that is not the case today. Now there are steels that run the gamut from simple to complex, from basic to superhigh tech. Having such a wide selection of top-quality steel available—something bladesmiths of old could only dream of—certainly facilitates knife making, but it still leaves one critical question unanswered for today's bladesmiths. How do you choose the right steel for the right blade?

This question is one of the oldest in bladesmithing. An ideal steel for every purpose would be extremely hard, highly flexible, and shock-resistant. That steel does not yet exist, so compromises must be made.

Any tool has a specific function that it was intended to perform. A pair of pliers wouldn't be expected to do double duty as a hammer, nor would a hammer be called upon to perform the duties of a paint brush. But a knife, on the other hand, often gets used as a pry bar, cold chisel, or screwdriver—among other things. This is the worst type of abuse. Yet, regrettably, owners expect this performance of just about every knife.

So how does one go about finding the correct alloy for a particular blade? The first question to answer is, what is the knife going to be used for? Is it a skinner that requires a sharp, fine edge for precise cutting, or is it a camp knife that is expected to perform a variety of functions, ranging from food preparation to chopping kindling? This make a difference in choosing the steel.

Another factor is blade style and length. The longer the blade, the more flexible it should be. A long stiff blade is easier to break than a long

25

flexible one. The ability of steel to absorb strains and shock should be an important factor in choosing the alloy.

Perhaps the most important questions for the bladesmith are, how do I know what's in these alloys, and what is the best alloy for each particular application?

Years ago, before the standardization of steel, the bladesmith had to rely on his experience and skill in smelting his own iron and steels to get the characteristics he desired. Today, the steel industry has developed a universal coding system to identify alloys currently in production. Along with this coding system, the industry has imposed a standard content of elements in each alloy that—for all intents and purposes—makes each alloy identical from melt to melt and mill to mill.

These codes allow the bladesmith to look at a particular alloy's specification sheet and decide what the steel can be used for, how it is best worked and heat-treated, and how the blade will function in its proposed form. But before we go into this coding system, you must first know what each element is and how it affects the alloy in question.

ALLOYS AND THEIR EFFECTS ON STEEL

Iron (Fe)

The most common element in steel is iron. Iron is the second most common metal found on Earth, second to aluminum. It is abundant in the various forms of ores, but it is never found in a natural state as is copper, gold, and silver. It must be smelted and refined before it can be used. During these processes, other elements are added to bring about profound changes in the performance of the alloy. The most common alloying element is carbon.

Carbon (C)

Carbon is the major reason that steel gets hard. Iron forms carbides that cause the surrounding steel to get hard—and brittle as well. Cast iron has approximately 3 percent carbon content; tool steels from 0.95 to 1.75 percent carbon; spring steels from 0.50 to 0.90 percent; mild steels less than 0.20 percent.

The carbon content of an alloy is usually expressed as a point of carbon, with each point containing 0.01 percent of the alloy. So a 35-point alloy contains 0.35 percent carbon.

The term carbon steel is used to describe any steel that contains carbon and is not a stainless steel. (Stainless steel is described later on in this chapter.)

The table below gives the points of carbon and their uses.

Points of Carbon	Uses
5-10	Nails, wire. Not hardenable.
10-20	General uses. Not hardenable.
20-30	Screws, some machinery parts. Not hardenable.
30-40	Machinery parts. Hardens slightly.
40-50	Gears, axles. Hardenable to a degree if properly treated. Results in a very tough blade.
50-60	Crowbars, hammers. Hardens enough to take an edge if properly heat-treated. Makes a very tough and flexible blade.
60-70	Swords, axes, cleavers. Blades for heavy chopping.
70-100	General cutlery uses. Choose a lower-carbon content for a tougher blade; a higher-carbon content for a harder, longer-lasting edge.

As you can see, the carbon content varies widely, and the purpose of the blade should dictate the appropriate carbon content. A good rule to follow is the more carbon, the harder and brittler the steel becomes.

Chromium (Cr)

Chromium increases the depth penetration of the hardening processes and also their responsiveness to heat treatment. It is usually added with nickel in stainless steels. Most of the chromium-bearing alloys contain 0.50 to 1.50 percent chromium. Some stainless steels contain as much as 20 percent. It can affect forging, causing the steel to crack.

Lead (Pb)

Lead increases the machinability of steel but has no effect on the other properties of the metal. It is usually added to an alloy only upon request and then in quantities of 0.15 to 0.30 percent.

Manganese (Mn)

This element is normally present in all steel and functions as a de-oxidizer. It also imparts strength and increased responsiveness to heat treatment. It is usually present in quantities of 0.5 to 2.0 percent.

Molybdenum (Mo)

Molybdenum causes the steel to harden more uniformly (deep hardening) and increases toughness. It also makes the steel more resistant to higher temperatures. An alloy with below .020 percent molybdenum can be worked without much difficulty.

Nickel (Ni)

Nickel increases toughness and strengthens the steel, but it is ineffective in increasing hardness. It is generally added in amounts ranging from 1 to 4 percent. In some stainless steels, it is high as 36 percent.

Phosphorus (Ph)

Phosphorus is present in all steel. It increases yield strength, reduces ductility at low temperatures, and is believed to increase resistance to atmospheric corrosion. It is, however, treated as an impurity in most alloys.

Silicon (Si)

Silicon has a beneficial effect upon tensile strength and improves hardenability. It has a toughening effect when used in combination with other elements. Often added to improve electrical conductivity, its average concentration is between 1.5 to 2.5 percent.

Sulphur (S)

Sulphur is usually considered an impurity in most alloys because it is damaging to the hot-forming properties of a steel. However, it is added to screw stock because it increases machinability.

Tungsten or Wolfram (W)

Tungsten is often used as an alloying element in tool steels because, when used in relatively small quantities, it imparts a tight, small, dense grain structure and keen cutting edge. It also causes steel to retain its hardness at higher temperatures and hence has a detrimental effect upon the steel's forgability (red hard).

Vanadium (V)

Vanadium retards the grain growth of steel even after long exposures at high temperatures. It also helps to control grain structures during heat treating. It is usually present in small quantities of 0.15 to 0.20 percent. Tool steels that contain this element usually absorb shock better than those that don't.

Of course, these are not the only elements that are used in alloying steels, but they are the ones most commonly encountered in the alloys you are likely to use.

How do you know what is in a particular alloy? To aid the industry in knowing the content of a given alloy, the Society of Automotive Engineers (SAE) has developed a numerical code for the available steels with certain standards for each alloy. This code is *usually* a four-digit number. The first two digits identify the basic elemental content of the alloy; the last two are the carbon content. (Some of the newer alloys may have 5 digits, in which case the *third* digit can refer to various elements, such as chromium, vanadium, and so forth.)

STEEL TYPE	SERIES CODE NUMBER
Plain carbon (nonalloy) steel	1xxx
Manganese steel	13xx
Nickel-alloy steels	2xxx
3.5 percent Ni	23xx
5.0 percent Ni	25xx
Nickel/chrome steel	3xxx
Molybdenum steels	4xxx
Carbon/moly	40xx
Chrome/moly	41xx
Chrome/moly/nickel	43xx
Moly/nickel	46xx or 48xx
Chromium-alloy steels	5xxx
Low-chromium content	51xx
Medium-chromium content	52xx
High-chromium content	53xx
Chrome/vanadium-alloy steels	6xxx
Nickel/chrome/moly-alloy steels	86xx or 87xx
Manganese/silicon-alloy steels	92xx

For example, alloy 1095 is a plain carbon (nonalloy) steel with 0.95 percent carbon, while 5160 is a low-chromium, medium-carbon content alloy steel. In addition to the above SAE numerical code, the American Iron and Steel Institute (AISI) has devised a letter/number code based either upon the alloy's hardening medium(s), content, or use.

AISI CODE	STEEL TYPE
A	Air-hardening steels
D	Die-steel alloys
F	Carbon/tungsten alloys
H	Hot work
L	Low alloy
M	Molybdenum alloys
O	Oil-hardening steels
P	Mold-steel alloys
PH	Precipitation-hardening alloys
S	Shock-resistant alloys
T	Tungsten alloys
W	Water-hardening steels

The numbers that follow the letter codes are standard alloy designations for the industry. This way the alloy content is standardized.

The hardening mediums are another factor in alloy selection. There are three basic families of steels: water-, oil-, and air-hardening alloys.

Water-hardening steel (W-1, WHC, W-2) tends to have a harder and longer-lasting edge, although it is somewhat brittle. Oil-hardening steels (O-1, 5160, 1095) do not get quite as hard as water-hardening ones, but they are usually tougher and more durable. The air-hardening steels (A-2, D-2) are the toughest alloys. They do present some forging problems, which will be discussed in Chapter 3. They are not a good choice for the novice smith, but they can make a well-forged blade even better if you know what you're doing.

STAINLESS STEELS

Bladesmiths have given stainless steel a bad reputation, and, frankly, I cannot see why. Maybe it is because they are considerably harder under the hammer than most carbon steels, but, then again, D-2 is just as hard to move as most cutlery-grade stainless. Stainless does make a first-class blade with excellent cutting ability as well as rust- and corrosion-resistance.

The stainless steels are either oil- or air-hardening and are best for blades that are used around water. They are forgeable and produce a sound blade when properly worked. Although they do require a different method of working, the techniques are within the grasp of the advanced forger.

SIMPLE-ALLOY STEELS

The alloys listed below are the most common ones used for today's custom blades. Some are easier to work with than others, but all of them—when properly worked—produce a far superior blade to one simply ground out of a bar of the same material.

Simple alloy steels are easy to work under the hammer and are very forgiving in terms of overheating/red shortness. Most of the simpler alloys withstand a greater amount of heat-treating stress without cracking than the richer-alloy steels.

The 10-series steels are the most usable of the readily available bladesmithing alloys. They are stable and easy to form under the hammer. One thing bladesmiths should remember about these steels is that for our purposes they are not water-hardening, despite mill specification claims to the contrary. While they may be so in the cross sections with which mills deal (measured in inches), any attempt to water-harden them in knife-making sections (fractions of inches) will result in broken or cracked blades.

The composition of the common alloys:

1050   Carbon: 0.48 to 0.55 percent
        Manganese: 0.60 to 0.90 percent
1060   Carbon: 0.55 to 0.65 percent
        Manganese: 0.60 to 0.90 percent
1070   Carbon: 0.65 to 0.75 percent
        Manganese: 0.60 to 0.90 percent
1080   Carbon: 0.75 to 0.88 percent
        Manganese: 0.60 to 0.90 percent
1095   Carbon: 0.90 to 1.03 percent
        Manganese: 0.30 to 0.50 percent

Wear-resistance: Medium
Toughness: High to medium depending upon carbon content
Red hardness: Very low
Distortion in heat treat: Very low
Forging: Start at 1750 to 1850° F
Austenite forging: Yes
Hardening: 1450 to 1550° F
Quench: Oil
Tempering: 300 to 500° F
Rc hardness: 62 to 55 (depending upon carbon content)

W-1

W-1 tool steel is an excellent general-purpose steel with a high degree of hardness to a rather uniform depth. Although it is a water-hardening steel, I strongly suggest that you oil-quench it, as this helps to prevent warpage, cracks, and distortion. W-1 has the following characteristics:

Carbon: 0.60 to 1.40 percent
Wear-resistance: Medium
Toughness: Medium
Red hardness: Very low
Distortion in heat treat: Low to medium
Forging: Start at 1800 to 1900° F
Austenite forging: Yes
Hardening: 1400 to 1550° F. Has a slight tendency to crack
  under certain conditions.
Quench: Water or oil
Tempering: 350 to 650° F
Rc hardness: 64 to 50

W-2

W-2 is similar to W-1 and has the same forging and heat-treating requirements. The only difference is in the alloy content, which is as follows:

Carbon: 0.60 to 1.40 percent
Vanadium: 0.25 percent

WHC

WHC tool steel has slightly less carbon and resists shock and impact better than either W-1 or W-2. Although difficult to find, it is great to use in pattern-welded blades.
It has the following characteristics:

Carbon: 0.75 percent
Wear-resistance: Medium
Toughness: High medium
Red hardness: Very low
Distortion in heat treat: Low
Forging: Start at 1850 to 1900° F
Austenite forging: Yes
Hardening: 1400 to 1550° F
Quench: Water or oil

Tempering: 350 to 650°F
Rc hardness: 64 to 50

5160

5160 is a medium-carbon spring steel with excellent toughness and high ductility. It is quite flexible and resists heavy shocks, making it well suited for swords, axes, big Bowies, and other cutlery on which a larger, flexible blade is desired. The characteristics of 5160 are as follows:

Carbon: 0.56 to 0.64 percent
Manganese: 0.75 to 1.00 percent
Phosphorus: 0.035 percent maximum
Sulphur: 0.04 percent maximum
Silicon: 0.15 to 0.35 percent
Chromium: 0.70 to 1.05 percent
Wear-resistance: High medium
Toughness: High
Red hardness: Low
Distortion in heat treat: Low
Forge: Start at 1800°F
Austenite forging: Yes
Hardening: 1450 to 1550°F
Quench: Oil
Tempering: 300 to 450°F
Rc hardness: 62 to 55

L-6

L-6 is a low-alloy steel used in large saw blades and similar tools. Although it is a good steel, it is somewhat red hard due to its vanadium content. Blades fashioned from it have a nice balance of toughness and wear-resistance. The characteristics of L-6 are as follows:

Carbon: 0.70 to 0.90 percent
Manganese: 0.35 to 0.55 percent
Phosphorus: 0.025 percent
Sulphur: 0.01 percent maximum
Silicon: 0.25 percent
Chromium: 0.03 percent
Nickel: 1.4 to 2.6 percent
Vanadium: 0.15 percent
Wear-resistance: Medium
Toughness: Very high
Red hardness: Low

Distortion in heat treat: Low
Forge: Start at 1800 to 2000°F
Austenite forging: Yes
Harden: 1450 to 1550°F
Quench: Oil
Tempering: 300 to 500°F
Rc hardness: 63 to 55

HIGHER-ALLOY STEELS

These richer-alloy steels have a tendency to be red hard when compared with lower-alloy steels. Some of them are a bit more complicated to work with than others, but all of them make high-quality blades.

These alloys offer a variety of features that the simpler steels cannot. These features range from enhanced edge-holding capability to extended wear-, rust-, and corrosion-resistance. This can be a great aid in the field or anywhere you do not have ready access to a sharpening stone and the blade is subjected to moisture and other adverse conditions.

O-1

O-1 is classed as a cold-work die steel and for a long time has been the standard carbon steel for forged or ground blades. It is suitable for all but the largest blades (such as swords) and those that require superflexibility. It is somewhat forgiving when it comes to heat-treating and warping, but its forgiving attitude doesn't extend to overheating. Very red short, it cracks and fractures at the higher temperatures. O-1 has the following characteristics:

Carbon: 0.90 percent
Manganese: 1.00 percent
Chrome: 0.50 percent
Tungsten: 0.50 percent
Wear-resistance: Medium
Toughness: Medium
Red hardness: Low
Distortion in heat treat: Very low
Forging: Start at 1800 to 1950°F
Austenite forging: Yes
Quench: Oil
Tempering: 350 to 500°F
Rc hardness: 62 to 57

Notes on forging O-1: bring up to temperature slowly and start forging at 1850 to 1950 degrees F. Do not forge below 1500 degrees F because this can cause stress buildup and possible cracking. Harden and temper immediately in oil for best results.

S-1

S-1 is a steel designed to absorb shocks rather than resist abrasion or wear. Its primary use is in hand and pneumatic tools designed for chipping and riveting. S-1's characteristics are as follows:

Carbon: 0.50 percent
Chromium: 1.50 percent
Tungsten: 2.50 percent
Wear-resistance: Medium
Toughness: Very high
Distortion in heat treat: Medium
Red hardness: Medium
Forging: Start at 1850 to 2050°F
Austenite forging: Yes
Harden: 1650 to 1750°F
Quench: Oil
Tempering: 400 to 45°F
Rc hardness: 58 to 55

S-5

S-5 is used for the same basic tools as S-1, but its molybdenum content makes it considerably tougher and somewhat harder. It is also a bit red hard. S-5's characteristics:

Carbon: 0.55 percent
Manganese: 0.80 percent
Silicon: 2.00 percent
Molybdenum: 0.40 percent
Wear-resistance: Medium
Toughness: Very high
Distortion in heat treat: Low
Red hardness: Medium
Forging: Start at 1650 to 1800°F
Austenite Forging: Yes
Harden: 1600 to 1700°F
Quench: Oil
Tempering: 350 to 450°F
Rc hardness: 60 to 55

Vasco Wear

Vasco Wear is another steel for the advanced forger. It is very tough and highly wear-resistant. Abrasives barely cut it, and once an edge is put on a blade, it simply doesn't get dull. Much like L-6, it is easy to forge. Its main difficulty comes after hardening. It gets superhard, tough, and difficult to work. Because of this, you must do 90 percent of the work hot before heat treating to work this steel into a blade. Otherwise, you eat up a lot of belts, and that gets a bit on the costly side. Vasco Wear characteristics are as follows:

Carbon: 1.12 percent
Silicon: 1.2 percent
Manganese: .30 percent
Tungsten: 1.10 percent
Chromium: 7.75 percent
Molybdenum: 1.60 percent
Vanadium: 2.4 percent
Wear-resistance: Highest
Toughness: High
Red hardness: Medium
Distortion in heat treat: Low
Forging: 1800 to 1900° F
Austenite forging: Yes
Hardening: 1550 to 1600° F
Quench: Oil
Tempering: 300 to 500° F
Rc hardness: 62 to 58

AIR-HARDENING STEELS

These steels demand stringent temperature control throughout the forging process. They also tend to be a bit red hard and require greater skill and much more force to move under the hammer.

A-2

A-2 is not for the novice smith, but it has some very desirable properties. It is tough and wear-resistant. A-2's characteristics:

Carbon: 1.00 percent
Chromium: 5.00 percent
Molybdenum: 5.00 percent
Wear-resistance: High
Toughness: Medium

Distortion in heat treat: Very low
Red hard: High
Forging: 1850 to 2000°F
Austenite forging: Yes
Hardening: 1700 to 1800°F
Quench: Air
Tempering: 350 to 1000°F
Rc hardness: 62 to 57

Notes on forging A-2: preheating prevents stress buildup and allows annealing to occur before reaching final forging temperatures. Hold at a dark red (about 1200 degrees F) for approximately 5 minutes and then slowly raise to 2000 to 2050 degrees and start working. At no time should forging be continued after the steel has dropped below 1700 degrees F.

Anneal immediately after forging by taking the temperature up to 2000 degrees F and placing the steel in a hot box. Allow to cool slowly.

A-6

A-6 is a low-alloy chrome/molybdenum, air-hardening steel with a good balance of strength, hardness, and toughness. Like A-2, it is a bit red hard, but it makes a great blade. The characteristics of A-6 are as follows:

Carbon: 0.70 percent
Manganese: 2.10 percent
Silicon: 0.30 percent
Chromium: 1.00 percent
Molybdenum: 1.40 percent
Wear-resistance: Medium
Toughness: High
Distortion in heat treat: Low
Red hard: Hard
Forging: 2175 to 1800°F
Austenite forging: Yes
Hardening: 1550°F
Quench: Air
Tempering: 300 to 600°F

D-2

D-2 is an air-hardening steel, which may present a problem. On the other hand, it does not warp when quenched. It is very wear-resistant and somewhat red hard and difficult to forge. I do not recommend it for the beginner. D-2 has the following characteristics:

Carbon: 1.50 percent
Chromium: 12.00 percent
Molybdenum: 1.00 percent
Vanadium: 1.00 percent
Wear-resistance: High
Toughness: High
Red hardness: High
Distortion in heat treat: Medium
Forging: Start at 1850 to 2000° F
Austenite forging: Yes
Harden: 1800 to 1875° F
Quench: Air
Tempering: 400 to 1000° F
Rc hardness: 61 to 54

Notes on forging D-2: for best results, preheat to 1250 degrees F and hold for 5 minutes. Slowly bring up to forging temperature. Anneal immediately after forging by bringing it up to forging temperature and placing it in a hot box.

M-2

M-2 is a high-speed tool steel, wear-resistant, tough, and well suited for blade making. It is not for the beginner because it takes considerable skill to forge, and it is prone to cracking during low-temperature forging. M-2's characteristics are as follows:

Carbon: .85 percent
Manganese: .35 percent
Silicon: .30 percent
Chromium: 4.15 percent
Vanadium: 1.95 percent
Molybdenum: 5.00 percent
Tungsten: 6.4 percent
Wear-resistance: High
Toughness: High
Red hardness: High
Distortion in heat treat: Low
Forging: 1750 to 1800° F
Austenite forging: Yes
Harden: 1700 to 1750° F
Quench: Air/oil
Tempering: 350 to 500° F
Rc hardness: 62 to 58

S-7

S-7 is a chrome/molybdenum alloy that has excellent shock properties, which makes it ideal for larger blades. Its high molybdenum content makes it difficult to move under the hammer. The characteristics of S-7 are as follows:

Carbon: 0.50 percent
Manganese: 0.70 percent
Silicon: 0.25 percent
Chromium: 3.25 percent
Molybdenum: 1.40 percent
Wear-resistance: Medium
Toughness: High
Distortion in heat treat: Very low
Forging: 1700 to 2050° F
Austenite forging: No
Hardening: 1725° F
Quench: Air
Tempering: 300 to 600° F
Rc hardness: 58 to 53

Notes on forging S-7: preheat to 1200 to 1300 degrees F for 5 minutes. Raise to forging temperature slowly and start to forge from 2050 to 1700 degrees F. Anneal immediately by heating to forging temperature and placing in a hot box.

STAINLESS STEEL ALLOYS SUITABLE FOR FORGING

As I mentioned before, I cannot understand why most modern bladesmiths look down on the stainless steels. When properly forged, the stainless alloys really shine in terms of their ability to hold an edge, remain durable, and, of course, resist rust and corrosion. Stainless alloys are a bit red hard and tend to move very slowly under the hammer, but if you work slowly and carefully, you can use the alloys listed below to forge blades that are far superior to a stock-removal (nonforged) stainless-steel blade.

440 C

440 C is a high-carbon, chromium stainless steel that has become a standard in the knife-making industry. In my opinion, it is unsuitable for big blades and in uses that require flexibility, but it does make some very fine blades. 440 C has the following characteristics:

Carbon: 0.95 to 1.20 percent
Manganese: 1.00 percent maximum
Phosphorus: 0.04 percent maximum
Sulphur: 0.03 percent maximum
Silicon: 1.00 percent maximum
Chromium: 16.00 to 18.00 percent
Molybdenum: 0.65 percent maximum
Nickel: 0.75 percent maximum
Copper: 0.50 percent maximum
Wear-resistance: High
Toughness: Medium
Distortion in heat treat: Medium
Forging: Start at 1900 to 2100° F
Austenite forging: Yes
Hardening: 1850 to 1950° F
Quench: Oil (and air in very small sections)
Tempering: 350 to 500° F
Rc hardness: 62 to 57

Notes on forging 440 C: by using a subzero quench after the hardening quench, you can achieve an extra degree of hardness.

154 CM

154 CM is a very good stainless steel that benefits from the same subzero quench used for 440 C. It is one of the most difficult to forge because it doesn't move under the hammer. 154 CM's characteristics:

Carbon: 1.05 percent
Manganese: .50 percent
Silicon: .30 percent
Chromium: 14.00 percent
Molybdenum: 4.00 percent
Wear-resistance: High
Toughness: Medium
Red hardness: High
Distortion in heat treat: Medium
Forging: 1800 to 1950° F
Austenite forging: Yes
Quench: Oil
Tempering: 350 to 500 F
Rc hardness: 62 to 56

RECYCLED MATERIALS

The ability to recycle materials, to change the shape and size of various steels, is a great advantage to the bladesmith. You can salvage many high-quality materials from automotive and machinery scrap piles or salvage yards. And, since the automotive industry utilizes a standardized material for specific purposes, you know for which uses they are suitable.

I am not recommending this practice for high-quality blades, but recycled steels make great material for getting the pattern down, learning new techniques, or training others. For your finished blades, you owe it to yourself and your clients to use only the finest materials.

Since items are recycled, you have no idea of the condition of the crystalline structure within the steel. Hence, they could be highly crystallized, affected with microscopic cracking, or otherwise fatigued to the point of failure.

You can use these recycled materials for pattern-welded blades because the repeated welding and forging processes would refine any crystalline weaknesses the materials might have. Below are some of the uses to which certain recycled steels can be put.

ITEM	STEEL
Leaf springs	5160
Plowshares	1060 or 1065
Improved plowshare	1084 or 1095
Clock spring steel	1095
Files	W-2 (on the older files)
Saw blades	L-6
Air-hammer bits	S-5
Truck coil springs	5160

These are but a few of the alloys available to the bladesmith, and new alloys seem to come out every day. Some of the new alloys are useful to the smith, while others are so highly specialized that they have very limited applications. Feel free to try new steels. After all, learning is what this is all about, isn't it?

HOW TO CHOOSE THE RIGHT STEEL

Choosing steel is one of the most difficult choices a bladesmith must make. Most smiths have favorite alloys that they use for everything. This works about 90 percent of the time, but that leaves 10 percent that requires a special steel.

The primary factor in choosing steel is the blade's function. Flexibility is most important in a big or long blade, so a steel that gets really hard (above 57 Rc) is not the answer. Now, on the other hand, a steel that is highly flexible but doesn't get harder than 53 Rc would be a poor choice for a skinning knife that is expected to do a lot of work before it needs a touch-up sharpening. And a blade that is going into a moist or saltwater environment needs corrosion- and rust-resistance, or the user will end up with a piece of rust in a very short time.

Another subject that needs to be considered is the shape and cross section of the blade. Some alloys tend to adapt to radical cross-sectional changes better than others. Usually the simpler alloys are more versatile than the richer ones. But the richer alloys tend to be a bit more shock- and wear-resistant than the simpler plain carbon, lower-alloy steels.

Length is another important consideration. Not all steels are available in longer lengths, and some of the ones that are available have a strong tendency to warp, sometimes severely in long sections unless everything in the heat-treating/tempering process is perfect.

All of these factors must be taken into consideration when selecting steel for a blade. Not all steels work for all situations, and the ability to know what a steel alloy will do by reading mill specifications is one every bladesmith should have.

For more serious students of the forge, I strongly urge you to take a metallurgy course at a local college or vocational school. You'll be surprised at how much you already know about the subject, but more importantly, you'll gain additional knowledge in basic metals and alloys, and how they react under various conditions.

With this knowledge, you'll have the confidence to advance further in your mastery of the forged blade.

ADVANCED FORGING
TECHNIQUES

Most of the techniques described in this chapter are not for the beginning smith. They are for the advanced student who is already familiar with the basic forging techniques of upsetting, drawing out, packing, and shaping. These techniques show how to use hand forging, tooling, jigs, and other mechanical aids to turn out top-quality blades. You'll learn how to use the tools described in Chapter 1.

Although most of the richer alloys are forgeable in a coal-fired forge, I prefer not to have to deal with the clinkers, fire maintenance, and other hassles that accompany a coal fire. So I suggest using a gas forge for almost all of these richer alloys.

GAS FORGES

In Chapter 1, you learned how to set up a gas forge, and now you're going to learn how to operate one safely and effectively. As with other fired heat sources, gas forges put out vast amounts of carbon monoxide gas. This gas is quite deadly. Learning how to get rid of carbon monoxide is perhaps the number-one safety concern with gas forges. So make certain that your work space has more than adequate ventilation before the forge is lit.

I strongly urge you to install a venting hood, which can easily be fabricated from light-gauge sheet metal and vented through the roof of the shop. To keep the carbon monoxide gas and other noxious fumes from flooding the shop, the venting hood channels them out of the room. As a matter of fact, some local fire codes require such a hood and sometimes a powered ventilation fan as well, and the penalties for noncompliance can be severe.

Regardless of your venting methods or gas-forge design, there are certain precautions that you must follow entirely to ensure safe and effective operation. Remember that you are now dealing with a pressurized, highly flammable gas that is very safe when used properly. Haphazard operation, however, can lead to property damage, serious injury, or loss of life.

Starting up is the most hazardous part of using a gas forge. To prevent any explosions, you should learn how to safely ignite your forge by following the correct operating procedures.

Venturi Gas Forge

Venturi forges have no blowers. They are designed to operate on gas pressure and the Venturi effect, which uses constriction to regulate gas flow and gas pressure. Follow the manufacturer's instructions for starting up. More than likely, this is simply lighting a piece of newspaper, putting it inside the forge, leaving the door (if there is one) open, and slowly turning on the gas. The gas ignites, and the Venturi effect causes the gas and air to mix properly in the Venturi burner, resulting in a very hot but somewhat adjustable flame. To hot-start a Venturi forge, slowly turn on the gas again, and the heat will trigger ignition. (Hot-starting occurs when a forge is restarted while it is still hot after being temporarily shut down—for whatever reason. It is easiest to hot-start when the inside of the forge is still glowing red/yellow.)

The simplest Venturi forges to ignite are the ones with a piezoelectric (push-button) start. Simply turn on the gas, press the button, and it's going. If your forge doesn't have a push-button starter, you can easily install one on it. The starters are available from most of the better blacksmith/farrier suppliers.

Blower-Powered Gas Forge

Cold-starting a blower-powered gas forge is simple. Crumple up a piece of newspaper, light it and place it inside the forge, and leave the door open. Next, while the paper is still burning, turn on the blower(s) and slowly turn on the gas. When the gas ignites, adjust the air/gas as required.

Warning: Always remember to turn the air on first and then the gas. Failure to follow this extremely important safety rule will likely result in an explosion.

If the forge doesn't light, turn off the gas at once. Leave the blowers running for 3 to 5 minutes before attempting to relight. This 5-minute delay evacuates all of the gas from the inside of the forge and allows any exterior gas to dissipate, thereby preventing any explosion. When the 5 minutes are up, turn the blowers off and try again.

To hot-start, turn on the blowers and then the gas, and the tremendous heat inside the forge will instantaneously ignite the gas. If the forge isn't still glowing inside, simply place another piece of crumpled newspaper inside to see if it is hot enough to ignite the paper. If the paper ignites and while it is still burning, follow the correct start-up procedure for the forge you are using.

Warning: If the forge isn't hot enough to glow, never turn on the gas without a piece of paper burning inside it.

As you can see, there are some serious dangers in using a gas forge, but if the proper safety practices are followed, then there should be no serious problems.

Once the forge is lit, you must make some adjustments to the fire. There are three types of fires or atmospheres commonly found in a forge: oxidizing, neutral, and reducing. Of these, the least desirable (but, unfortunately, the most common) is the oxidizing atmosphere. Most smiths, when first starting out with a gas forge, do not know how to adjust the inside atmosphere to prevent the steel from scaling up and burning off. To adjust the flame, you must first understand what is going on inside the forge.

Adjusting the Atmosphere inside a Forge

Gas is flammable, but it needs air to burn. When an excessive amount of air is mixed with the gas, there is extra oxygen left over. This oxygen, in turn, oxidizes the steel inside the forge. The degree of oxidation can be gauged by the amount of scale produced on the steel. This scaling can be virtually eliminated by using a neutral atmosphere.

A neutral atmosphere contains just enough oxygen to allow total consumption of the gas and any extra oxygen. Since the fire consumes all of the oxygen, there is none left to oxidize the steel and cause scale and decarburization.

To get a neutral atmosphere, adjust both the gas pressure and the air flow into the forge until there are equal amounts of gas and oxygen present, and the forge is at its hottest point. There is no excess gas burning outside the forge, and the forge should emit a steady, well-tuned "hum." The interior of the forge should be a bright red/yellow. Steel placed inside a neutral forge should have minimal (if any) scale and an even heat.

You should monitor the amount (volume) of gas and air to maintain the smooth operation of the forge and allow quicker adjustments as the inside temperature changes. The correct proportions run approximately 12 to 1 air to fuel, depending on the particular design and type of forge and its temperature at the time. As the forge heats up, less air blast is required to sustain combustion and heat.

Warning: When operating a neutral atmosphere, do not exceed the manufacturer's recommended pressure or, if you are using the plans outlined in this book, do not exceed 7 to 9 pounds per square inch (psi) of gas or LPG pressure. Serious health hazards or injuries can result if you fail to follow this or any other safety outline. These forges are only as safe as those who operate them.

A reducing atmosphere is difficult to establish and use safely. It produces a far greater amount of carbon monoxide gas than the neutral atmosphere because of the combustion of excess gas outside the forge. If you foresee using a reducing fire on a regular basis, your ventilation system must be able to take care of the carbon monoxide.

For a reducing fire, first get a neutral fire and then introduce a little more gas into the forge. This should result in a small blast of red/orange flame from the forge opening. This is fine. If there is any straw yellow flames or if you smell unburned gas, turn down the gas pressure immediately! You are introducing far too much gas, and this is dangerous.

In a reducing atmosphere, there is no oxidation of the steel, and while it isn't as hot as the neutral setting, there is more than enough heat for most forging operations. I use this setting when working steels that oxidize more than normal, such as Vasco Wear and L-6.

Now that you are familiar with the safe and sane operation of a gas forge, we can proceed to the forging processes.

FORGING RICHER ALLOYS

As I mentioned before, you must master all of the basic hand-forging processes before using advanced techniques effectively. These advanced techniques include fullering—both single- and double-grooved—upsetting, jump welding, forging high-speed tool steels, stainless steels, air-hardening steels, and other processes that are difficult in a coal-fired forge.

Don't get me wrong; I'm not trying to sell coal forges short. Smiths have used them for centuries with great results. But a gas fire has no fire maintenance, clinkers, or other problems that are common with coal. I love my coal-fired forges. In my opinion, there is none better for pattern-welding and general smithing. The contorted heat in a small area has its advantages over the larger, evenly heated areas in a gas forge.

But before we cover advanced techniques, let's cover how to forge the more sophisticated alloys available These alloys include the richer high-speed tools steels, the air-hardening steels, and the stainless steels. All of these produce a first-rate blade that can outperform the simpler carbon steel alloys more commonly used by smiths. However, the price for this superiority is measured in time spent and difficulty in forging.

Perhaps the most difficult alloys to forge are the air-hardening alloys, followed closely by the stainless steels. Both of these families can produce top-quality blades, but the process is considerably slower than with a simpler carbon steel. The richer tool-and-die steels make wonderful blades, and they work more easily than the stainless or air-hardening steels.

Warning: Some of the richer alloys contain chromium and other metals that—when heated to the temperatures we will be working with—emit toxic fumes. A well-vented and properly installed hood in a well-ventilated shop area is a requirement for working with these metals, and I strongly recommend a respirator rated for fumes. Also, proper face/eye protection should be worn at all times.

Forging Air-Hardening Steels

Air-hardening steels, such as A-2 or D-2, are best worked very slowly. These alloys tend to be red hard and resist moving under the hammer. This is because most of the alloys were designed to be used in either hot-cutting or other operations where heated materials are worked. For the smith, this means that the steel remains harder at a higher temperature, and it gives a finer cutting edge on a knife.

When forging air-hardening steels, there are three things to remember.

1. *Do not rush the process*. Where it may take 15 minutes to forge a blade from carbon steel, it may take 45 minutes to an hour to do the same amount of work on an air-hardening alloy.

2. *Working time, or the time the steel remains in the working temperature range, is reduced*. Because the working ranges are narrower, these alloys are much more exact in terms of actual forging time versus heat loss.

3. *Most importantly, working temperatures of these alloys are quite different than those to which most smiths are accustomed*. There are two ranges, one on each side of the critical temperature. The low-temperature ranges are from 1200 to 1500 degrees F, depending on the particular alloy (check the mill specifications on the melt you are using for further information). This is the austenite forging range (aus-forging), and, while it does produce the finest blade in most alloys, some cannot be forged using these temperatures. Here again, check mill specs. The upper forging range runs from 2200 down to 1700 degrees F, again depending on the alloy. Become familiar with the alloys so you will know the temperature ranges of these steels.

The temperature ranges are determined by the hardening process of the alloys, which are air-hardening. The normal hardening process for these alloys is that carbide (cementite) forms austenite and then crystallizes into martensite when the critical temperature is reached. This can cause problems when hot-working these alloys. Having a blade harden up under the hammer can be very hazardous. To prevent this from occurring, work within the ranges of the alloys you have chosen.

If you are aus-forging, never let the steel reach or exceed the critical temperature for the alloy you're working with. If you are working in the higher ranges (general forging), never let the temperature decrease below the critical temperature while you are working the steel. This causes the steel to start hardening, and that can be damaging to your blade, your anvil, and you.

When forging an air-hardening steel, you should warm your tools and the anvil surface because these alloys tend to be touchy when it comes to being brought out of a hot forge, placed down on a stone-cold anvil, and hit with a cold hammer. The preheating can be done with a thick (1 inch or so) square steel plate (mine is 1 x 6 x 6 inches) that is heated to a dull red, laid onto the anvil surface, and left there to warm it. After the plate has cooled a bit, I place my hammer on top to warm it as well. You do not want to burn or scorch the handle, so be careful as to how you place the hammer.

Even a slight amount of warming is better than none at all. Since the sheer mass of the anvil will act as heat sink to prevent it from overheating, there isn't any reason not to preheat prior to any forging operations. I preheat just prior to removing the steel for the first time and then start to work. This prevents any excessive thermal shock from occurring when the steel is placed on the anvil. If the room temperature is below 60 F, the air should be heated or the work postponed until it is a bit warmer. I have had blades warp and crack when pulled from the forge on a cold (40 F) day and exposed to the chilly air.

The ability to maintain consistent temperature and heat is a major advantage of gas forges over coal-fired ones when heating air-hardening steels. You do not want excessive hot or cold spots in an air-hardening alloy because these cause stress in the steel. While the thermal sensitivity of air-hardening alloys may seem like a major drawback, it can be dealt with once you are accustomed to working with these materials.

In forging, the steel may oxidize and scale. To prevent this from occurring, use a neutral atmosphere and a nonscaling compound. These compounds are available from most industrial tool steel suppliers, or they can be made from ground anhydrous borax and applied like welding fluxes. Even easier, you can dissolve laundry borax (20 Mule Team Borax) in water to form a saturated solution and then dip and air-dry the steel until it is well coated. Do not use the water/borax solution on hot steel because this can cause cracking. Use it for the starting coat and then apply a little anhydrous borax as required to keep the metal coated.

These compounds form a barrier between the atmosphere inside the forge and the surface of the steel, thereby preventing any oxidation from taking place. Their use does not affect any forging processes; in fact, they reduce excessive decarburization and surface scaling to the point that the final forging appears cleaner and easier to finish.

NOTE: This and other nonscaling compounds can eat into the refractories used in gas forges. To prevent these compounds from making contact with the forge's interior, place a small section of kiln shelf under the work. It's easier to remove a piece of shelf than to reline the entire forge.

After the forge has heated to a neutral atmosphere, preheat the anvil and hammers and then heat the steel by holding it against the open door of the forge while it progresses through the lower tempering color ranges into the black range. Put the steel inside the forge and bring up to the working temperature. By doing this you prevent thermal shock from occurring.

Some alloys require soaking at a given temperature to enable them to reach a uniform temperature throughout. Originally, this step allowed for the thicker industrial-sized steel stock to be worked without fear of cold-shears or crystalline cracks that often result from improper heating. Some alloys require a soak of 1 hour for each 1 inch of thickness. Generally for knife-maker sizes, a soak of 1 to 3 minutes is enough, given the same surface area versus volume. Since most of these richer air-hardening alloys contain elements that prevent or prohibit grain growth, this soaking in no way damages the steel. I think that soaking is a good idea, but some smiths get good results with no soaking at all.

When working with air-hardening steels, you will notice that the amount of force needed to move them is considerably greater than that used for carbon steels. This is especially true with D-2, which is infamous in bladesmithing circles for being hot-hard and difficult to forge.

Remember to keep the steel in the proper working ranges and do not rush the processes. There are no real shortcuts in the forging of an air-hardening steel. This is hard, dirty work that is best done on a power hammer for the most part. Save your arm for the finer finishing touches of hand forging. All in all, most of the techniques used in bladesmithing can be used with good results on the air-hardening steels.

Annealing these steels is a bit more difficult than with most other alloys simply because they are air-hardening. Most annealing processes result in a hardened blade, so simply letting the blades air-cool is out of the question.

The standard industry method for annealing these steels is a furnace-cool process that takes a considerable amount of time, usually at a rate of 20 degrees an hour down to 900 degrees F. And since this method requires a thermostatic control on the forge, it is beyond the capabilities of most bladesmiths. But there is a way to get annealed air-hardening steels, and that is by using what I call a hot box.

Hot Box

A hot box is a heavy sheet iron/mild steel box with a secure lid, filled with clean, sifted hardwood ashes, demarcation lime (used for marking playing fields), or a fine-powdered charcoal. Some smiths swear that they get a better anneal with charcoal than with anything else. How this works is beyond me, but I suspect that the charcoal may smolder and hold a greater amount of heat longer. I haven't tried it, but it should work.

The box is made from 1/8-inch thick plate welded together to form a box. Mine is 8 x 8 x 24 inches with a hinged lid and is filled with lime.

A hot box holds in the heat for a long time. This prevents the steel from making contact with the surrounding air, resulting in a gradual reduction in temperature and a proper annealing. It is also advisable to anneal other alloys in a hot box. This slow cooling prevents any possible stresses from building up in the steel and causing problems later on.

To use, heat the steel to the proper temperature and then bury the blade in the box, completely covered by the insulating medium. Leave it undisturbed until the steel is cool. It may take 12 to 18 hours or longer for the steel to cool enough to be handled barehanded, and this has to be taken into consideration when planning work schedules.

Forging Stainless Steels

There has been much controversy over stainless versus high-carbon steels. Smiths have debated the attributes of each for decades, with no real victory on either side of the argument. There is no perfect steel for every application, so comparing a stainless steel to a carbon steel is like comparing apples to oranges.

For some reason, stainless steel has received a bad reputation. Of course, not all stainless steels are suited for cutlery applications, but neither are all carbon steels. And you don't hear the same complaints against carbon steels that you hear about the stainless ones.

I believe that the prejudice of a select vocal few, who over the years have spoken out against stainless steels, has made almost everyone believe that stainless is the kiss of death for edge-holding and forging. Nothing could be further from the truth. Metallurgically speaking, if an alloy has enough carbon to properly harden, then it can hold an edge. Carbon steel is a simple alloy that holds an edge, and most of the cutlery alloys have a carbon content of 0.60 to 1.25 percent.

There is no reason that a high-carbon, stainless-steel alloy with the same amount of carbon shouldn't take at least the same degree of sharpness and hold it for just as long—if not longer—as a simple carbon steel. Actually, in theory, since stainless steels tend to be higher in corrosion-resistance, the edge should hold up better because microscopic rusting does not take place as quickly or as severely as it does on a carbon-steel blade.

For most applications, no discernable difference can be found between the performance of stainless and high-carbon steels. Stainless does have a tendency to be a bit on the brittle side, and it doesn't withstand shocks and vibrations as well as some carbon steels. But carbon steel in a wet, damp, or saltwater environment doesn't take long to become a piece of rust with a nice grip on it.

Forging Peculiarities of Stainless

While I wouldn't use 440 C for a broadsword, neither would I use 5160 for a diving knife. The steel must suit the purpose of the blade, and whether to use a stainless or a carbon steel is a matter of choice and practicality.

Forging stainless does present some new problems for the smith. Mostly these involve cracks, working temperatures, and grain growth. Also there is a strong tendency for stainless to absorb impurities from the surrounding fire, so a clean coke, charcoal, or gas fire should be used when working this material.

There is another important factor that is peculiar to stainless: the shape of the bar and the condition of the surface prior to forging. Stainless has a tendency to be touchy when it comes to square corners and abrupt changes in cross sections. Square corners of the bar should be broken or rounded (slightly radiused) to prevent overheating. Also, when forging, slightly rounded corners prevent overstressing of the steel.

As for the surface condition, if you are using hot-rolled material (I cannot see using any surface-ground stock because it is too expensive), you have to deal with the bark, or the outer surface that has to be removed from the outside of the bars. These hot-rolled bars can have numerous flaws on the surface, such as skin rollovers, roller markings, and maybe even grain separation of the outer surface. These can cause serious problems and have to be removed prior to forging. It takes only a few minutes to remove these imperfections, and a smooth surface is a must in order to prevent any cracking. Cracking is better prevented than corrected later.

Tooling

Cutting stainless steel to length presents a problem unique to this family of alloys. Most stainless steels do not cut well with a cutting torch. So use either a band saw or abrasive cut-off saw, or score the bar and break it under a power hammer or in a vise. Regardless of the cutting technique, the cut surface has to be smoothed to prevent cracks.

The condition of the hammer and anvil faces is important when forging stainless, as any nicks or sharp corners can set up stresses, and cracking results from these as well. Your hammers must be properly crowned, and no sharp anvil corners should come in contact with the steel while it is being worked. The anvil surface must also be smooth, with no bad nicks to cause surface irregularities or cracking.

When starting out, you should preheat the anvil and tools just as you did to prevent stress-cracking in air-hardening steel. The surface must be preheated to a higher degree than for air-hardening alloys. I strongly suggest that the hammer and anvil be warmed regularly on the warming plate throughout the forging process just to be safe.

Temperature Ranges

Another peculiarity of stainless steel is the working ranges. While most of the mill specifications give a forging range of 2100 to 1900 degrees F, depending on the exact alloy, these are too high for hand forging. These temperatures are used for drop forging where the steel is struck by power hammers weighing several tons or more. These hammers strike only a few times, with the steel flowing into the shape of the hammer dies from the tremendous forces involved. For hand forging, the repeated impact of the smith's hammer adversely affects the steel's structure, while the higher temperature encourages excessive grain growth. These problems can be prevented by working at a lower temperature.

I have had good results working in the 1700 to 1900 degrees F ranges (the cherry red to orange ranges). While this means that the material will be on the red-hard side, it is no worse than working D-2 or a similar alloy.

Working in these ranges does take considerable effort and time, but you avoid most of the inherent problems with stainless.

To work the steel, preheat before placing it into the forge. This prevents any excessive shocks from damaging the steel's structure. Bring the temperature up slowly and soak for 3 to 5 minutes at approximately 1400 degrees F prior to starting.

Forging a Stainless Blade

I suggest that the blade be forged first, starting with the tip and working back toward the tang. Do not completely forge to shape because this is asking for problems. Rather, leave a nice rounded shape to the blade's tip, making certain that the corners are completely forged down. Take care here to avoid any piping or overlapping that could result in a ruinous longitudinal crack. With the blade forged to shape, proceed to the tang.

Forging a narrow tang on a stainless blade must be done with great care, making certain that there are no sharp corners, nicks, or other sudden changes in section. There must be an even radius at the junction between the ricasso and tang to prevent any stress buildups from occurring.

The next step is forging in the edge bevels, making certain that they are smooth and even. Stainless does have a tendency to warp in heat treating if the bevels aren't even. Since temperature control is vital to the successful forging of this steel, I heat the blade edge-up in my forge or from the back (spine towards the burner) in a gas forge in order to keep the edge from becoming overheated. This works for a single-edged blade, but on a double edge, the edges heat up before the thicker center, which causes problems.

To deal with this, I suggest that the blade be worked carefully and heated evenly to prevent any grain separation from occurring. Grain separation is where each individual crystal of the steel starts to pull apart from the ones surrounding it. It can range from very small separations that appear as a frosted effect to severe pits and holes. It can be prevented by working carefully at the proper temperature.

Annealing Stainless

After the forging is completed, begin annealing as soon as possible to prevent stresses. Annealing stainless takes a higher temperature and a more even heat than the richer alloys do. The temperature involved is in the 1400 to 1550 degrees F range, and a soak of 1 to 3 minutes is advised at this temperature to ensure an even, deep heat. If required, the blade should be straightened prior to the soaking heat. After soaking, place the hot blade into the hot box and allow to cool slowly and undisturbed.

FORGING HIGH-SPEED STEELS

High-speed tools steels, such as M-2, are easier to forge than the other two steel families, but they still present some difficulties. This is primarily because these alloys were designed to resist softening at higher temperatures and tend to be red hard. They were alloyed for tooling used in heavy machining, and a great deal of heat can build up in machining operations. This means the smith has a harder time working these steels, but they do result in a better blade.

Most of the working ranges are in the cherry red colors, although some of the alloys, M-2 especially, benefit from aus-forging. This lower temperature working refines an already superior grain structure even further, resulting in excellent edge-holding capability.

Alloys like the O series tend to be sensitive to excessive heat, and they may be a little red short. (Red short is where the steel falls apart at a light cherry to red/yellow heat, which is common in the richer alloys and wrought.) Care must be taken to avoid excessive heat and working in the higher ranges.

While the O alloys tend to be crack-prone, others seem to hold together no matter what. Cracks and warpage can be prevented by:

1. preheating properly;
2. avoiding radical changes in sections;
3. working within the proper ranges;
4. keeping a slight radius on all corners of the forging.

You can deal with the red-hard problem by two methods. The first is to use a power hammer. The second, if you prefer to hand forge entirely, is to use a slightly heavier hammer. Going up 1 pound from a 3-pound hammer can help overcome the problem. This can be tiring to those who are not accustomed to using a heavier hammer, and it may take some getting use to. But it does move steel.

The actual working of tool-and-die steels is like a cross between working stainless and air-hardening steels. Some scale rather badly, so an antiscaling compound should be used. To prevent stress from building up, forge in the same radii as for a stainless blade and work the blade as little as possible. Overworking these alloys damages the grain structure.

Anneal as you did for air-hardening steels, place in a hot box, and allow to cool undisturbed.

All in all, the richer alloys are not for the beginning smith. Some of these alloys are a pain to work, while others are a pleasure. Almost any steel can be forged to some degree, and mostly it is the smiths themselves who make the difference. Since smithing is, for the most part, instinctive, the ability to read the steel is a key asset. Knowing each alloy's limits and knowing when to keep going are part of being a good bladesmith.

Now that you are familiar with working the higher-alloy, cutlery-grade steels, we can proceed onto other, more advanced techniques.

ADVANCED TECHNIQUES

Although a few basic techniques will be used (drawing out, upsetting, edge-forming, and packing), the emphasis here is on new techniques. These new techniques include the distal taper, offset and in-line fullering, median rib-in blades, and others. You'll learn how to use them to forge better, lighter, and more refined blades, while allowing a greater degree of diversity in design and execution.

Distal Taper

There has been a great deal of excitement in the custom cutlery community about the distal taper in a hand-forged blade. This is simply a tapering in thickness from the blade's ricasso to its tip. This taper may also extend from the ricasso back into the tang.

In theory, this taper allows for a lighter blade while still maintaining a great degree of strength and flexibility because of the steel taper's tendency to distribute the strains of a bend along an arc, similar to the way a fishing rod bends.

In practice, while it does work, it is a moot point. In my opinion, no one in his right mind would even try to place that much strain on a blade. I put a distal taper in most of my blades simply because it makes them lighter and easier to balance. The less weight on the end of a knife (or sword for that matter), the easier it is to balance and handle properly. Regardless of the reason, a distal taper is a nice extra on a custom blade—

DISTAL/NONDISTAL BLADES

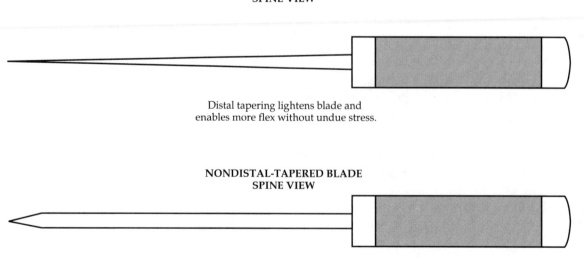

DISTAL-TAPERED BLADE
SPINE VIEW

Distal tapering lightens blade and
enables more flex without undue stress.

NONDISTAL-TAPERED BLADE
SPINE VIEW

A nontapered blade is heavier, more
difficult to balance, and a bit more prone to breakage.

one that is often expected by sophisticated cutlery enthusiasts.

The taper is not easy to forge in because it requires a great deal of practice with a hammer to get the taper even and equal on both sides of the blade without leaving hammer marks.

When forging the distal taper, it is best to do so before the blade is forged to shape because this process lengthens the steel. Usually, this lengthening is between 10 and 25 percent or more, depending on the degree of taper and the thickness/width of the steel. This should be taken into account when cutting steel for blade length. I start my distal taper prior to the basic shaping of the steel. This way it is to length before I start on the tip and bevels.

Starting with the point (which usually thickens while forging to shape because the steel compacts during this process), taper the blade toward the point. A smooth hammer face makes finishing up easier. The hammer blows should be well placed, leaving few if any marks on the steel surface. There is some tendency for the blade to taper on one side (the hammer side) more than the other. To even out the taper, lift the blade at a slight angle to compensate for this effect. Working back toward the ricasso, strike even, overlapping blows with the hammer face. If there is a great deal of material to be moved, a light series of blows with the cross peen, followed with blows by the hammer face, makes this quicker to accomplish.

This process can be done using a normal forging heat, as the blade is still, for the most part, unfinished. Any grain growth will be refined as the blade is worked.

The blade should now appear to have a basic taper extending from the ricasso toward the point. The taper should stop a short distance above the guard area to facilitate a tight fit of the guard and blade without any unsightly gaps.

If you wish, the same process can be used for tapering the tang as well, giving a slimmer look to the finished knife. This is best on a full tang knife because there is no reason to do a distal taper on a hidden tang. As with the blade, the taper should be even and equal on both sides of the tang. The taper should start at the guard and work back (there is no need for a tight, even fit on this side of the guard, as any gaps will be covered by the grip scales).

A distal taper works well with a hollow-ground blade but is best with a flat-ground cross section. Both types benefit from the taper—it gives a lighter blade while still maintaining a great deal of strength.

Fullering

Fullering (grooving) was used for centuries to lighten and stiffen blades. (It reinforces or stiffens the blade in much the same way as an I-beam does in building construction.) Fullering also helped to conserve materials. Today, conservation of steel/iron may not seem like a necessity, but back when bladesmiths smelted their own iron and made their own steel, every bit saved was that much more to use on something else.

Today, not many fullered blades are being made, be they factory or custom. Most people fail to realize how much a well-done fuller improves the look of a blade.

Yet some makers agree with me about fullers and use them to accent and lighten their blades. Mostly, these grooves are simply ground in with a small-diameter wheel on a belt grinder. This isn't the best way to go about doing this, but it is the easiest. Nevertheless, to be at its best, a fuller has to be forged in. (One exception to this is the Japanese blade, which had the fullers—"hi," pronounced hee—scraped into the blade with a tool similar to a draw knife.) There are several ways to go about fullering a blade, using various fullering tools. (These tools were described in Chapter 1.)

Fullering is a middle step in blade forging that takes place after the blade is forged to shape and before the edge bevels are forged in and the edge packed.

Forging in a single groove is probably the easiest one to do, and there are several ways to accomplish it. If you do not have top/bottom tooling, you can obtain the same effect by using a top tool and a piece of round stock. With this method, you make the groove by simply placing the top fuller where you wish the groove to start at the ricasso and lightly hammering the tool into the steel, resulting in a shallow depression. Move the tool down the blade, slightly overlapping the depression, and strike again. Work down the blade until the fuller is to the desired length.

Work carefully to get the fuller centered and straight in its length, or the resulting groove will result in an off-center blade and severe warpage. Some minor corrections can be made when the fuller is forged full width and depth—but only minor ones—so get the groove right the first time.

After completing the lighter forging, go back over the groove with the fullering tool and strike the fuller to full depth, approximately 80 percent of the desired depth of the fuller. Remember, you will be fullering the other side of the blade and that will also thin out the webbing between the bottoms of the fullers.

The thickness of the steel at the bottom of the groove is very

Damascus dagger with fullered blade made by the author. Photo by Stephen Jacobson

SINGLE FULLER USE

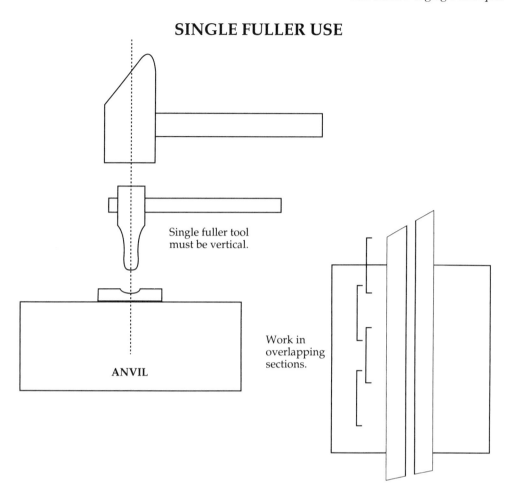

Single fuller tool
must be vertical.

ANVIL

Work in
overlapping
sections.

Fuller must remain properly centered.

important. If it is too thin, you may break through the web into the fullering when the other side is grooved. There is also the possibility that when the groove is smoothed and cleaned, you could cut through then as well. I suggest that one-third of the starting blade thickness be left between the bottom of the groove and the opposite (unfullered) side. This allows enough thickness for the opposite groove to be forged in with little danger of breaking through. This translates into 3/32 inch for a 1/4-inch blade, 1/16 inch for a 3/16-inch blade, and so forth. Also, if you are planning on fullering a distal-tapered blade, make certain that there is enough steel present for a good fuller to be forged in.

When the fuller is completed on one side, forge one on the opposite side. This fuller is the same length and width of the first one. One situation that will confront you immediately is how to keep the finished fuller from collapsing when the second one is forged in. After all, you have no bottom tooling to back up the fuller and prevent its flattening out.

The answer is simple. To provide extra support, use a section of round

ROD/FULLER

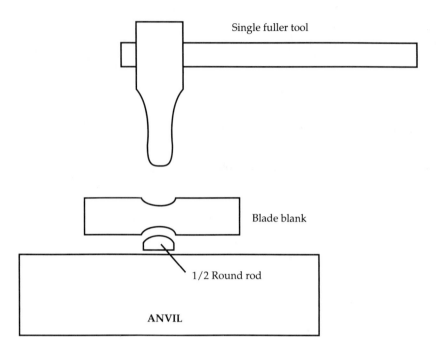

Single fuller tool

Blade blank

1/2 Round rod

ANVIL

Again, make certain that the fullering
tool is in the proper position.

bar stock, either ground or cut in half lengthwise, that is the same radius as the fuller. Place the rod flat side down on the anvil and position the blade, fullered side down, on top of the rod, with the rod resting inside the finished fuller. Cool off the rod regularly so it doesn't overheat and soften, which would defeat its purpose. I cool off the rod every time the steel is returned to the fire. This way I know that the rod is always cool enough to do its job.

The rod should be the same length as the fuller it supports, but if this isn't possible, a good rule to follow is the length of the rod should equal the length of the area to be worked in a single heat plus the length of the fuller being used. For example: if the tool is 2-inches long and the working area is 4 inches, the rod should be 6 inches in length. Of course, you have to advance this sectional rod down the blade so that it is under the section being forged.

As the fuller approaches final depth and width, make sure there is enough steel left between the bottoms of the grooves to allow you to blend and clean up either by hand or with power tools. The steel thickness should be at least 1/16 inch to remove tool marks, scale, or other surface irregularities.

This same basic technique can be used for forging in off-center fullers,

FINISHED FULLER CROSS SECTIONS

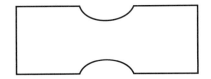

Finished, fullered cross section prior to edge forming
(centered fullers)

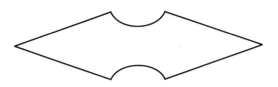

Fullered and edge-packed cross section
(centered fullers)

OFF-CENTER FULLER CROSS SECTIONS

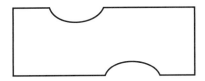

Off-centered, fullered section prior to edge packing

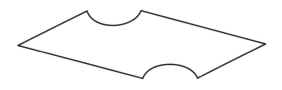

Off-centered fullers w/edges formed

such as those used in the Persian *qama* or the Caucasian/Georgian *kindjals*. Actually, this is the only way that I know to make off-center fullers without elaborate tooling.

If you are planning on doing several fullered blades, you should use a top/bottom tool, which is not as tricky as the process above. Since these tools work both sides of the blade at once, it not only speeds the process but automatically aligns both grooves. The disadvantages of using this tool are that it requires dexterity and timing, and it has a tendency to wave around from the effects of the fullering blows. You can easily correct the effects of this waving after the fullering is completed or, if they are severe enough, as the blade is being worked.

To use the top/bottom tool, place it upon the anvil as required by your particular tool's design, position the blade between the top and bottom die, center the top/bottom tool in position, and strike a light blow to set the tool and indent a guide mark.

To make aligning the fuller easier, draw a centerline down the blade with a soapstone marker. This helps you in positioning the blade between the dies. The soapstone marks should last long enough to indent the length of the blade being worked.

After the lighter indenting marks are forged in, start at the base of the blade and use full-power blows, forging the fuller to its full depth. For a smooth fuller, you must overlap the work areas. Also, check the depth of the groove and the thickness of the web between the grooves to ensure that there are no breakthroughs. Here, as well, there should be approximately 1/16 inch of thickness.

Fullering makes blades lighter, stiffer, and better looking. Fullered blades should be appreciated not only for their function, but for their beauty as well.

Median Ribs

For one or more reasons, bladesmiths from all cultures have put median ridges in their blades throughout time. The Arab *jambiya,* the European spear, and even some later-period swords had median ribs running the length of their blades.

Some smiths don't like to put them in because blades with median ribs are more difficult to forge, and they require special tooling. These tools are the tenon tool described in Chapter 1 and the rib/ricasso tool described below.

The rib/ricasso tool is similar to the tenon tool, but it is narrower to make a sharper incision at the point where the rib is to start. This allows for a smooth and even cut in where the ricasso joins the cutting edge. By using this tool, you can forge a smooth transition from a flat ricasso into

FULLER TOOL

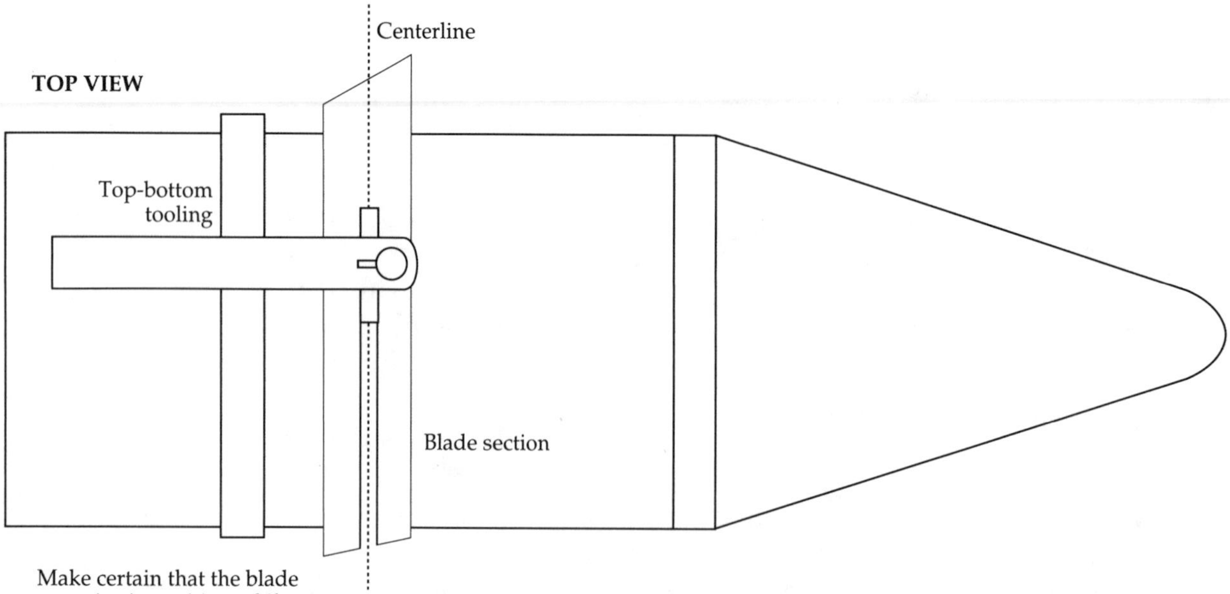

TOP VIEW

Centerline

Top-bottom tooling

Blade section

Make certain that the blade remains in position while fullers are being formed.

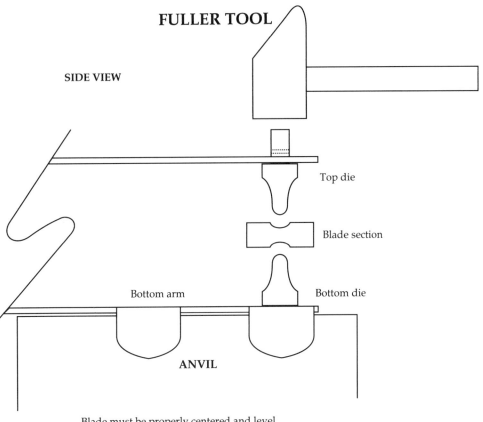

FULLER TOOL

SIDE VIEW

Top die

Blade section

Bottom arm

Bottom die

ANVIL

Blade must be properly centered and level
to form the fuller properly.

the blade bevels and center rib as well. To form a ribbed blade, I strongly suggest that you start from round stock and forge in a tenon die.

For most medium width/thickness swords, 1- to 1 1/4-inch round works very well. For daggers, use either 3/4- or 7/8-inch round. For the center rib, use a 3/16-inch diameter tenon tool for daggers and light swords, and a 1/4-inch tenon for full-sized swords and larger blades. Actually, you can use any size you want but make certain that you have a corresponding rib/ricasso tool for whatever size you choose. The tooling sizes the steel as it is being worked.

To forge, start with a full cherry red heat on a section of the round stock. Start flattening the bar at one end and work down the bar in sections as it is flattened. Do not completely flatten the sections, as this can ruin the blade. Flatten the steel until the rib is seen and move on to another section. Continue until you have formed the length of the bar to the ricasso area. Next, use the rib/ricasso tool to form the ricasso and work on the tang until it is 90 percent finished. Then return to the blade. Using the previously forged rib as a guide, resume work at the point and work back toward the ricasso until the blade has a center rib and a thickness of 3/32 to 1/8 inch. It should have a cross section as shown above.

Make certain that the rib remains centered and the areas are smoothly

RIBBED CROSS SECTION

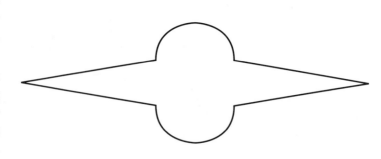

Center-ribbed cross section

blended into one another. This blending is crucial, especially for the ricasso/edge-bevel area.

The point can be formed during the forging or after the rib has been forged. Either way works, but I prefer to form the point as the rib is formed, as this eliminates reworking the rib, which is required if the point is forged after the rib.

Since the edges of a ribbed blade are already considerably thinner than the center section, you don't really need to pack the edges. Actually, I think it would be useless because the heavy forging used to shape the blade from a round bar should have made the crystalline structure very fine already. But if you feel that the blade must be packed, protect it from hammer blows by making a packing plate that fits over the anvil's face.

These plates can be made from any steel, although one made of carbon-tool steel (such as 1060) properly hardened and tempered to a blue color lasts longer than a softer, unhardened mild-steel plate.

To use the plate, place it onto the face of the anvil and position the blade so that its edge is on the plate and its rib is alongside the edge of the plate.

When packing the edges, make certain that the blows are equal in number and placed on both sides of the edges and that none land on the center rib, which can severely deform the rib and ruin the blade. Throughout the packing, hold the blade straight.

Although the radius (half-round) rib is the most common, you can use octagonal or triangular center ribs if you choose. Simply make the tooling to form these shapes and work them as described above.

In conclusion, center ribbing works best with the simpler, more forgiving alloys, such as 5160, the 10xx series, and S-type steels. I have had some success with the richer steels, but I don't recommend your using them for ribbing until you have become more familiar with their working peculiarities. If overworked, the heavy center section and the thinner edges can cause warping and cracking.

Cleaning up a center-ribbed blade involves a good deal of hand labor. While some power tools could be used, it is best to hand-sand the blade using various grits of wet/dry paper and a lot of time. You can save yourself a great deal of trouble by coating the steel with antiscale

PACKING PLATE

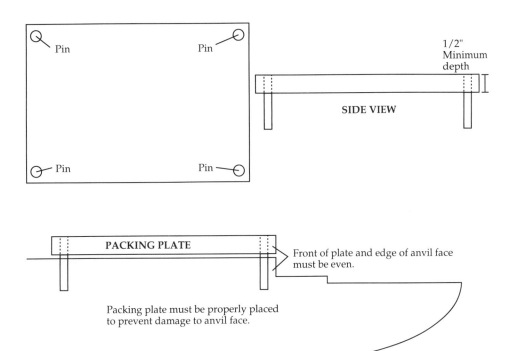

compound while it is being worked. Since this prevents most surface imperfections from occurring, the surface is easier to clean.

Forging Curved, Double-Edged Blades

Forging a double-edged blade is easy, but forging a double-edged blade that is curved takes considerable practice and skill. But it is not impossible. As with most difficult tasks, the right tools make the process easier and more effective. One such tool is a smaller anvil stake that fits into the hardy hole on your anvil. This stake is simply a smaller anvil face used when forming the inside curve edge. For best results, forge the stake from either 1060 or 5160, and harden its face by drawing it to a spring temper. Of course, you can purchase a stake from a blacksmith supply, but they are expensive and difficult to find.

As for the size of the stake, I use several different sizes. The most commonly used size is a 2- x 2-inch square, and the second most used is a 2- x 4-inch rectangular-faced stake. The small stake works better on the more radical curved blades, while the longer-faced stake works better on a gentler curve in a longer blade. You'll probably end up with a selection of stakes as your studies advance.

The first step in making a curved, double edge is the rough shaping of the blade. These blades can be symmetrical or nonsymmetrical. Most of the classic curved blades have a more-or-less symmetrical curve on both sides of the evenly tapered blade. To start on one of these, forge much as you would for a double-edged dagger blade.

With the blade tapered, start packing and curving the edge. This is a critical segment of the forging, and it remains a hit-or-miss situation until you get the feel for this type of blade.

Remember that the blade should be curved, and the steel stretches away from the hammer on the side being worked. This stretching works to your advantage because the steel forms its own curve during the edge-packing.

To form the edges and the curve, start with a slight curve. (Deciding how much curve to use is trial-and-error at first until you have become more experienced at this.) Working the outer edge of the blade first puts more curvature into the blade. Do not worry about having too much curvature because working the inside bevel removes most of it. Work the outside edge until it is about half completed.

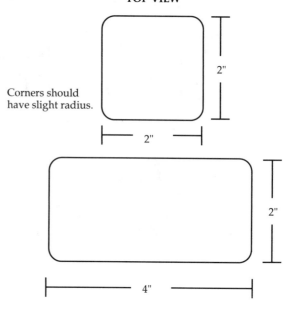

ANVIL FACE STAKE
SMALL FACE STAKE
TOP VIEW

Corners should have slight radius.

2"

2"

2"

4"

LARGE FACE STAKE
TOP VIEW

BOTH SIZES
SIDE VIEW

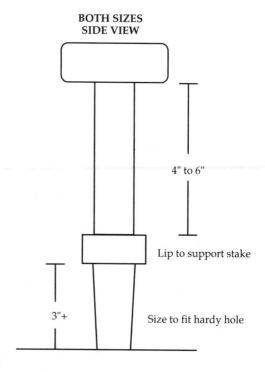

4" to 6"

Lip to support stake

3"+

Size to fit hardy hole

Then work on the inside bevel, using an anvil stake of the appropriate size, until it is about 75 percent finished. This leaves you enough steel on the edge to blend everything until the curves and the edge bevels are even and shaped.

With the inside edges packed, go back to the outer edge and prepare it for final packing. This curves the blade a bit more, but not as severely as the first course of heat. With the outer bevels forged, return once more to the inner edge for completion. You must move the blade around the surface of the stake until you have the best advantage with the hammer on the inner edge. As you are working, the steel stretches, slightly straightening the blade. When completed, the blade should have a nice even curve, with evenly forged edge bevels.

Putting a curve on a double edge takes considerable practice, but once you have become used to the tools and the techniques, it isn't that hard. You may have to do some further refining of the shape, and this can be done in one of several ways.

The first and most effective is to simply hammer on the inside or outside edge bevels, depending on which way you want the steel to move. By doing this, you can change the curvature or the shape.

The second method involves working the blade edgeways on the anvil face or pad, depending on the desired effect. This is effective for cross sectional changes, but I do not advise it for radical changes in curvature.

The third method is working the blade over the anvil horn. I do not recommend this method except in extreme circumstances.

Forging Clipped Points

Making clipped or swaged points (such as on a Bowie knife) seems easy, but it requires a great deal of finesse and the right touch. Depending on the design and function of the blade, the clipped point can be short and stocky or long, even, and graceful.

When you start to forge in a clip, you will notice that the steel tends to fold over at the end of the bar, causing an overlapping pocket to form at the end. The steel behind the corner of the bar is compressed while the steel at the corners remains more or less unworked. This pocket is not only ugly, it also causes stress cracking and other difficulties. It can be prevented by radiusing the bar corners (removing the sharp corners so they don't thicken or bend into a fold), which makes moving the steel easier in this area.

For an even, graceful clip, such as that found on a Sheffield Bowie knife, I begin by working the spine edge of the bar into a taper (see above). You should make this as even and smooth as possible because the more refined the shape is at this stage, the better the results will be. I usually leave a "rounded square end" of 3/4 inch at the tip end of the bar to form a point later.

With the clip formed, flip the blade over and start to point the blade. NOTE: Keep the the clip taper flat against the anvil, or the forging will cause the clip to straighten and separate into two tapered sections, one on each side of the blade.

CLIPPED POINTS

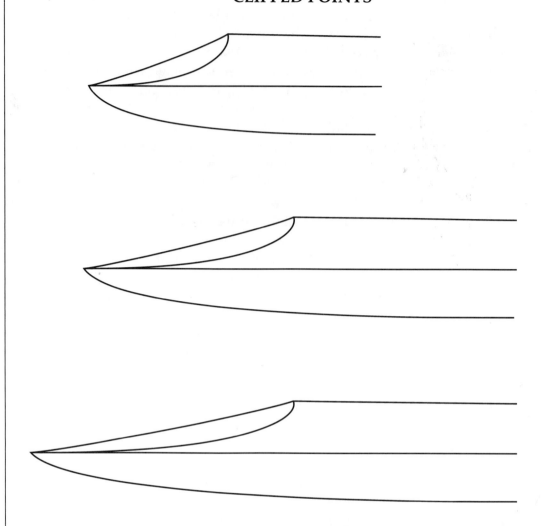

Clipped (swaged) points can run from short and stout
to long, slender, and graceful.

Working near the edge of the anvil to prevent any anvil scars, forge in the curved point, working from the corner of the bar, up the edge, and then back down again. You should round this edge, making certain that the clip taper remains in contact with the anvil.

Some upsetting of material occurs in this area, resulting in a noticeable difference in thickness between the spine and the worked tip area. You must correct this to form a proper tip. You can do this by using a hammer face, or, in severe circumstances, a light cross peening, followed by smoothing blows with a light hammer face.

By this point, you should have a nice profile of a clipped point blade, and final forging can be done at any point after this. Two factors to keep in mind are that the clip should be even and smooth throughout its entire length, and the bottom edge should meet the clip in a smooth arc that

SPINE TAPER

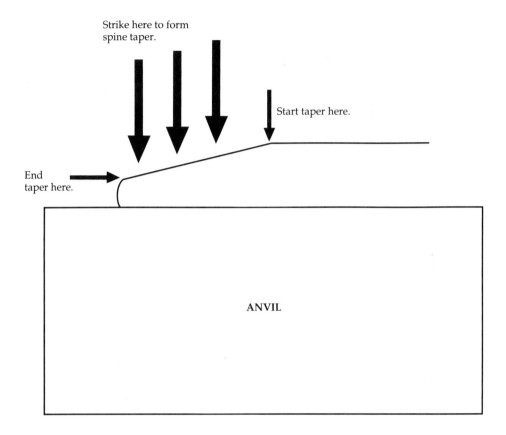

Strike here to form spine taper.

Start taper here.

End taper here.

ANVIL

forms a point in the center of the blade. After forging in the clip, pack the edges by the standard techniques.

Flame Blades

This is the most difficult blade design for any smith to do well. I know smiths with a lifetime of experience who will not even consider doing one. The wavy edges and even, sinuous curves are difficult to forge in evenly—and how do you pack the edges?

I have no idea how the sixteenth-century German *landscknechts* forged their flame-bladed *zweihander* (two-handed) swords, but I have developed some methods that are relatively quick and give a decent flame effect. The German mercenary soldiers believed that their flame blades inflicted more grievous wounds on their adversaries. Granted, they do have a larger cutting edge because of the blade's curves, and the curves themselves tend to make the blade bite deeper into the wound channel, but against armor I doubt that they gave any additional advantage.

To form the flame blade, shape a piece of steel into a slight taper and point. Start at the ricasso of the blade and form the first curve over a

BICK

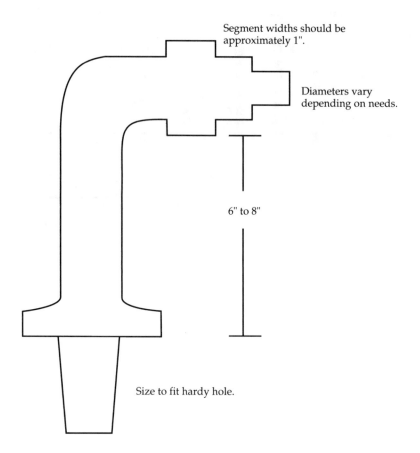

Segment widths should be approximately 1".

Diameters vary depending on needs.

6" to 8"

Size to fit hardy hole.

This bick allows for sizing various curves, bends, and other shapes.

small round section. I do not recommend using the conical horn of the anvil because its shape causes problems in the forming. I use a customized bick hardy (I put steps in the diameter so I can use it for different things) in the hardy hole.

After forming the bick, start on the first curve. Use light-to-medium blows to bend the blade over the bick. Heavy blows deform the steel. Turn the blade over and do the next curve on the opposite side. Take a small local heat to prevent the deformation of the first curve; again, use lighter than average blows to form this curve. Turn the blade back over once more and use a small local heat to forge in the third curve. Continue alternating the curves until completing the length of the blade. At the point, the tip should be centered with the line of the blade.

Straighten the blade and anneal prior to hardening. There is no need for further forging. The stretching of the steel during the forming of the blade accomplishes much the same thing.

Bending Forks

The easiest and most effective way of making a "flame" blade is by using bending forks. Bending forks are wrench-like devices that use hand pressure to bend and form steel. They can be easily made from medium-carbon steel. You should have a variety of sizes, and the tines should be heavy—3/8- to 1/2-inch round—so they won't bend. The longer the handles, the easier the bending is.

To use the bending forks, simply take a heat and place the forks on the blade. The forks should be wide enough to allow for the blade to be contacted in an offset manner. Position the fork and then bend the blade. You may have to clamp the blade in a heavy vise to get a solid hold and the desired bend. Work the forks up and down the length of the blade, evening out the flame effect and forming the blade as desired. This takes practice and you must know the limits of the steel that you are using.

NOTE: Don't use an alloy that is prone to warpage or other deformation during heat treating/tempering because these blades are difficult to correct once they are heat-treated.

A properly proportioned flame blade is both beautiful and deadly. Easier to balance than you'd expect, it is one blade I wouldn't want to face in the hands of a determined and motivated man. Flame blades are rare today, for reasons I don't understand. They have a long history, ranging from the Malaysian *kriss* to the Swiss *flamberge*.

Kopis Blades

Kopis are curved, double-edged swords of ancient Egypt and Greece. These blades are the all-time champions at chopping through just about anything. These classic close-combat blades handle extremely well and have extraordinary impact at close quarters. *Kopis* blades include the Indian *kukri* (made famous by the Nepalese Gurkha mercenaries who fight for the British Army), the Turkish *yataghan*, and others too numerous to mention.

These close-quarter blades are an effective compromise between a knife and a hand ax. The design has survived thousands of years of evolution and refinement into what I consider the ultimate close combat/survival knife. You can chop, cut, sever, and even dig holes with these blades. Look at the effectiveness of Alexander the Great's troops or the Gurkhas in the British Army, and you will see for yourself that in the right hands, a *kopis* blade is something to respect.

Lately, the modern knife world has rediscovered this ancient design. A look at the "new" blades being touted by some manufacturers shows them to be slightly modified copies of the old *kopis* blades. This should be an indication of how well this design works.

To forge this blade, simply widen the tip area as shown on the facing

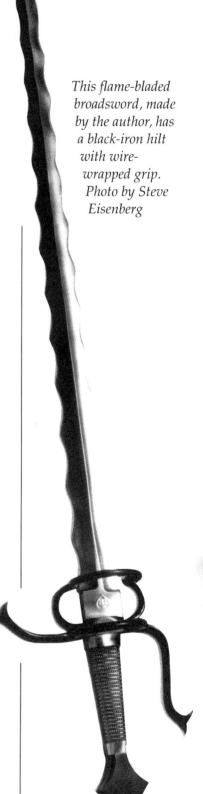

This flame-bladed broadsword, made by the author, has a black-iron hilt with wire-wrapped grip. Photo by Steve Eisenberg

This pair of kopis-style blades—one traditional, one modern—was made by the author. Photo by Stephen Jacobson

page. Keep the back edge as straight as possible because this should be straight when the blade is finished. You must pack the edges at this point because it is too difficult later. After widening the tip and straightening the back edge, forge the area where the inside curve will be. Make this area thinner than normal because it will thicken when the curve is formed. Heat the area to be curved and forge the curve in by forming over a bick or the anvil horn. The tip should be slightly forward of the centerline to bring the center of gravity forward and improve the chopping action for which these blades are noted. When the curve is completed, straighten if needed, anneal, and finish.

In closing, the techniques described in this chapter can be used as is or modified to make numerous other blades. The limits are up to the imagination of the individual smith. But no matter what you decide to make or how you choose to make it, make it the best that you can.

These little tricks or secrets (how I detest that word!) are useless if they are not properly executed. The mark of a good craftsman is not in how much he knows, but how well he knows how to do it.

WIDENING TIP

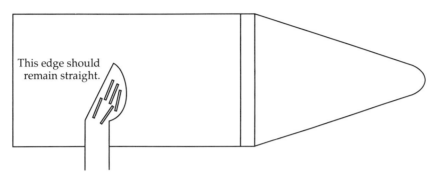

This edge should remain straight.

To widen tip, use peen of cross peen hammer and strike as shown.

FORGED CURVE AREA

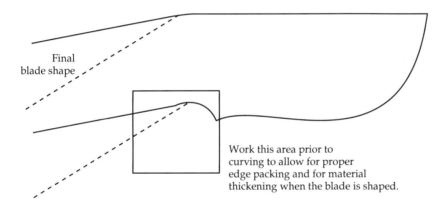

Final blade shape

Work this area prior to curving to allow for proper edge packing and for material thickening when the blade is shaped.

THE POWER HAMMER

The invention of the power hammer several centuries ago was a terrific labor- and time-saver for smiths. The older hammers ranged in size from small, one-man operations to the water-powered giants depicted in late medieval/early Renaissance woodcuts. But they all have one thing in common: they move a lot of metal very quickly. Even the smaller ones can do a lot more work than a smith working alone, while the larger ones can actually do more work in one day than a trained team of strikers can do in a week or more.

Although not for beginning smiths, a power hammer can be a great aid to the advanced craftsman. But, while it can reduce the amount of labor and time, it should not be viewed as a replacement for the basic skills needed in hand forging. There is no replacement for craftsmanship and pride in your work.

A smith does not have to have a power hammer, but it is a viable alternative to a trained apprentice—especially for those who work alone. Of course, you can do all of the work by hand, as I did for many years. But, if you have the space and the desire to get a power hammer, by all means do so. As with any machine, the key to using a power hammer is learning to operate it safely and efficiently.

Some forgers out there (and for the longest time I was one of them) believe that using a power hammer is, in a sense, cheating. Yet, these same forgers use electric belt grinders, drill presses, buffers, and other modern devices. So where do you draw the line? I believe that using a power hammer for heavy, monotonous work and doing the more delicate, skilled work by hand constitutes a hand-forged blade. A power hammer—or any tool—lets you save your time, energy, and skill for the more important steps in forging a top-quality blade.

There are many designs, makes, and models of power hammers from which to choose. These range from the old-fashioned mechanical ones to the state-of-the-art air-powered (pneumatic) machines that do a much better job than the older, less-efficient iron bangers. The pneumatic hammers are very expensive and not many people can afford them. So I shall deal with Little Giant mechanical hammers. While the design of these hammers may be different from the one you use, their shape and dies are all similar.

I use a 25- or 50-pound Little Giant for heavy grunt work, and they have saved me from endless hours of swinging a hammer. I still forge to shape and do all the other important steps by hand, but when it comes to drawing out tangs and lengthening Damascus billets prior to welding, I reach for a power hammer.

A power hammer can be intimidating to the uninitiated. I remember hearing all

LITTLE GIANT POWER HAMMER

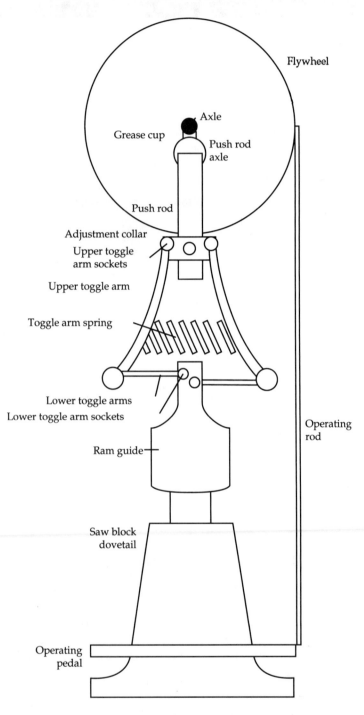

sorts of horror stories about blacksmiths who crushed fingers or lost hands and/or other body parts to these machines. Even after finding, restoring, and setting one up in my shop, I actually feared using it. Up until the time that it was serviceable, I felt safe. But when it was ready to be turned on, I had to come to grips with my fears—take the bull by the horns and go at it hammer and tongs (a little bladesmith humor). After all, I had my reputation to consider. So girding my strength, I turned to face the cause of my anguish.

So there I was, standing in front of "The Beast," whose face was glowing a rich, vibrant red, his hammer's motor whirring, and I squeamishly placed a glowing bar between the dies and timidly depressed the foot pedal. The hammer struck the steel, flattening it out in the blink of an eye. To my amazement, I was still alive! Looking at the still glowering machine, I no longer felt it was a mechanical demon from Hell awaiting its next victim. Nevertheless, I immediately checked all of my important parts. We had forged a new relationship.

While you should be very respectful and cautious when operating these (or any other) machines, you do not have to fear them. Granted, using one for the first time can be a bit scary, but any fear and intimidation you might have soon turns to satisfaction with the realization that this device can save you hours of labor. Plus it enables you to do work you couldn't consider doing by yourself. But no matter how well you know how to use a power hammer, never lose respect for it and act carelessly. This can lead to serious injury.

POWER HAMMER PARTS

To become familiar with a power hammer, you must first know what the various parts are and their uses.

Clutch

The clutch transfers the power from the rotating outer ring to the axle, which, in turn, rotates the flywheel, and that powers the ram, which does all the work. Clutches are wear-adjustable, and the adjustment levers are found inside the spider, which is attached to the axle. The clutch is activated by the tie rod, which is located on the side of the frame and extends down to the foot pedal.

Axle

At the back of the axle is a grease cup that must be filled with a top-quality grease to keep the machine running smoothly. I use a lithium grease, but just about any high-grade grease should work.

Oil Wells

The oil wells are located on the top of each journal block. These must

POWER HAMMER

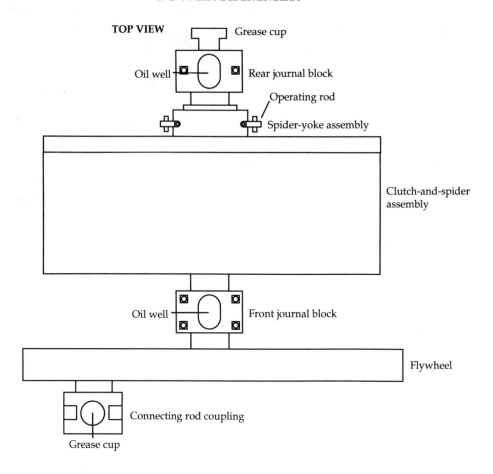

be filled with a heavy-weight motor oil, such as 30-weight, to keep the machine from seizing up. To keep the oil from running out, place a piece of felt in the bottom of the well. This felt acts as a wick and delivers a small amount of oil in a constant flow to the axle.

Flywheel

This part converts the axle's rotation to vertical movement, much like a piston rod running to a crankshaft. The grease cup at the junction of the flywheel and the push rod must be greased.

Push Rod

This heavy-duty, cylindrical rod attaches the flywheel to the toggle arm assembly. It also allows you to adjust the height of the machine's stroke. To adjust, loosen the nut that secures the push rod in a split collar at the top part of the upper toggle assembly. After adjusting, retighten the

POWER HAMMER

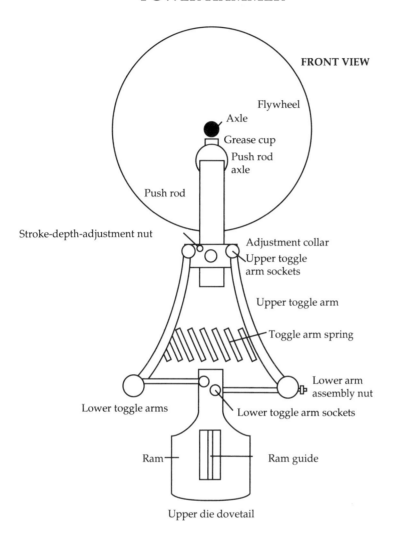

FRONT VIEW

Flywheel

Axle

Grease cup

Push rod axle

Push rod

Stroke-depth-adjustment nut

Adjustment collar

Upper toggle arm sockets

Upper toggle arm

Toggle arm spring

Lower arm assembly nut

Lower toggle arms

Lower toggle arm sockets

Ram

Ram guide

Upper die dovetail

UPPER POWER HAMMER ASSEMBLY
(FRONT RAM GUIDE REMOVED)

nut, and the hammer will operate at that setting unless otherwise adjusted. Most hammers have a range in which they operate without any adjustments needed. Any deviation is compensated for by the toggle action of the arms and spring.

Toggle Arms

The top toggle arms are held apart by the compression spring and should be kept well-oiled for smooth operation. There can be no adjustments to this section of the machine. The bottom toggle arms attach to the top arms and the ram below. These also should be kept well-oiled and require no adjustments. (NOTE: There are small oil wells in the tops of both toggle arms that should be oiled periodically while the machine is being used.)

Ram

This part holds the dies that strike the steel, and it should be kept well-lubricated in its keyway guides and toggle-arm junctions. I use a heavy grease in the keyway, as this cuts down on oil dripping onto the hot piece beneath. On the ram's bottom is the upper-die dovetail. The dies are held in place by wedges driven between the die and the dovetail.

UPPER/LOWER DIE DOVETAILS

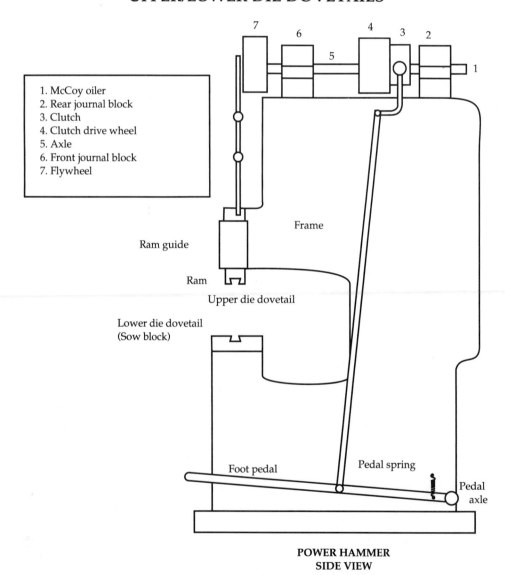

1. McCoy oiler
2. Rear journal block
3. Clutch
4. Clutch drive wheel
5. Axle
6. Front journal block
7. Flywheel

Frame

Ram guide

Ram

Upper die dovetail

Lower die dovetail
(Sow block)

Foot pedal

Pedal spring

Pedal axle

**POWER HAMMER
SIDE VIEW**

Sow Block

The sow block holds the lower die in place by the same dovetail/ wedge arrangement as the ram dovetail.

Foot Pedal

Depressing the foot pedal activates the power hammer. The pedal attaches to the tie rod that runs alongside the machine to the clutch assembly. This, in turn, causes the rotating outer wheel of the clutch assembly to move forward into the spider, which catches the outer wheel and sets the entire mechanism in motion. The foot pedal also regulates the speed and strength of the blows delivered, ranging from light and slow to fast and hard.

Dies

But what is it that makes power hammers so useful to the bladesmith besides striking the steel so hard? The answer lies in the dies used by the machine. The dies are the part of the hammer that actually comes in contact with the piece. They are available in different designs for different purposes. Some designs are highly specialized, while others can be used for a myriad of purposes.

Planishing Dies

The most common dies are called planishing (also anvil or flattening) dies. They look like hammer faces, with a slight dome to them and a radius on the edges to keep them from forming sharp shoulders from extended use or marking the work. These dies are used for minor drawing operations and flattening cross sections and should be used with other tooling such as fullers, swages, cutters, and so forth. They can be used as a replacement for the sledge hammer/striker for almost any piece that can be fitted between the dies. They leave a smooth, flat, and almost mark-free finish.

Drawing Dies

The next most common dies are drawing dies, and there are two types: regular and severe. The only difference is the degree of taper in the dies. Drawing dies look like the peen end of a cross-peen hammer and are used for the same basic operations as the tool they resemble. The regular dies are a bit slower than the severe, but they are also easier on materials because they don't place as much strain on the work.

Although severe drawing dies move a great deal of metal, they can cause shearing and/or weld separations in some combinations of pattern-welded materials. If you are going to use these severe dies, I suggest working any laminated materials at a higher-than-normal heat.

Drawing dies operate like a cross-peen hammer, drawing down the thickness of the material while keeping width expansion to a minimum. They are quick because they draw down simultaneously from both the top and bottom.

NOTE: Severe drawing dies may exhibit a tendency to grab and pull the work into or push it out of the dies, depending on the direction of the draw-out. Make sure your work piece is secured when using these dies.

Drawing dies leave a slightly wavy pattern on the work surface that must be dealt with. But, even with this, they save a lot of labor.

There are many more highly specialized die designs, but planishing and drawing dies are the most common and useful for bladesmiths. Of course, you can make your own dies, and I suggest using either D-2 or a 10xx series steel such as 1060 to 1084. If you use D-2, which was designed for this type of application, draw it down to about 900 degrees F and let air cool. If you use a 10xx steel, draw down to a medium-hard (dark brown) temper. This keeps them from overhardening and being dangerous when you use set or spring tooling. Yet, they can withstand the impact of the hammer.

Changing Dies

To change the dies in a sow block, look to see if there are already dies in place. If so, drive out the wedge that's between the die and the dovetail. Use a brass hammer to prevent any peening on the wedge. You

PLANISHING/DRAWING DIES

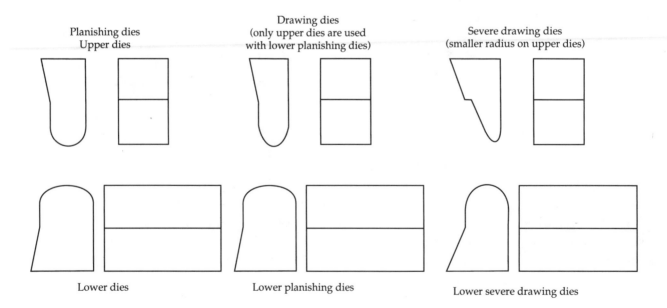

Planishing dies
Upper dies

Drawing dies
(only upper dies are used
with lower planishing dies)

Severe drawing dies
(smaller radius on upper dies)

Lower dies

Lower planishing dies

Lower severe drawing dies

may have to use a drift (also brass) to get at the wedge. When the wedge is out, the die should simply slide free of the dovetail without any further hammering. If not, use a brass or aluminium punch to move the die.

No matter how jammed a die may be, never strike any die with a steel hammer. Always use a brass, lead, or plastic hammer, or a brass (or some other "soft" material) drift on the die. Using a steel hammer can either damage the hammer, or chip or destroy the die. To remove a die in the ram, the procedure is the same as for the sow block.

There is an easier way to remove wedges, but it takes a slight modification to the wedge itself. Drill a 25/64-inch diameter hole near the end of the large end of the wedge. This lets you place a 3/8-inch hook in the hole. I use an automobile dent puller that has been modified to take a 3/8- x 16-inch thread, and I fashioned a hook that fits the dent puller and the wedge.

A few blows from the dent puller is usually all it takes to get any stubborn wedge free. Besides being faster and easier, you don't have to worry about mushrooming the small end of the wedge. Most automobile supply stores sell dent pullers, and they are relatively inexpensive and easily modified.

Replace the old dies with new or different ones. The same operation works for the top and bottom. The easiest way to insert new dies is to slide the bottom die into the sow block and center it. It is very important for the die to make proper contact with the dovetail. Depending on the design of the die, this contact should be either on both of the top sides of the dovetail or on the bottom of the dovetail channel. Most dies use one or the other method, but some use both.

When the dies are properly centered and seated, drive a wedge between the die and the dovetail until it is tight—but not too tight. This can cause a fracture of the sow block and break the dovetail. Snug is all that's needed. Be sure to remember if the wedge is in front of the die or in back. This is important in aligning the top and bottom dies.

When the bottom die is installed, lower the ram by hand enough to insert the top die. The die must make proper contact with the ram, and it must align perfectly with the bottom die. When the dies are aligned, drive in a wedge on the same side as the wedge on the bottom die, making certain that the top die isn't moved during the process.

The wedge must tighten the die and clear the ram guides, or the machine may be severely damaged. If needed, the wedge can be cut to length to facilitate this. You need only enough wedge to hold the die securely in place. I usually leave about an inch of extra wedge extending beyond the ram just in case I have to "snug up" the die during use.

You can make wedges out of just about anything, but I prefer 1045 steel, hardened and tempered to a full spring temper. This way the steel has some give to it but won't deform under the hammer as badly as a piece of mild steel.

WEDGE

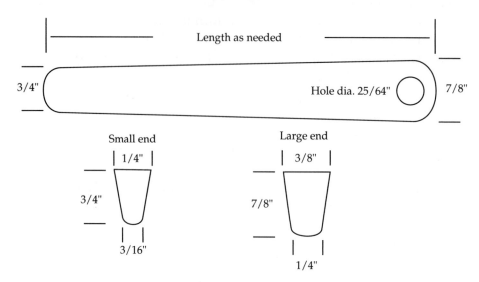

Wedges should be sized according to
the size of dovetail and the die so the wedge
fits snugly between the dovetail and the die.
Remember, the dies must be snug and secure but
not overly tight, as this can damage or break the dovetail.

There are two tapers on two separate planes. The first is a distal taper, along the length of the wedge, while the other one is a sideways taper.

Safety Precautions for the Power Hammer

Now that you understand the basic operation of the power hammer and the different dies, I want to go over the most important step of all before we learn how to use the hammer: safety.

Power hammers have a well-deserved reputation for causing serious injuries. Even a small 25- or 50-pound hammer can seriously injure or cripple you. But injuries can be easily avoided if the proper procedures are followed.

1. *Wear the proper clothing.* These machines can throw a great deal of spatter, spraying hot scale and molten flux all over a 360-degree range. So dress to use these machines: leather shop apron (bib apron); long-sleeved cotton (no polyesters or blends) shirts and pants; leather boots (with the pant legs on the outside); leather gloves; and proper face/eye protection must be worn at all times when operating the hammer. Various types of face shields are available, and I strongly recommend that you wear one. Mine is made from heavy-duty, fine stainless-steel screen that provides

protection yet allows me to see. The steel screening doesn't melt, scratch, or fog up and, when worn with didymium safety glasses, provides excellent protection to your face and eyes.

The spray of scale and flux can get pretty heavy, and it comes off the machine at a high speed and high temperature. You must keep this in mind when operating the hammer. You might want to don welder's leathers. This medium-weight leather jacket-like garment can prevent you from getting "berry burns" from the hot slag. While these burns aren't life-threatening, they do make your arms look like you've got some strange tropical disease.

2. *Do not turn the motor on until you're ready to use the hammer.* And once finished with the heat, turn it off.

3. *Never make any adjustments when the hammer's motor is running.* This includes changing dies or oil.

4. *Never at any time place any part of your body under the ram while the motor is running.* If you must wipe away scale or debris, stop the motor first, then clean it away with a brush, not you hand.

5. *Make certain that the area around the hammer is free of clutter and there are no distractions while you are operating the machine.*

6. *Never operate the machine when you are off-balance.* It can cause you to stumble into the ram and that can cause serious injuries.

7. *Never dry fire the hammer without something between the dies.* This causes undue strain on the dies, ram, sow block, and frame, and it can destroy the hammer. If you must check the alignment of the dies, use a piece of scrap lumber.

8. *Keep the hammer well lubricated.* This makes operation smoother and prevents any premature wear from occurring.

9. *Always make certain that the work is level with the plane of the bottom die.* If not, the work can be wrenched out of your hands or forcibly thrown out of the dies. Work that is thrown out usually strikes the operator anywhere between the groin and the sternum, which is a very painful experience.

10. *Also, make certain that the work is securely held in box-end tongs or in some other fashion that allows no lateral movement.* Never use vise grips! These can let go at any time. The type of tongs used for hand forging are haphazard at best when it comes to a power hammer. Rather, properly fitted box-end, box, or lipped tongs are best. (See below for instructions on how to make your own.) This prevents any lateral slippage that can cause the work to move under the dies and damage you or the machine.

I cannot overemphasize safety when using a power hammer. Of all the power tools used by a smith, this is the most dangerous. It does not forgive lapses into stupidity. But if you follow these simple guidelines and use your brain, you have little, if any, chance of getting hurt. Using a power hammer safely is an art that every smith should master.

TOOLING FOR A POWER HAMMER

Tongs

Box tongs are simple to fashion from existing tongs. All you need is a piece of 1- x 3/16-inch scrap of mild steel long enough to form into a sharp-edged "U" to fit the width of the piece to be held. Weld this "U" onto the end of one of the tong jaws, and you're all set. The U-shape prevents any lateral movement from occurring that could cause the work to be thrown out of the machine. However, you'll need several different sizes of box tongs because, unlike regular tongs, they are not adjustable.

The next alternative, which I like a lot, is adjustable and will hold different thicknesses of materials. These adjustable tongs have a deeper box end than most on one jaw, while the other one has a curved and slightly narrower jaw that fits down into the bottom of the U-section. Make these of heavy stock, and they will hold a large range of thicknesses securely in place.

TONG PLANS

Regular Box End Tongs

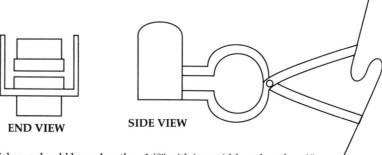

END VIEW   **SIDE VIEW**

Jaw thickness should be no less than 1/8" with jaw width no less than 1".
Box width should be as required by the stock size. The height and width of the "ears"
should be at least 1".

Adjustable box end tongs

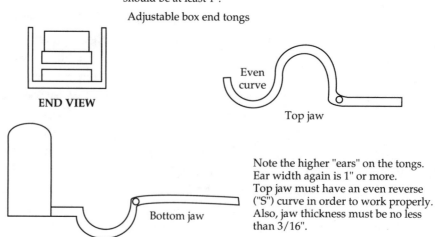

END VIEW

Even curve

Top jaw

Bottom jaw

Note the higher "ears" on the tongs.
Ear width again is 1" or more.
Top jaw must have an even reverse
("S") curve in order to work properly.
Also, jaw thickness must be no less
than 3/16".

Set Tooling

If you are using a hammer in the 50-pound range, you can use either set or spring tooling. Set tooling is similar to the type of tooling used in hand forging or with fullers, cutters, swages, and so forth. Place the tools on top of the work, and the hammer (outfitted with planishing dies) does the work.

Spring tooling is similar to hand-held top/bottom tools. They also are placed between the dies to allow the hammer to do the work.

There are many different types of set and spring tooling ranging from fullers, tenons, and ornamental finial tooling to more elaborate designs used in ornamental iron work. The set and spring tooling used under a hammer are simpler and easier to construct than those used in a hardy hole on an anvil.

As mentioned before, set tools are simply placed on top of the work and struck by the top die of the hammer. There are many different types of set tools, and the following are the most common used for bladesmithing.

Hack

This cutting tool is similar to a hot chisel used in hand forging. It is of heavy cross section with a radiused top face to prevent any damage to the hammer dies. The cutting edge is not sharp but rather has a slight flat on the tip to withstand more rugged use and to lessen the effect of the heat absorbed from the work.

Place the hack on the work to be cut and center both vertically and midline in relation to the dies. Strike it several light blows in the power hammer to set it into the work, and then strike with full-power blows until the cut is almost completely through. Remove the hack and place a piece of scrap steel (square stock works well for this) underneath the cut in the work to protect the bottom die. Then strike the work with the top dies, causing the work to break apart.

Round Fuller

This is simply a section of round rod attached to a handle. This tool is used to reduce cross sections where an abrupt change is not required. Its use results in a radiused separation of material. These radii correspond to the diameter of the rod used to make the fuller. To use, place the round fuller upon the work and strike several light blows to prevent the fuller from shooting out of the hammer, and then strike full-power blows until reaching the desired depth.

Side Fuller or Checking Tool

This is a triangular tool used for drawing down narrow portions on wide material. It is used to form the separation between the main section of the forging and the area to be drawn down. This helps to reduce any mistaken blows that could mar or ruin the finished product.

It has one sharp and two rounded corners. To use, drive a rounded corner into the work with the flat top of the fuller meeting the upper hammer die. This causes a triangular separation on the work. By removing, rotating, and reapplying the tool, you form an opposite but identical depression on the other end of the work.

This tool is a great aid in drawing out tangs or other processes that

HACK TOOL AND ROUND FULLER

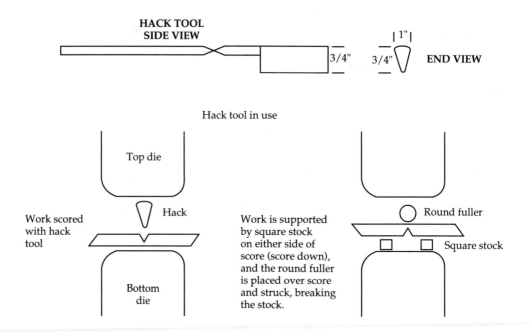

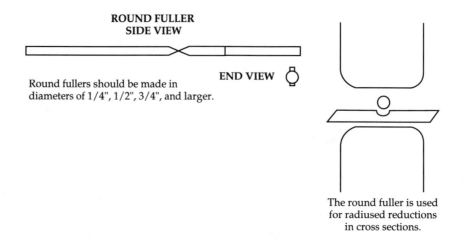

The round fuller is used for radiused reductions in cross sections.

CHECKING TOOL

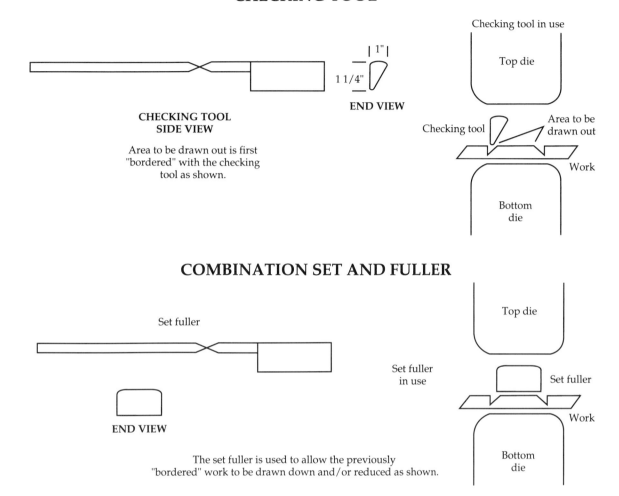

COMBINATION SET AND FULLER

require a heavy change of cross section. This depression can be either worked down with a round fuller or the combination set and fuller.

Combination Set and Fuller

This rectangular tool has two equal large and small faces. There are two sharp corners on one end and two radiused corners on the other. When placed in contact with the work, the sharp corners cause a slight cutting effect of the grain structure, while the rounded corners forge aside the metal, leaving no cuts in the grain structure.

This tool is also a great aid in forging down sections separated by the checking tool, as it helps to prevent any "cold shuts" or lapover on the material being worked. Simply use the tool with the large flat area on the piece to be worked.

Set Blade Fuller

This is similar to the round fuller described above, but the rounded working section is at 90 degrees to the handle, allowing forging of a lengthwise groove. The radius on the tooling should be from 1/4 to 1/2 inch or more, depending on the depth and width of the desired groove.

To use, place this tool onto the section of the blade where a groove is desired, and strike lightly until the tool is set into the work. Then use full-power blows until reaching the desired depth. To lengthen the fuller, place the tool so that it slightly overlaps the previously forged area; 1/2 to 3/4 inch usually suffices. This tool works best on blade designs that require fullers on one side only. (For tooling for two-sided fullers, see below.)

Regardless of the type of tooling, whether set or spring, the dies should be fashioned out of medium-point steel (such as 1040 to 1060) and tempered very soft to the blue ranges to prevent damage to the hammer dies.

The handles of the set tools should be constructed of a mild steel in the 20- to 25-point carbon ranges and either flattened out (from top to bottom) for single-use tools, such as the hack, or twisted slightly behind the working area for multiple-use tools, such as the fuller and set. This helps to absorb the shocks transmitted by the hammer and prevent any undue punishment from reaching your hand and arm.

Spring Tooling

These are simply double versions of the above tools. They should be fastened to mild-steel handles that can be fabricated from one or two pieces. Spring tools are better suited to hammers that have a higher throat between the bottom dies and the ram.

These tools cut down on forge time and help smooth the processes

BLADE FULLER

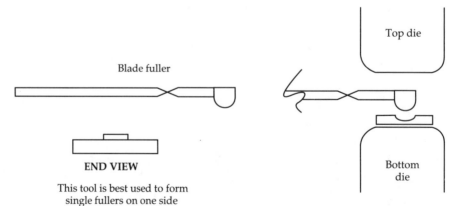

Blade fuller

END VIEW

This tool is best used to form single fullers on one side of the blade only.

Top die

Bottom die

The blade fuller is simply struck down onto the work once it is in the proper position.

involved with their use. Since they work both sides of a piece simultaneously, the amount of time under the hammer and the number of heats can be reduced to a minimum

Double Round Tang Fuller

These tools are used for drawing out tangs and/or reducing cross sections requiring a radiused transition from wider to narrower. The radii can be 1/2 inch or greater, but anything smaller than 1/2 inch tends to do less work than it's worth. This tool works best when the work is inserted between the dies prior to placing the tool in the hammer. Use light blows to set the tool, making certain that the tool is centered and vertical between the dies. Once the tooling is set in the work, strike full-power blows until the desired effect is achieved.

Double-Blade Fuller

This tool allows you to forge in grooves down both sides of the blade at the same time. It is the same tool that's used on an anvil with a sledge, but it has been changed a little for a power hammer.

The working section of the tool has the rounded fullering section set at 90 degrees to the spring handles. The radii on the tooling can be from 1/4 to 1/2 inch or more, depending on the desired fuller. The fullering sections should be no longer than 2 to 2 1/2 inches in length because this prevents difficulties in positioning the tooling and allows for the maximum use of the hammer.

This is perhaps the trickiest spring tool to use. To use, position the tool between the dies and hold the blade between the fuller's jaws, with the fuller running lengthwise down the blade parallel with the edges. As with most other power-hammer tools, the first blows should be lighter than normal to set the tool into the work, followed by full-power blows.

To lengthen the fuller, overlap the work area by 1/2 to 3/4 inch, working down the length of each section to even out the fullering.

Cross-Sectional Tooling

These tools are more difficult to fashion than the ones above, but they make blade forging much easier and more precise. And once made, they last a long time.

This tooling consists of a set of dies that work to form the bevels on the blade, much like hand-packing edges. The big advantage to using this tooling is that you can make the bevels far more exact and even than those done by hand. Also, the dies form both sides of the blade at once, forging in the cross section for which the particular die was designed.

There are several ways to make these dies. You can make a dummy blade and temper it to a full spring temper and use that as the master to form the top and bottom tooling.

TANG FULLER

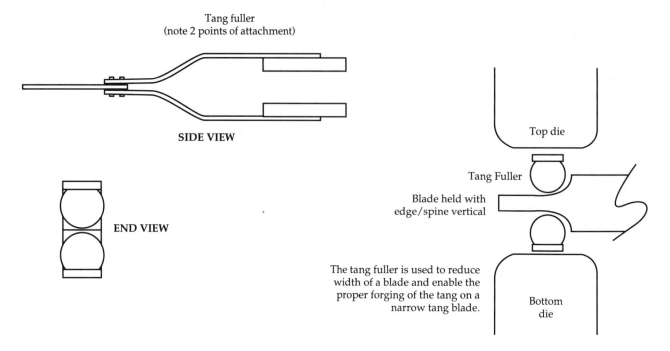

Tang fuller
(note 2 points of attachment)

SIDE VIEW

END VIEW

Top die

Tang Fuller

Blade held with
edge/spine vertical

The tang fuller is used to reduce
width of a blade and enable the
proper forging of the tang on a
narrow tang blade.

Bottom
die

To make the dies, attach two pieces of appropriate-sized tool steel to a spring handle, as you would any spring tooling. Take an even, full cherry red heat on both the dies and place the dies between the power hammer dies. Make certain that you have planishing dies in the hammer. When this is done, place the master between the hot dies and fire the hammer once or twice to force the hot dies down onto the master. It is critical that the master be held level between the tooling to prevent damaging or shattering it. Remove the master and cool it down to preserve the temper. This process must be done quickly, or the heat from the dies will soften the master, and it will not be hard enough to form the dies.

If all goes well, you should have a set of matched top and bottom spring tooling that has the same cross section, in reverse, as the master. If you only got a partial strike (the dies aren't fully formed), reheat and strike again under the power hammer, making certain that the master is in the exact position that it was the first time. If you don't align it correctly, you may ruin the dies and be forced to start over.

When the dies are fully struck, let them air-cool and harden. Temper to a full spring temper so they can withstand both the heating during use and the cooling between heats.

To clean them up, hand-sand or use a flexible shaft machine and small cratex wheels on an arbor. These dies do not need a perfect mirror

DOUBLE BLADE FULLER

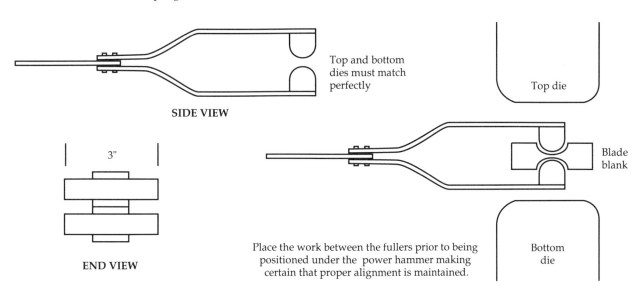

Spring double blade fuller

SIDE VIEW

3"

END VIEW

Top and bottom dies must match perfectly

Top die

Blade blank

Bottom die

Place the work between the fullers prior to being positioned under the power hammer making certain that proper alignment is maintained.

polish, but they must be smooth and free of pits, marks, or bumps that can be transferred to the work surface.

To use, place the dies between the top and bottom dies of the power hammer (or they can be used with a sledge hammer and striker), put the work between the spring dies, and fire the hammer. The metal that is being forged should be slightly hotter than normal because the hammer forces the metal into an entirely different shape. Also, since the edges of the work are thinner than the center, they tend to cool more quickly, thus shortening the working time.

It takes two or three strikes with the hammer to form the cross section. These dies require absolute precision in aligning the work and striking evenly. But they save a great deal of time in the forging and grinding.

Those are the basics of power-hammer forging. I could write volumes on what these machines can do. They are labor-savers par excellence. You have to see the amount of steel these machines can move in a single heat to believe it. Although they can be hazardous to the unwary, with the proper safety precautions, these beasts tame down to a controllable and highly useful machine for the advanced bladesmith.

GRINDING

Grinding a blade is a basic skill, but it is one that must be mastered to get the best results in a finished blade. Bladesmiths today primarily use two different types of grinding: the flat grind and the hollow grind.

FLAT-GROUND VERSUS HOLLOW-GROUND

For the most part, flat-ground blades are heavier and stronger than hollow-ground blades, but this additional strength probably will never be noticed. The bevels of flat-ground blades are ground in on a flat platen or filed in by hand. They take a good, sturdy edge and are prime candidates for the cannel edge so often touted by knife experts as the ultimate in edges.

Hollow-ground blades are lighter and thinner, and their sides are hollowed out on a contact wheel. The thinner edges translate into a sharper cutting surface. How much to hollow out the sides is determined by the thickness of the steel and the diameter of the contact wheel. Both types of grind work, and it is up to you which one to use.

By now, experienced bladesmiths should be familiar with all the basic aspects of grinding. We'll work on the final refinements. A good grind consists of even bevels; an absence of scratches, dips, bumps, or wavy edges; and even choil plunges where the edge meets the ricasso.

WHEN DO YOU GRIND?

A good blacksmith must know when to grind and how much to take off. Some smiths grind after heat treating, which does reduce warpage, but it also presents the hassle of grinding a hardened and tempered blade. Trying to do this can cause overheating and warping problems during grinding. Others grind after forging and before heat treating, leaving the edges a little thick to prevent or at least lessen warpage. Either way works, as long as you are careful in your techniques. I generally grind before heat treating, but since my blades are more or less to shape from the forging, the rough grinding is minimal. Mostly it's to even out the bevels and do the final profiling before heat treating.

If you grind after heat treating, you have to remove a lot of hardened steel. So keep the blade cool to prevent overheating and damaging the temper. This, plus the fact that you are grinding a hardened

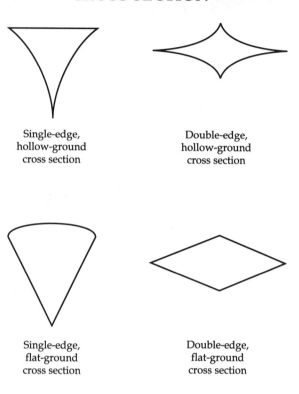

HOLLOW/FLAT-GROUND CROSS SECTION

Single-edge, hollow-ground cross section

Double-edge, hollow-ground cross section

Single-edge, flat-ground cross section

Double-edge, flat-ground cross section

material, takes more time (and belts) than grinding an unhardened blade. And some steels, such as Vasco Wear, are nearly impossible to grind when hardened, so the material may dictate which way you grind.

If you grind prior to hardening, you must leave the edge bevels a little thicker to prevent warping, rippling, and cracking during hardening. This way, you can easily grind the blade, smooth out the profile, and remove any flaws with little concern for the blade's temperature prior to hardening. When the blade is hardened, the amount of clean-up grinding is minimal. You should only have to reduce the edge to its final thickness and refine the grind lines.

What you want is an edge thickness of 0.030 to 0.060 (thirty to sixty one-thousandths) of an inch. The smaller the blade, the thinner the edge can be with little threat of warpage. Larger blades should have thicker edges because of their longer blades, which can cause excessive stress, resulting in warping and/or cracking. Also, to lessen the chances of cracking during heat treating, the grind marks on the cutting edge should run lengthwise along the edge, not across it.

Flat-ground blades can be ground a little thinner than their hollow-ground counterparts. They have more steel backing up the edge than the hollow-ground blades. Flat grinding is also more forgiving in terms of warping and cracking, so rough grinding can be taken a bit further without worrying about these.

Final grinding of hardened and tempered blades should be minimal to even up the grind lines and reduce the edge to a sharpenable thickness.

Whichever grind you choose, the important thing to remember is to keep the grind even and the grind lines sharp. While the grinding basics can be applied to most blades, the most troublesome blades to grind are those with fullers and inside curved edges.

GRINDING INSIDE EDGES

The inside curved edge can be a real pain to grind, especially on a tight curve. The best way is to grind on the corner of the wheel or platen and use that narrow area to do the work. Positive belt tracking is a necessity when doing this.

Again, grind edge-up so you can see what is going on. Grinders have a tendency to "hog out" steel at the bottom of the curve and at both ends, so watch these areas. Work slowly and carefully so you don't burn the steel or overgrind the edge. Hollow grinding an inside curve is a little easier than flat grinding, but both result in a well-ground blade.

CORNER USE OF WHEEL

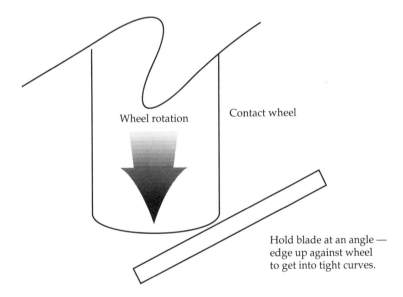

Wheel rotation

Contact wheel

Hold blade at an angle — edge up against wheel to get into tight curves.

By holding the blade at various angles to the contact wheel, you will be able to grind inside curves of different radii.

Grinding Flame Blades

Flame blades, while beautiful to behold, are a nightmare to grind. They present a variety of problems that, with proper consideration, can be easily solved.

A flat grind is easiest for flame blades. Instead of using a platen, you use a contact wheel. Hold the blade lengthwise against the wheel, with the grind running down the length of the blade as shown below. You can follow the forged bevels and the centerline by simply tilting the blade to the left or right as required. You get a wavy centerline that follows the waves in the blade. This requires thought and practice to get it right, so make a few dummy blades to practice on before you do a real one.

Keep the blade against the wheel at an angle that grinds in the bevels from the centerline to the edge and allows you to see what is going on. You must be able to see where the grind needs to curve and where additional grinding (if any) is needed. Be certain that you maintain the same angle with which you started to prevent any bumps or dips in the grind.

Grinding a long blade (such as a sword) can be tricky if the blade is longer than the height of the grinder. You work vertically the entire

BLADE IN POSITION

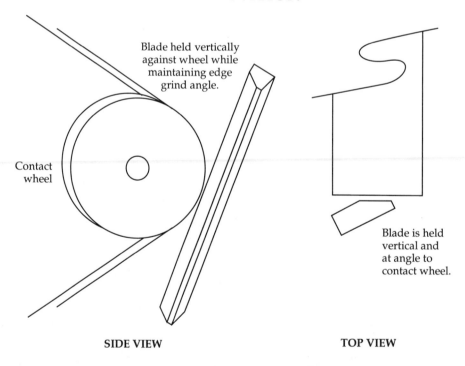

Blade held vertically against wheel while maintaining edge grind angle.

Contact wheel

Blade is held vertical and at angle to contact wheel.

SIDE VIEW   **TOP VIEW**

While blade is being ground vertically along the wheel,
it is also "canted" into the wheel, thereby grinding the edge bevel.
Care must be taken to ensure that this angle, once established,
is constantly maintained to get an even grind.

length of the blade. On the longer pieces, this can get tiring. I suggest that you work in sections and blend the grind until it's even.

This method of flat grinding isn't limited to flame blades. Almost any type of blade can be flat ground in this fashion with excellent results.

Grinding Fullered Blades

Fullered blades can be either flat or hollow ground, depending on the style or design of the blade. Fullered blades can be troublesome because the edges of the fuller dictate where the grind bevels end. Also, the ends of the fuller must be met in such a way that the fuller runs out evenly on both bevels and both sides of the blade.

At the ricasso end, if the fuller runs full-length under the grip, you only have to make certain that the bevels are even and straight from edge to edge and side to side. If the fuller starts at the ricasso/choil area, the edge bevels should also begin there so they will be even with the fuller.

When grinding the blade, the edge bevels start to cut into the fuller at the tip—if the blade is tapered and the fuller width is uniform throughout the length of the blade. This is normal. In fact, on a distal-tapered blade you actually want this to happen. This means you are thinning out the blade as well as grinding in the edges. Just make certain that the edge bevels and the fuller/bevel junction are straight. This takes practice, patience, and time. Work slowly and carefully, making certain that the blade is evenly ground and that the fuller isn't undercut and partially erased in the grind.

FLAT/HOLLOW FULLERED CROSS SECTION

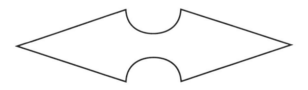

Flat-ground cross section with fuller
Note the heavy cross section along the
edge, making a better "chopping" edge.

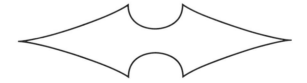

Hollow-ground cross section with fuller
Note the thinning of the edge, allowing
for a lighter and sharper blade.

FULLER RUN OUT AT BLADE TIP
(CROSS SECTIONS)

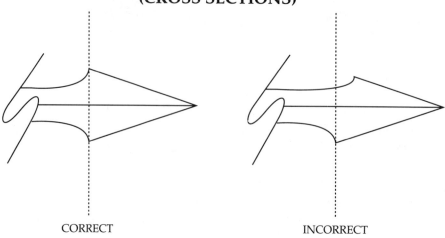

CORRECT   INCORRECT

Fullers must be of equal depth and length,
ending in the same spot on both sides of the blade
to form the proper tip cross section.

If you find that you have begun to erase the fuller, grind it a bit deeper if you have enough steel left (and the proper diameter contact wheel). If not, there is little that can be done other than chalking it up to experience and starting all over again.

Most smiths have a tendency to overgrind the edges, in part because of the short edge bevels. You must watch this, or you can quickly ruin your blade. The steel may become overheated, as well. Cool off the area you are grinding at regular intervals to prevent this.

You may end up with an unground flat area at the tip. This can be left as is, or it can be ground to a sharp centerline. If you are going to leave it, simply even up the grind until both bevels are the same. If you are going to grind in a centerline, raise the edge bevel up toward the spine in this area, making certain that you do grind out the fuller. You want the centerline to align with the center of the fuller. This reinforces the tip, as it is slightly thicker than the rest of the blade. This looks great and is correct for some daggers and most of the later-period swords.

Grinding a fullered blade takes some practice, but it goes very quickly because the bevels are shorter than usual. A well-ground blade looks and cuts better. Grinding is the most difficult step to master in bladesmithing, and one that few smiths enjoy. But once you do get accustomed to it, you'll find that grinding enhances the grace and beauty of a well-forged blade to the eye and the touch.

FULLER/BEVEL START

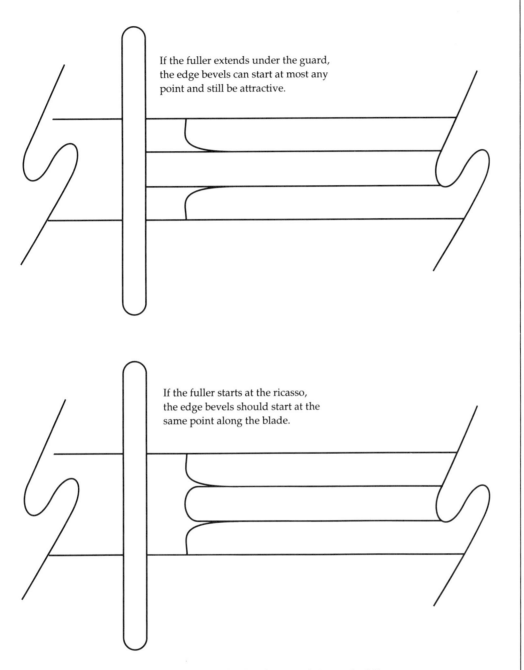

If the fuller extends under the guard, the edge bevels can start at most any point and still be attractive.

If the fuller starts at the ricasso, the edge bevels should start at the same point along the blade.

An attractive edge bevel cut in relation to the fuller will improve the looks of the blade.

HEAT TREATING

AND TEMPERING

The basic skills of hardening and tempering carbon steel can be enhanced to include air-hardening alloys, stainless, and other high-alloy steels.

There is more to hardening steel than simply heating it and then sticking it in oil or water. This may work for some alloys, but it isn't the best way. The main rule is to remember that you do not quench an oil-hardening steel in water, nor an air-hardening steel in water or oil—but you can quench a water-hardening steel in oil.

The heart of the blade is its temper. The hardening must be completed properly or problems arise. The blade may not take or hold an edge, or it may warp, crack, or even break under the slightest amount of stress. Also, the actual tempering is just as important as the hardening. If the blade is undertempered, it will hold a very good edge, but it will be brittle. If it is overtempered, the blade will not hold an edge very long. So the temper must suit the intended purpose of the blade. Since you should already have mastered the basic skills of hardening the simpler alloys, we'll review these only briefly before going on to more difficult steels.

BASIC OIL- AND WATER-HARDENING TECHNIQUES

Hardening carbon steel alloys is, in itself, simple. You bring the steel up to the critical temperature, hold it there until the steel is evenly heated—but not long enough to allow grain growth—and then quench it in the proper medium: oil for oil-hardening steel and strong brine for water-hardening alloys.

Even heating of the steel reduces warpage, which can be a problem in hardening, especially with water-hardening steels. To prevent warpage during the quench, use a very light oil quench for water-hardening alloys. They harden satisfactorily in oil, and, since the oil quench isn't as hard on them as a water quench is, the steel better resists the tendency to warp during the rapid cooling that it is subjected to during the hardening process. If you prefer to use a water temper on water-hardening alloys, then use a hot-brine solution, which is less severe than a plain water quench in terms of thermal shock.

To make a brine bath, simply dissolve as much salt as possible in warm water. I add water-softening salt to the water until I can get no more to dissolve. Although this doesn't sound very tasty, the steel seems to enjoy it. The salt raises the boiling temperature of the water above the normal 212 degrees F (100 C). This higher boiling temperature means less shock on the steel. It also helps to preserve a degree of toughness in the hardened blade.

For the quench, heat the water to approximately 100 degrees F, which reduces the thermal shock for the steel. Quench the blade vertically as quickly and evenly as possible to reduce warpage.

TEMPERING

Once the blade is hardened, the tempering process should begin as soon as possible to prevent excessive stress buildup. Clean one side of the blade until you can see clean metal. This brightening allows you to more easily read the oxidizing colors during tempering.

Slowly heat the blade until the color starts to change. As steel gets hot, the surface oxidizes from silvery gray to black. The colors occur at more or less constant temperatures, and this lets you temper to a color and know the hardness of the steel. The following colors, which are usable for most carbon (nonstainless) steel alloys, should serve as a guide.

Pale yellow	200 degrees F
Bright yellow	300 degrees F
Straw yellow	350 degrees F
Dark straw yellow	425 degrees F
Brown	450 degrees F
Purple	475 degrees F
Violet	500 degrees F
Blue	550 degrees F
Bright blue	575 degrees F

Gauging these colors is subjective, and some errors occur. To eliminate guessing, you can temper in an oven set for the desired temperature. Bake the blades for at least 2 1/2 hours to ensure that the temper is thorough.

What temper do you use for what blade? It depends on the blade's intended use. A lighter temper results in a harder blade, and a heavier temper gives a slightly softer but somewhat tougher blade. Remember that the harder the steel, the better the edge, but toughness is sacrificed in favor of the better edge. A softer blade is tougher, but it won't take or hold as good an edge as a harder blade. So there are trade-offs to be made when tempering a blade.

For most cutting blades—including hunters, skinners, and fighters—I suggest tempering to a pale to bright yellow (300 to 350 degrees F).

For light chopping/utility blades—including Bowies, camp knives, and big fighters—I have good results using a slightly softer temper, straw yellow to dark straw (400 to 425 degrees F).

Swords and other big knives or blades that must withstand shocks and other abuse should be tempered first for toughness and then for edge-holding. I use a brown-to-purple temper (450 to 475 degrees F) to ensure that the blade holds together when used.

Springs and highly flexible blades—such as rapiers—use a full blue temper (525 to 550 degrees F). Here the emphasis is on flexibility, not the edge-holding capabilities of the steel.

When the blade reaches the desired color, quickly quench the blade to stop the tempering process.

This is the basic technique for most water- and oil-hardening steels. Although you can experiment with this technique, using it as given produces a fully hardened and tempered blade.

Sand Temper

This is an easy method to get a uniform temper on blades. You simply bury the blade in a box of heated sand and let it absorb heat from the sand. For the bath container, I use a heavy, mild-steel sheet-metal box sitting on a hot plate to heat the sand. Mine has a lid, but one really isn't required.

The best way to gauge the temperature of the sand is to use a candy thermometer or some other thermocouple device. When taking the temperature, make certain that the sand is mixed well and there are no hot spots in the bath. Also, make certain that the blade is completely degreased prior to placing it in the sand. If not, then the sand gets oily and clumps together, thereby causing an uneven heat and possibly warping the blade as well.

When the sand is ready, bury the blade and leave it until it reaches the proper temperature. Make certain that the sand doesn't overheat and damage the temper. If you are doing more than one blade, bury them all, remove the sand from the heat, and let cool slowly.

This hot-sand bath is useful for larger blades that are too big for an oven temper. Simply make a bigger box to fit the blades.

A variation of this technique using molten lead was used for centuries to temper springs and other resilient steel items. While controlling the temperature of molten metal is easier than with sand, the chance of toxic metal poisoning is so great that I strongly advise against using this method.

Progressive Temper

Everyone is very excited about this hard-edge, soft-back temper right now. Granted, it works quite well—when properly done.

Simply stated, the back (the spine) of the blade is drawn to a softer temper than the edge; using a hot plate to temper the blade is easiest. Heat the plate, place the hardened and brightened spine down onto the plate's surface, and watch the color change along the spine. The colors bleed into the edge at a slower rate; hence, when the spine is purple, the edge should be in the straw ranges. When the edge turns to the desired color, quench the blade to prevent further softening and go on to the next step.

Progressive tempering works well on a single-edged blade, but what about a double edged one? This question has plagued bladesmiths for many years, and I have finally developed a solution to this age-old problem. As with many so-called difficult problems, the answer is simple: use a heated rod instead of a plate to run a progressive temper.

To do this, use 1/4- to 3/8-inch round rod for small blades, such as daggers, and 1/2- or 3/4-inch round for swords. Heat the rod to a dull red and place it down on the anvil's face. Next, hold the hardened blade by the tang and place the blade down on top of the rod, with the rod running down the length of the blade along the spine. This transfers the heat from the hot bar to the blade, along the spine, and outward toward the edges. Practice on several dummy blades before attempting it on an actual blade.

When the edges reach the desired color, quench the blade to prevent overtempering.

AIR-HARDENING STEEL ALLOYS

Air-hardening alloys are easy to harden. Bring the steel up to its critical temperature (usually in the 1600 degree F range, but check mill specifications), making certain that the steel is evenly heated all the way through to prevent warpage. Allow to cool undisturbed. Do not lay the blade down or lean it against anything. Doing so can cause the blade to warp or harden improperly or unevenly because any areas that come in contact with other surfaces cool at a different rate than the rest of the blade.

Rather, hang the blade up so there is free air space around the hot sections of the blade. When using these alloys, I simply place a heavy wire hook on the tang end prior to heating, and, when the blade is heated, I hang the blade on a steel rod to cool in a corner of my shop. Air-hardening works well with A-2 and D-2, resulting in a tough, durable blade.

HEAT-TREATING STAINLESS STEELS

Stainless steels are quite unique. They have some peculiar properties that make them touchy when it comes to heat treating. Chief among these is their tendency to build up stress and to warp. As with many other forging processes, the key to preventing these unfortunate occurrences is an even heat. This may or may not be an easy task, depending on the length, width, and thickness of the blade.

The condition of the blade surface is another factor in how well stainless steels heat-treat. Properly preparing the surface reduces or eliminates cracking, stress risers, and warpage. The blade surface should be free from scale, hammer marks, and drastic changes in cross sections. Any one of these can cause problems when quenching the blade. Grind the blade smooth to prevent most problems from occurring.

Most stainless steels harden quite well in a light oil, but some harden satisfactorily in air. I do not recommend an air quench for stainless, but it can be done.

The temperature of the oil also affects the hardening of stainless steel. If the bath is too cold, it can cause cracking and/or warping. If the oil is too warm, you may not get the proper degree of hardening. I start to quench stainless blades when the oil reaches 75 to 80 degrees F and stop when it reaches 110 to 120 degrees F. My oil quench contains approximately 50 gallons of oil, so I can heat-treat a sizable number of blades before I have to stop.

The blade should be heated to approximately 1650 to 1800 degrees F, depending on the alloy, and then quenched as soon as it reaches the proper temperature to prevent grain growth. (This can be a real problem with some stainless alloys.)

I prefer to quench the blade point down to keep the warpage to a minimum. There is much controversy as to whether a still bath or a circulating quench is better on stainless steel. Having tried both, I like a still bath better for my type of work. Other smiths feel differently, but as with everything else, try both and see which works best for you.

When the blade is cooled to the temperature of the bath, remove and degrease. Proceed either to the temper or the subzero quench immediately, as stainless is prone to stress-cracking.

For a subzero quench, use acetone/dry ice or liquid nitrogen, available from most industrial gas suppliers. Liquid nitrogen is more expensive, but it's safer, easier, and more effective than acetone. Most suppliers also have containers that are suitable for quenching blades. If not, you can make one.

You can easily make a stainless-steel bucket by welding 18-gauge sheet together, wrapping a layer of mineral wool around the sides and bottom, and adding a stainless-steel jacket that fits snugly around that. This more-or-less insulated container is serviceable for subzero quenches. Or you can use a small restaurant-style steam-table bucket if you can find one. Stainless steel is recommended for the container because it resists rust and corrosion. Mild steel can be used, but you have to degrease the inside every time you use it. Stainless steel, on the other hand, is basically maintenance free.

Warning: Liquid nitrogen is inert and nontoxic, but it is very cold. It is this severe coldness that gives stainless steel extra hardness without making it more brittle. Liquid nitrogen splashes and spills much like water, so always wear eye/face protection when handling it. This means a face shield and splash-resistant goggles, not glasses. Goggles protect the sides, top, and bottom of your eyes, not just the front. Liquid nitrogen can cause instant freezing of your hands or any other body part with which it comes in contact. Proper safety procedures must be followed at all times. Never handle any ultracold material barehanded, including pouring liquid nitrogen. Use the right kind of gloves and wear a heavy leather apron to protect your torso from the cold.

To subzero-quench stainless, degrease the blade thoroughly and—using a pair of long-handled, grease- and oil-free tongs—submerge the blade into the liquid for approximately 20 to 30 seconds. Allow crystals to cool to the ambient temperature and then remove. *Do not touch the blade!* It is very cold, and your skin can freeze to it. Also do not drop the blade because steel at this temperature is very brittle and can shatter into a lot of small pieces.

Stainless-steel tongs are recommended because stainless seems to withstand the shocks of the quench better than the mild steel so commonly used for tongs.

Let the blade warm to room temperature before you start tempering. Simply hang it up someplace out of the way. You can use forge-tempering techniques, but I recommend using an oven temper. Let the the blade bake for a couple of hours or more to get an even temper.

Stainless-steel alloys are a godsend to the smith who is making blades for wet, marine, or damp environments. Even though they are touchy when it comes to heat-treating, their corrosion resistance more than makes up for it.

The keys to successful hardening and tempering are knowing your materials and the specific processes involved, along with considerable practice, patience, and skill. Hardening and tempering make a blade cut and hold an edge. Don't rush or compromise any of the processes, although some take a long time to do properly. After all, it is your name on the blade.

The grip and hilt of a blade are among the most important features of any edged tool. If it isn't comfortable, durable, and controllable, what good is it? Chances are, if you don't like the way the blade handles, you won't use it very often, no matter how well it holds an edge.

But the grip is more than simply something to hold onto. While knife/sword grips can be as simple as a wrapped piece of rawhide, they can also be as elaborate as inlaid and fluted ivory or abalone or even a sculpted lost-wax casting in bronze, silver, or gold. The grip is the part of the knife that is most often seen, and hence, it should be attractive to behold as well as functional.

By now you should be familiar with assembling and fitting both the full tang and full hidden tang knives. But there are more traditional materials (and methods by which to use them) than simple wood, ivory, or horn.

LEATHER

One material that has been used for centuries to make hilts is leather. It is generally wrapped around the grip. Although leather can present some problems in terms of durability and serviceability, these can be overcome. There are several ways to wrap a grip, but first the grip core should be fitted and cut slightly undersized to allow for the thickness of the leather. You can use various materials for the grip core, but I prefer solid hardwood (such as ash or oak). Most plastics tend to resist the adhesives that are used.

Leather is available in various weights and grades. These run from heavy tooling leather used for saddles and industrial uses to ultralight lining leather used for expensive clothing.

I have had the best results with garment leather. An appropriate-sized piece for a blade hilt weighs about 2 to 2 1/2 ounces. It is available in many colors, but I prefer black or red. It is tough and stretchable, which is a desirable characteristic in wrapping grips. Although a full hide is expensive, you should get at least thirty normal-sized grips out of it. So compared to other materials, the cost is reasonable.

Wrapped Leather

There are two ways to wrap a grip. The first is to cut a long strip and wrap it around the grip core, spiraling down the length and then tucking the free end underneath—all the while hoping that it doesn't come loose. There are obvious disadvantages to doing it this way. The first is the grip's inclination to come loose. The second is that it doesn't look that great. Third, the ridges along the edges of the strip tend to curl up, which is unsightly and uncomfortable for the user.

Another and better method is to simply wrap a sheet of leather around the grip so that only one straight seam is present. Simply lay the grip on the leather and cut so the leather wraps around the grip with approximately 1/8 inch overlapping. When fitting the leather, remember that leather stretches. On most evenly tapered sword grips, the shape should be a trapezoid. Leave a little extra on the ends, which can be trimmed after securing the leather to the grip core. The seam (edges) should meet along the edge of the grip. This way the leather does not curl up with use and time.

The leather on this grip was wrapped around a fitted, smooth, wooden grip core prior to final fitting and assembly. Photo by Stephen Jacobson

Adhesives

You can choose from various adhesives ranging from traditional white glue to state-of-the-art cyanoacrylates that set in a matter of seconds. I have had the best luck with old-fashioned hide glues that have been used for centuries.

Hide glue is simply boiled-down cowhide. It is available at most art stores and some hardware stores. Hide glue is so effective because it is organic, and, since you are gluing animal hide to another organic substance, this stuff is almost venomous in its tenacity. Two other of its big advantages are that it sets quickly and wipes off leather with a damp cloth. If you cannot find hide glue, substitute yellow carpenter's glue. It holds like the devil when properly cured and cared for.

Follow the directions that come with the glue as far as mixing, curing, and storing. One important fact you should notice is the pot or shelf life of the adhesive, or how long before the glue becomes unusable.

Another adhesive you might consider is Leather Weld. It is available at most leather or hobby stores. It doesn't withstand temperature extremes very well, but for most uses you won't encounter these. Follow the instructions on the bottle, and you should have no problem.

Of course, most smiths are familiar with the various epoxies, which have been used for years in the custom-knife industry. You can use epoxy, but, while I have had good results with them, they do have a few drawbacks. They are hard to clean up, and they have a tendency to be brittle. You want some flexibility in the glue to help absorb some of the vibrations encountered.

Assembly

Prepare to glue the leather on the body of the grip. Coat the grip core and the leather with a small amount of glue. You do not need much, only a light coat. Any excess should be squeezed out and wiped off immediately to prevent any unsightly glue on the outside surface.

Position the leather on the core and glue down. Stretch the leather and work from the glued-down end toward the free end. If there are any bubbles under the leather, work them out by squeezing them toward the edge of the leather. Work quickly, but meticulously.

When you get to the end, smooth out the grip, squeeze a bit of glue out of the seam, and flatten the edges down to a smooth seam. Wipe off any excess glue with a damp, not wet, cloth. You have a smoothly covered grip core with a slight fringe around the ends.

Depending on the type of glue, it may set in a few minutes, a few hours, or overnight. If you used hide glue, wrap the grip with some sort of binding to make certain that the leather stays down. I use something called rubber banding. These are big rubber bands used in furniture making as a sort of clamp. They will not mark or scuff the leather, and they get tight.

Leave undisturbed until the glue is cured. Remove the wrapping slowly and carefully and check the grip. If all went as planned, you have a smooth, securely covered leather grip.

Using a new single-edged razor blade, trim the leather flush with the grip ends. Make sure the edges are cleanly cut, not frayed. Next, fit the grip back on the blade. The grip is completed, except for hard assembly.

Ribbed-Leather Grip

This is a variation on the wrapped-leather grip. The ribbed leather gives a more secure grip, and it looks prettier as well. The processes involved are much the same, but there are a few additional, easily performed steps. Make, shape, and size the grip core in the same manner as the nonribbed grip and start on the spiral.

The easiest way to form the spiral is with cotton twine. The glue will not adhere to synthetics, including nylon, rayon, or polypropylene. You need two strands of twine: one to wrap around the grip and glue down and another to act as a spacer while the first one is being wrapped. Secure the end of the wrapping strand with glue, lay the spacer strand alongside it, and start to spiral the two pieces down the grip.

Make certain that you have enough, but not too much, glue on the wrapping twine, and don't glue the spacer down. Continue until you have completed the spiral wrap. When at the grip, cut the wrapping strand and glue the end down. Next, *gently* remove the spacer strand, and you should have a grip that looks like the one on the left in the photo below.

Let the glue set until it is dry. Next, cut the leather to the appropriate size. Before gluing the leather down, stretch and secure it to the core. Next, while the glue is still wet, take another piece of twine (not the spacer piece used earlier) and wrap that around the grip tightly. You are wrapping the twine and the leather down into the groove formed by the spiral twine around the grip core.

Let the glue set (overnight is best), and then remove the twine. Trim off the excess leather, and you are basically finished. To improve the durability of a leather grip, coat the leather with one or two coats of high-quality lacquer to help seal and preserve it from skin oils, the elements, and other

This photograph illustrates the three stages of making a ribbed leather grip. On the left, the grip core has been wrapped with spiralled twine. The center grip shows the leather wrapping with twine spacer in place. The completed blade on the right is wrapped with spiral wire prior to final fitting to the blade. Photo by Stephen Jacobson

forces. Lacquer has preserved a lot of grips, as witnessed by all of the surviving leather-wrapped saber grips that were treated in this manner.

Turk's Head Braid

An interesting variation on this is to wrap a single strand of twisted wire between the ribbing and to secure the ends by placing them between the grip core and the guard/pommel or by tying the wire in a Turk's head knot. A Turk's head is a single-strand braid that is made by wrapping the loose end of the wire around and back onto itself as shown below. The photograph shows a simple version of this knot. Most of them are complicated and difficult to do without considerable practice, but they look great on the end of a grip.

To do this type of knot, simply wrap the loose end of the wire in a open spiral around the first loop and continue until the wire is tighter. The diameter enlarges as the wire is wrapped around the original loop. This is cheating, of sorts, but it does work. After reaching the end, simply cut off the excess as close to the loop as possible and tuck the loose stub back under the grip. This knot gives the appearance of a roped band.

If you do not want to use a Turk's head, you can place a band of bronze, nickel silver, or other metal over the end and secure it in place by pressure and/or a combination of pressure and an industrial adhesive.

This leather-and-wire-wrapped grip can also be lacquered to protect the leather and to prevent the wire from tarnishing or oxidizing.

Close-up of a Turk's head knot the author soldered to the bolster. Photo by Stephen Jacobson

JAPANESE SAME

This is a variation on leather wrapping using a particular type of ocean-ray skin. This skin is the material that was used underneath the silk braid wrapping on Japanese blades.

Same provides a good gripping surface because this material is very rough and tends to grab onto your hand for a secure hold. On some of the more aggressive pieces, it can actually abrade away some of your skin. That's a good grip.

Same is available from most of the Japanese sword collector's suppliers. The pieces aren't very big, usually around a square foot, more or less. The Japanese prize the larger nubs of the center section of the skin. You will only get one piece of this so-called prime grip material per piece. The Japanese believe this was the only piece worth using. To me, it is far from it. The entire skin is usable if you know how to work it.

When you first acquire same, it is hard, brittle, and stiff. You can soften it by soaking it in warm water until it becomes pliable. It reacts a lot like rawhide (which it is, sort of), becoming very flexible and moldable when wet. Same does not shrink, but it does stiffen and hold its shape when it dries. It can be cut while still wet with a sharp pair of scissors or razor blade. You work this material like leather but more quickly. Once it begins to dry, it stiffens. If you plan on gluing it down, use a hide glue, which is best suited for same.

No matter what you are doing with this material, it should not be used dripping wet—well soaked is fine. Traditionally, the Japanese used it for grip panels under the wrapping on swords. They also used it to cover scabbards. When it was used for this, it was lacquered in various colors until the spaces between the nubs were filled in. Then the whole was sanded down until the tops of the nubs were even with the lacquer and the whole was polished to a high luster. This is referred to as inlaid ivory. It gives an interesting effect that can also be used on grips.

As you are working with same, you'll find that it handles a lot like the shagreen (sharkskin) that was used on some of the U.S. naval swords from the nineteenth century.

After the piece is glued down, let it set to harden and solidify. I suggest that you wrap the grip tightly with either string or twine to hold it in place. Make certain that all of the excess glue is removed prior to doing this, or you may easily glue the wrapping down to the grip—an annoying thing to have happen.

The Japanese wrap their grips with silk braid, but there is no need to do this as long as the ends of the wrapping are securely glued down. An interesting variation on same is a ribbed wrap spaced with wire. This is similar to some of the martial wraps found on military swords from around the turn of the century. It makes a nice-looking and highly effective grip for almost any blade, but especially swords.

STACKED GRIP

This type of grip was used on the World War II U.S. Marine combat knives. The grips on these blades were formed from heavy leather washers tightly torqued down between the guard and pommel. This grip appeared on a lot of hunting knives from the 1940s to the mid '60s. Some production knives still use the stacked leather grips, while others use a grip stacked of other materials, including horn, micarta, amber, fiber spaces, and so on. Some custom blades used during World War II even had all-metal grips formed of brass or aluminum washers. A stacked grip can enhance the appearance (and value) of a custom knife.

There are several ways to make a stacked grip, and each has its advantages and disadvantages. While the materials used are pretty much up to the discretion of the maker, each individual piece should be uniform in thickness, unless you plan on making a special shape or pattern. This type of grip is best suited to the full, hidden tang blade with either a pinned or screw-down pommel/butt cap. You simply cannot do this type of grip on a fully exposed tang knife.

The materials should have a little give to them, although this isn't an absolute requirement. Whatever material you use, each piece of the grip needs to be fitted to the tang and between the guard and pommel.

You should do a rough shaping to the pieces prior to fitting them on the tang. By doing this, you reduce the amount of material that has to

ROUGH STACKED GRIP

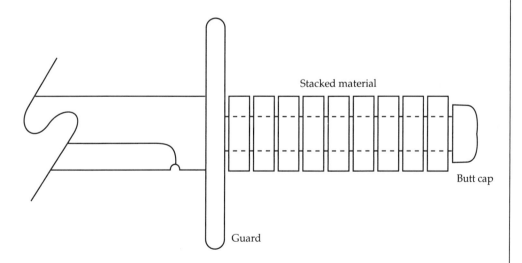

The stacked grip gives the maker the option to use
a variety of materials in various combinations.
Simply arrange the material on the tang
and shape as desired.

This utility blade of welded cable with stacked grip was made by Scott Sparapani. Photo by Scott Sparapani

be removed during the final shaping.

You can shape each individual piece separately and then assemble, which isn't that easy, but for some blade designs it is the only way it can be done effectively. Or you can put everything together and then shape the grip by using hand tools and a belt grinder, as the design dictates.

It is of utmost importance that each piece makes perfect contact with the piece next to it. This means no gaps or voids between the pieces of the grip. It takes time and practice to do this correctly. Also, the pieces should be as tight as possible and the pommel/butt cap snugged down to a high torque to hold each piece in place.

With the pieces fitted to the tang and everything tight, snug, and gapless, assemble using a high-quality adhesive. I use rifle-bedding compound for this. Some smiths use silicon rubber automotive gasket material. The choice of adhesive is up to you. A high-strength industrial epoxy is more than adequate for this purpose.

Apply the adhesive, assemble the grip, and wipe off the excess. Let the grip set until the adhesive cures. The time varies from a few seconds to 48 to 72 hours, depending on the adhesive.

When cured, start to shape the grip following your design. You can shape by using files, rasps, hand-sanding, or anything that enables you to do the work.

If you are using materials of different hardness on the same grip, such as horn separated by brass sheets, be careful that you do not undercut the softer material, which is removed considerably faster than the harder brass. So work slow and carefully so this does not happen. Also, the final sanding has a tendency to undercut, so watch it there as well. You must be careful during polishing, as well, because the buffing compound can cause the softer material to dish. This produces dips and/or ripples in the surface.

Stacked blades have been used for many years on a lot of different blades. They do take time and planning, but then again, what doesn't?

PANELED HORN GRIP

This type of grip was used mostly for swords. The available horn wasn't suitable for a solid grip (one piece) on a blade of that size. So to answer the need, bladesmiths formed the grips from panels of horn (one piece on either side) set into a framework giving the basic shape of the grip. The framework itself is illustrated on the facing page.

This framework is simply a guide that has the same thickness (or slightly thicker) as the tang of the blade with two small cross pieces on each side to keep the two pieces in place. The horn is then placed over this frame (the area of the cross pieces are relieved to allow a close fit) and held in place by various methods.

This grip style is elegant and also can be used with wood, ivory, stag antler, or any other material that can withstand vibrations. It wasn't uncommon for some precious stones to be used in this grip style, including jade or amber.

The secret of doing this type of grip is getting a close fit between the inside surface of the horn plates and the framework. This reinforces the horn and keeps breakage to a minimum.

To construct this grip, you must first make each half of the framework. These pieces are easily fabricated from mild steel, bronze, silver, or other material. As for shapes, these were traditionally the hock bottle, the straight taper, or a combination of the two as shown on the next page.

To shape the sides of the framework, you can forge, file, grind, or cast them. The technique is not that important. What is important is that the sides are identical. As for the thickness, they should be no thinner than the tang to be encased.

As for the width, the shape of the inside of the frame should be very close to that of the tang. This ensures that the whole assembly is tight and decreases the reliance on the epoxy/resin filling to firm everything up during final assembly.

The surface that the plates rest on also has to be flat and smooth. Everything has to match nicely for this grip to look good. This is the mark of a craftsman—nice fitting and precision hand work.

After completing this part of the framework, make the cross bars. These can be wire, small shim stock, or any stiff, metallic material. I suggest using 3/32-inch diameter brazing rod. Welding rod also works quite well. File or grind one side flat to give a good hold after the pieces are assembled.

GRIP FRAME

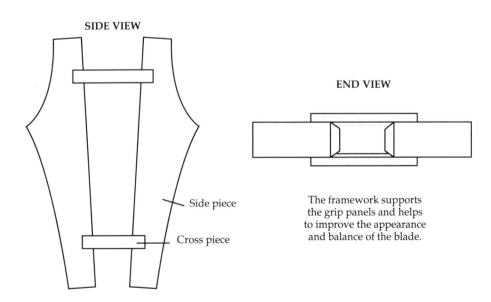

SIDE VIEW

END VIEW

Side piece

Cross piece

The framework supports the grip panels and helps to improve the appearance and balance of the blade.

GRIP SHAPES

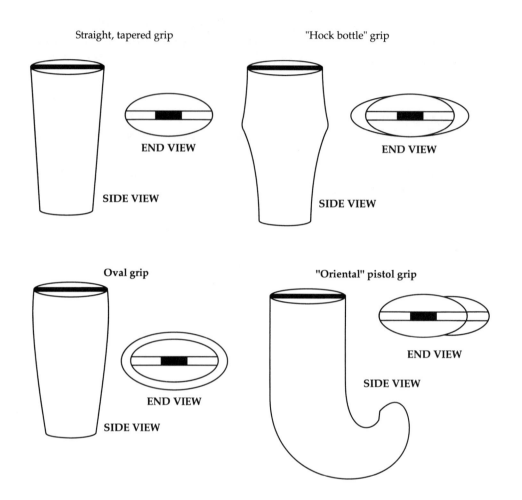

You need three or four pieces, and four is more secure. They should be either brazed or silver soldered to the framework. Silver soldering is a strong method of attaching the pieces, and they should hold for a long time, at least a few centuries (which is long enough for most people).

The positioning of the cross bars depends on the design of the grip. Your best results come from attaching the cross bars close to the ends of the framework, approximately 1/4 inch from either end. This slight space between the ends and the cross bars allows the grip panels to cover the cross bars so they are not visible. Also, leave approximately 1/8 inch from the cross bars to the edge of the framework so they are not visible from the side of the grip.

When the attachments are completed, fit the framework to the blade, guard, and pommel. This prefitting allows for a small degree (if any) of hand fitting after the panels are attached. After fitting, you can shape, relieve, and fit the grip panels.

CROSSBAR POSITIONS

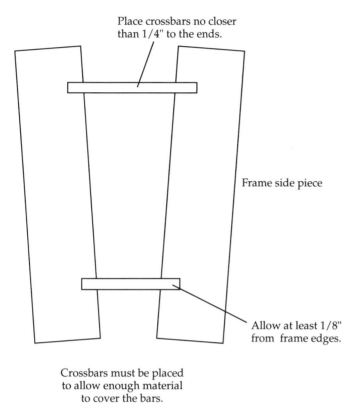

Place crossbars no closer than 1/4" to the ends.

Frame side piece

Allow at least 1/8" from frame edges.

Crossbars must be placed to allow enough material to cover the bars.

Regardless of the mounting method you selected, you still must make the panels. These need to be shaped exactly the same as the grip frame. The edges should be slightly radiused, as these radii prevent any chipping of the grip that would accrue if the edges remained squared. Also, if you are using the bezel attachment, the radius gives a surface that the bezel can be turned into, thereby securing the panels into the grip frame.

Panel thickness should be at least 3/16 inch, depending on the material used. Horn is tough, but it can crack—although it is not as prone to cracking as some types of ivory. For the brittler materials, I would go a little thicker on the panels, but no thicker than 3/8 inch. Panels any thicker than this would be too thick for a comfortable hold.

The panel shape must be as close to the frame as possible. When you have shaped the panels, smooth and polish them. The surfaces must be fully finished before the panels are mounted onto the frame.

There are two different ways of attaching the panels. The traditional method is to hold the panels on with adhesive and a top and bottom ferrule as illustrated here. While this isn't the most secure way to do this, it does work.

But if you wish to make a reproduction piece, form the ferrules from 18-gauge brass, copper, steel, or other sheet material the same way that you would for a wire-wrapped grip. Do the top ferrule first because this is the best way to get everything together. NOTE: Use a free-flowing hard solder to secure the ends of the ferrule together. The softer, low-melting point silver solders (the ones you use to secure the guard to the blade) aren't strong enough to hold.

When the top ferrule is completed, place the panels and the grip frame

together, secure the top ferrule, and then fashion the
bottom one.

The ferrules should be
snug but not so tight as to
prevent them from being
snugged up by a brass
punch. Move them up tight
with a brass or copper
punch. The bottom ferrule
is held in place by the
pommel, and the top one
remains in place by a very
tight friction fit. You can
use some sort of adhesive,
but the original blades
didn't, as far as I can tell.

While these ferrules are
traditional and quite
secure, I think there is a
better way of doing them.
The alternative method
looks great and securely
attaches the panels to the
framework. This technique
is the same basic method
used for mounting cabo-
chon-cut stones into jewelry. Form a bezel from 18- or
20-gauge fully annealed
brass or copper sheet,
leaving enough of a lip so
that the edge can be rolled
over the curve of the
panels. Solder this to the
edges of the grip frame

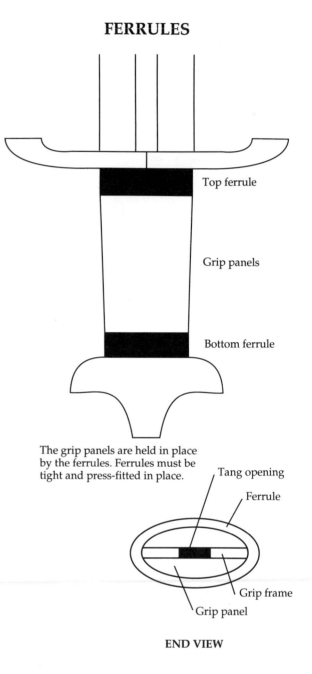

FERRULES

Top ferrule

Grip panels

Bottom ferrule

The grip panels are held in place
by the ferrules. Ferrules must be
tight and press-fitted in place.

Tang opening

Ferrule

Grip frame

Grip panel

END VIEW

with a soft solder. While this isn't the strongest solder available, it is more
than adequate for this purpose, if it is properly applied.

Solder this to the outside of the framework, following the shape of the
frame. Make certain that you use no more solder than absolutely necessary
to get a solid bond. Any excess solder can cause problems when you insert
the panels. If by chance you get too much solder, you can scrape the excess
away using a small chisel or a flexible shaft machine with a cratex wheel.

You need to have a nice, square joint on the inside of the bezel so that
the panels fit evenly against the framework. If there are any lumps or other

irregularities on the inside surfaces, the panels will not be set flush into the frame, which can cause the panels to fracture.

With the bezel soldered and the panels shaped, insert the panels into the framework one at a time. Take a burnisher and roll the bezel over the edge, starting at one end and working down the bezel toward the other. When this is completed, roll the other bezel to secure the first panel. Then go on to the second one.

Remember that the bezels must be tight and the panels must be centered in the framework. The tightness of the bezels is of the most importance because this is what holds the whole assembly together. It helps to have strong hands when you are doing this. You need to roll the bezel down onto the surface of the panels, and over the curve until it is a smooth, even bend without any kinks in the bezel. This can take two or three tries to achieve.

When the bezels are tight and the panels secured, assemble the grip to the weapon. To fit the grip to the blade, you can use careful hand filing or sandpaper and a level block, such as a piece of glass with the paper taped or cemented down to it.

The amount of hand fitting is minimal because of the prefitting before the panels were assembled. With the grip completely fitted, proceed with the final assembly.

Grips of this style were used late in the medieval period, and though not entirely traditional, they were seen on occasion.

Sandwich Grip

This is one of the oldest types of grips used on both daggers and swords. This grip is simply two separate pieces fitted together with a cavity carved into each half to allow for passage of the tang, as shown on the next page.

This is a tricky grip to make, as it involves fitting three different surfaces at the same time. To make this easier, hollow out each half and fit these together prior to fitting to the hilt. When these are fitted together, wrap them together tightly and fit the grip to the hilt. You must secure the two halves together. This can be very difficult when dealing with horn, as most adhesives do not stick to horn very well. So, to help keep things together, you need to make tight-fitting ferrules for the top and bottom of the grip. This is the most common method of attaching the two halves together on the sandwich grip.

After completing all of the fitting, do a final trial assembly, and if everything checks out, do the final hard assembly and secure the blade, guard, grip, and pommel together.

You can use any top-quality adhesive, but the traditional method is to use cutler's resin. This is the pitch of a type of pine tree that, when heated, softens and then liquefies. When liquid, the resin is poured into the grip, like any glue, and the whole quickly assembled before the resin

SANDWICH GRIP

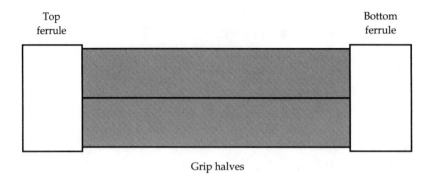

The grip halves must match perfectly—no gaps— and are
held together by adhesive and the ferrules.
Here again, the ferrules must have a snug, tight press-fit.

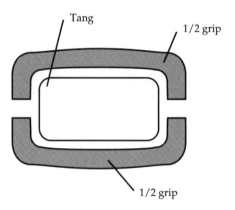

Both halves are inletted to allow the tang
to pass through and then fitted to a tight, even seam.

cools and hardens. It really does work, and while it isn't as strong as the more modern adhesives, I have several pieces in my personal collection that are more than 300 years old that were assembled with cutler's resin, and all of them are still tight and serviceable.

To use cutler's resin, heat it in a double boiler until it is hot and liquid. When liquid, pour or scoop the resin into the grip, being careful not to burn yourself. Next, place the grip on the blade, assemble, and squeeze out any excess resin. The resin can be cleaned up with an oiled cloth. After the assembly, place the blade where it can cool/harden undisturbed. The biggest difficulty in using cutler's resin is in finding it.

Some of the larger, better-supplied knife maker's supply firms carry it. Even though it is difficult to obtain, it is available, and it does work, especially on horn, stag, and ivory.

Fluted Grip

This is one of the prettiest grips that you can use on a blade. The fluting can be used on wood, stone, metal, or any material. It is especially beautiful on ivory. The secret of doing a fluted grip is to get the correct layout and twisting of the flutes so the grip looks balanced.

There are several ways to do this. The simplest way is to use string or a very strong thread (carpet thread) to aid in laying the flutes out on the grip surface.

Needless to say, the fluted grip works best on either a full hidden or a partial tang. While you can flute a full tanged knife, it must be exceedingly difficult to get the layout correct. But not having tried it, who's to say? That is the beauty of being a custom bladesmith. There is no one who can tell you that it has to be done a certain way.

The grip should be completely shaped and fitted before the flutes are cut in. The flutes themselves are formed by round files of various sizes. I have had good luck with triangular files, but the grips weren't as nice.

There are two basic ways to make a fluted grip: one that uses a twisted wire between the flute and one that doesn't. Both look great, but I like the unwired grip better on most blades.

Also, you must consider the thickness of the grip. Since these flutes are cut into the grip, the grip walls have to be thick enough to allow for the fluting without worrying about breaking into the tang channel. While this may not be a problem with larger pieces, such as swords and some larger daggers, smaller blades may have to be redesigned to accommodate the fluting.

Fluting can be done on just about any shape of grip, but the best results come from using a round or slightly oval grip shape. These are easier to lay out and cut than a rectangular or even a square shape.

As I mentioned before, if you get the layout wrong, the fluting will also be wrong. There are several ways to lay out these grips. For starters I suggest that you make a few practice grips out of clear pine or basswood. Both of these cut well, are inexpensive, and give you the needed experience before you get to the more expensive materials. Face it, doesn't it make sense to try out a new technique on a two-bit piece of scrap before you attempt it on a $300 chunk of ivory?

With the grip shaped, you are ready to proceed with the layout. The easiest way to do this is to drill four 1/16-inch diameter holes equally spaced around each end of the grip as shown above.

These holes are the reference holes for laying out not only the flutes themselves but also the rate of twist. You need four pieces of heavy

HOLE POSITIONS

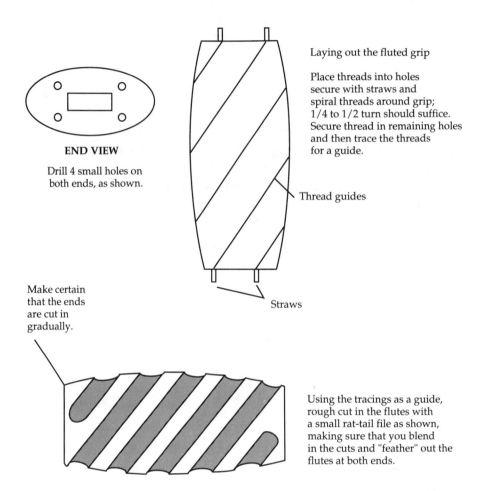

END VIEW

Drill 4 small holes on
both ends, as shown.

Laying out the fluted grip

Place threads into holes
secure with straws and
spiral threads around grip;
1/4 to 1/2 turn should suffice.
Secure thread in remaining holes
and then trace the threads
for a guide.

Thread guides

Straws

Make certain
that the ends
are cut in
gradually.

Using the tracings as a guide,
rough cut in the flutes with
a small rat-tail file as shown,
making sure that you blend
in the cuts and "feather" out the
flutes at both ends.

thread cut long enough to allow for each to wrap around the grip—6 to 7 inches should be more than adequate for most dagger/knife grips; slightly longer should suffice for most swords.

With the thread cut, insert one end into each hole and secure it with a straw or a splinter of wood. Now, wrap the thread around the grip as desired. This takes some thought as to the rate of twist. A one-quarter turn is a loose twist while a complete turn is a very tight one. Most twists work well with a one-half turn.

The threads are a guide for the flutes. Next, carefully trace along each thread with a contrasting colored pencil or marker. These lines serve as the cutting lines for the flutes. When the lines are drawn, remove the threads and get ready to cut the flutes.

You cut the flutes with a rat-tail or round file, though the taper on the rat-tail makes it the better choice. The taper makes starting and ending the flutes neater and easier to cut.

To cut the grooves, start at one end and lightly score the pencil line to give you easier-to-follow marks in case the pencil lines are obscured during the cutting process.

By following the scoring, cut the grooves approximately two-thirds of the way down, leaving the last one-third to allow for clean up after all the grooves are cut. If you make any minor mistakes, this allows enough material for minor corrections.

While you are cutting, the files will fill with material and must be cleaned regularly. As far as I know, there is nothing that works to keep this from happening. I have tried chalking, oiling, and just about everything else, and nothing worked well enough to recommend. So clean the teeth with either a file card or a fine wire brush as required.

Continue cutting until all of the flutes are scored. After that, go back over the fluting and blend in any irregularities that may be present.

When this is done, you can either cut another set of flutes for setting a twisted wire into the grip or go on to sanding and polishing the flutes and finishing the grip. If you are going to add a strand of wire, you need to drill additional holes to terminate the wires and hold them in place when the grip is assembled.

As for the depth of these smaller grooves, they should be at least two-thirds as deep as the wire is wide. Three-quarters is better because the grip tends to hold the wire better if it is deeper.

To smooth and polish the grooves, start with a medium-grit sandpaper. I have had the best results using wet/dry paper because it tends to be tougher under the circumstances.

Wrap the paper around a piece of dowel to maintain the shape of the flutes and to prevent distortion of the grip. Sand with progressively finer grits until you get to 320 and then hand polish. The wire grooves need some sanding to smooth the surface but not as much as the fluting because the wire covers the surface of the smaller grooves. The sanding merely prevents splinters from raising and causing problems later on.

When the grip is sanded, seal and finish as required. If you are going to wire the grip, now is the time to insert the wires. To place the wire in the grip, epoxy and wedge one end into the hole drilled for this purpose and allow the epoxy to set and cure. When this is done, simply lay the wire into the groove and pull it tight (being careful not to pull it loose from the other end), and then tuck the end into the remaining hole on the end. Again, epoxy and wedge the wire into the hole, let set, and cure.

With the wire in place, secure the grip to the blade, and do your hard assembly.

These grips require a certain amount of practice, but they are not all that difficult once you get used to doing them. There is a great deal of artistic allowance in this type of handle. A well-done fluted grip makes a great grip on most blades.

WIRING THE FLUTED GRIP

SIDE VIEW

SIDE VIEW

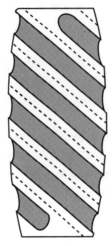

With the grip fluted,
lay out the wire grooves
between the flutes, as shown.

Cut the wire flute
between the "main"
flutes to a depth of at least one-half
the diameter of the wire used.

END VIEW

END VIEW

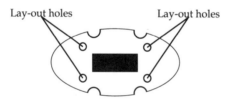

Cut the wire flutes
over the edge of both
ends of the grip.

When the wire flutes are cut,
inlet (groove) a pathway from the
wire groove to the lay-out holes so
the wire lies flush with the end surface.
Secure the ends of the wire in the lay-out
holes. Enlarge these holes as required to fit
the diameter of the wire.

Processing Bone

Bone is another material that has been used on blades since they were made from stone. Bone is very beautiful and tough when properly handled and treated. More than likely, the bone you use will have to be processed prior to using on a blade.

The raw material can be any leg or shank bone from any animal. Of course, the bones themselves should be large enough to fit a good-sized handle. But you can cut handle slabs from larger beef shank bones, depending on the size of the bone and the slab. As for other bones, most are unsuitable. I use various beef and lamb shank (leg) bones on full hidden tang knives and daggers.

Regardless of the type of bone, if you are using fresh bones from a butcher, rendering firm, or slaughterhouse, you have to deal with unwanted material clinging to or inside the bone. This has to be removed.

Depending on the condition of the bone, clean off any remaining meat, cartilage, or other residue. Next, cut off the knuckle portion of the bone to expose the marrow. The marrow is the soft, pithy center of the bone. When removed, the marrow channel perfectly accommodates a hidden tanged blade.

With the surfaces cleaned off and the knuckles cut, there are two ways to proceed. The best way is to place the bones atop a large ant hill and wait for nature to take her course. Granted, this is a slow process that can take several weeks to a couple of months, but the ants do pick the bones clean, inside and out. Plus the sunlight bleaches them to a pleasing off-white color. But not everyone has access to anthills, nor would everyone want to take the time.

The quick way is to boil the bones in a pot of water until the fat rises to the surface. It usually takes two or three hours to boil out all of the fat. When this is done, remove the bones and dump the water.

The bones now look a sort of yellowish/off-white and, while they appear to be clean, they are not. To bring out a nice bone color, boil the bones again in a mild solution of water and household chlorine bleach. Add 1 cup of bleach to a quart of hot water and boil the bones for another 45 minutes to an hour. Do not be alarmed if a great deal of foam appears or a dark brown scum forms. These are additional fats and oils being removed from the bone that the first boiling didn't remove.

When the bones are white, remove them from the bath, rinse well in cold water, and let dry. The bones should now be bone white and clean of any oils, fats, or other materials. They are ready for final processing.

Bone make a durable grip but must be handled correctly to eliminate splintering, cracking, or otherwise falling apart. The additional processing comes after the bones are fitted as a handle.

Working the bone is a lot like working any other animal material. Proper care must be used when grinding to keep the bone from overheating or burning, and you should wear a respirator at all times to protect your lungs from the dust. Bone dust can eventually kill you.

Fitting bone can be done prior to or after the bone is stabilized. Since the stabilizing material is a cyanoacrylate, I strongly suggest stabilizing after fitting the bone. Why take any chances?

Because of the nature of bone, it is brittle, especially at the ends. To get around this, simply band the ends by placing ferrules at the guard and butt-cap/pommel. These do not need to be made from heavy sheet; 20- to 22-gauge material is more than adequate to prevent any splintering of the bone. Roll the ferrules as close to the bone surface as possible.

If the design you are using protects the ends, such as butting up at the guard and pommel, the bands aren't necessary, but they do look nice and dress up the grip.

Press fit the bands to the bone after it has been stabilized to prevent any health hazards from the cyanoacrylates. Also, use an adhesive to help hold things in place (cutler's resin works well for this).

With the bone fitted and shaped, you are ready to stabilize the bone. Stabilizing bone is like stabilizing ivory and stag antler—except it takes a good deal longer because of the excessive porosity of the bone. Apply as many coats as needed and vacuum as required for the sealant to penetrate. It is not unusual for this to take up to ten applications.

After the bone is stabilized, finish as you would ivory or stag. Bone makes a beautiful grip that can stand the passage of time and gains a patina that few other grip materials can emulate.

Using natural materials on a top-quality blade is, in my opinion, the only way to go. The man-made materials, while stable, simply do not measure up to the beauty of a prime piece of coco-bolo, ivory, or even bone. After all, natural, organic materials have a beauty all their own.

There is something else about natural materials: they have a special feel that man-made materials do not have. By using organic materials, you are adding a beauty to your work that plastics can never achieve. Wood, ivory, bone, and stag are unrivaled in beauty and deserve a place on a quality hand-forged blade.

METAL AND WOOD FINISHING

Finishing metal and wood is a highly needed skill and one that is easily mastered. The principal factor in learning to finish is patience, and the second is attention to detail. Both play a major role in the outcome of the finished product.

Most of the techniques described in this chapter take time to do and present some hazards if done improperly. In metal finishing, the most hazardous techniques involve the toxic solutions and compounds used to color metals. Some of the "proven" old-time processes (such as the ancient art of mercury gilding with gold and silver) are so poisonous that even attempting them is sheer stupidity. In wood finishing, the primary danger comes from inhalation of vapors produced by the drying finish. Use wood-finishing products in well-ventilated spaces only.

Regardless of whether you are finishing metal or wood, you are risking your life if you do not follow the proper safety procedures. These safety measures include—but are not limited to—the use of a respirator, eye/face protection, protective clothing, and excellent ventilation.

METAL FINISHING

Metal finishing goes beyond polishing, although this is an important part of it. The ability to polish a piece of metal is a basic skill that most knife makers do not fully understand.

I am not a fan of the full-mirror polish. In fact, I think that it is a waste of time. The first time you cut anything with the slightest bit of acidity, the blade turns colors, wasting all of the time and effort you put into getting the beautiful mirror polish.

Final Grinding

If you want a full-mirror polish, however, preparations begin in the final grinding. All of the coarser grit scratches must be removed with a finer grit. If not, no amount of polishing can make up for it.

The grinding is done in stages, using progressively finer grits. Start with a 220/240 grit, followed by a 320/360 grit. Make certain that you are removing 100 percent of the coarser grit marks. Follow the 320/360 with a 400-grit polish.

At this stage, you should really be able to see the coarser grit scratches that you failed to remove with the 220 grit. If these show up, go back to the 220 grit and start all over again. Follow the 400-grit polish with a 600-grit polish. After this, you can either continue on into the micron grit sizes or go on to the buffing. Micron-size belts are ultrafine and ultraexpensive. I do not see any advantage in using these, yet some makers swear by them.

Buffs

There are several types of buffing wheels to choose from: sisal; sisal/cloth; hard-sewn muslin; loose muslin; and soft, medium, and hard felt.

Sisal buffs used with a coarse grease-based compound remove light scratches, rust, and a lot of flaws. These wheels should be used carefully, as they "roll over" or dull grind lines very easily.

Muslin buffs come in sewn (hard) and loose (soft) types. The hard wheels work best for fine grits because they are hard enough to remove most surface scratches. Care should be taken with these also.

Loose buffs are simply a stack of muslin sheets sewn together at the center. The loose buffs are less rigid than the harder sewn buffs and, hence, produce a softer cutting action well suited for finer finishing compounds.

Felt wheels are available in soft, medium, and hard. Though expensive, they are well worth their price when you consider they don't roll over grind lines as severely as muslin or sisal wheels.

I prefer felt wheels for fine finishing, used with extra-fine compounds. Some knife makers use felt from start to finish.

Finishing Compounds

There are two basic types of compound, greaseless and grease-based. Greaseless compounds, also known as glue compounds, are applied while the wheel is idle and allowed to dry on the wheel. Available in various grit sizes, these compounds are easy to use once you get used to them.

Grease-based compounds are more common and come in grades ranging from coarse to extra-fine. Coarser compounds work best for clean up and removal of rust and scratches on sisal or hard-felt wheels. Medium compounds are not as aggressive and work best on hard-muslin buffs. Fine compounds remove the smallest amount of material and leave the highest degree of polish. Although they can be used with hard buffs, they work best with the loose-muslin or soft-felt wheels.

Polishing

The first step is the setup polish. This is done when you have a good deal of blending or removing of rust or small pits to do. Use a sisal wheel and coarse compound. Work carefully and make certain that you do not blur the grind lines. The cutting action of the grease-based compounds can be enhanced by coating the piece with a light oil as you polish.

As you work, polish on the lower one-third of the wheel to lessen the chances of the blade being snatched out of your hand. Also, never buff a blade with the edge up. This is asking for problems. The blade could easily jam into the wheel, be torn from your hand, and fly off the wheel in any tangent. Chances are, it will make a half rotation on the wheel, and spin off at a high speed directly at you!

After completing the setup buffing, proceed to the next finer grit. Remember, using different compound grits on a wheel contaminates it. Also, wipe off any leftover compound from the piece being buffed to prevent the wheel's being contaminated from it.

For the next-to-final polish, use finer compounds. With these grits, I suggest using hard-sewn muslin buffs until you get to the final finishing polish. Don't overheat the blade because this can melt the solder or, in the worst cases, anneal the blade and destroy the temper.

As you are buffing, remember to keep the grind lines sharp, as these are rather easy. Improper polishing has turned many expensive blades into less valuable knives. So pay attention! Using felt wheels can also reduce the dulling of grind lines. The felt, due to its inherent hardness, does not fold over and cause excessive wear on the grind lines. These wheels maintain their round shape under pressure, thereby giving a highly buffed surface and maintaining sharp grind lines.

For the final grit, change to a soft-sewn buff, the best buff for a mirror polish. This soft buff and the ultrafine, green, chrome-oxide abrasive compounds produce a glassy smooth, reflective surface on steel, stainless steel, bronze, brass, or silver.

A mirror polish can be achieved on most metals, some more readily than others. Silver, while soft in comparison to steel, shines to an exquisite, mirror-like polish. Alas, it also tarnishes quickly. Bronze, brass, and other cupric (copper-containing) alloys take a full-mirror polish—and they hold it for a long time as well.

A mirror polish is beautiful on a knife, but it is totally out of place for a "user." I use a mirror finish on some sword fittings, especially blued ones, as this really brings out the beauty of the blueing.

METAL COLORATION

The ability to color metals—by chemical action, heat, or both—opens up many wonderful combinations to the smith. Some coloring processes are simple, involving a minimum of tools and equipment, while others can be quite complex, requiring a great deal of specialized tooling. Common coloration techniques include hot-bath blueing, charcoal blueing, plating, and gilding.

Hot-Bath Blueing

Almost everyone is familiar with the blueing used on firearms. This same finish can be used to enhance a custom blade, either by blueing the blade itself or using it as an accent color on fittings. A set of highly polished, deeply blued fittings on a sword or dagger enhances the blade's overall appearance.

Blueing is a chemical process that uses caustic sodas and heat. Nonstainless steels generally blue better, although some formulas do a decent job of blueing stainless steel. Blueing salts are the key to the process. You can make your own or use the premixed salts available from gunsmith suppliers. The commercial salts are easy to mix and use, and they produce excellent results when used correctly.

Warning: These salts are caustic and can cause severe burns. They are used at temperatures above 275 degrees F, and adequate protective clothing, including eye/face protection, must be worn during all the steps involved in blueing. Also, the fumes can be hazardous so work only in a well-ventilated space. Since the fumes are base compounds, keep a bottle of 50 percent diluted household vinegar to counteract any spills or spatter.

Blueing Tanks

To do a proper job of blueing, you need vessels able to withstand the extreme temperatures and blueing salts yet won't poison you. Most gunsmith suppliers sell blueing tanks, but these are usually at least 2-feet long, and you don't need such a long tank.

Aluminum, zinc, plastic, Pyrex, and stainless steel cannot be used. These either break, melt, react with the salts, or poison you. Stainless can be used for parkerizing, as the nitrides used in this process are largely unaffected by the blueing action.

So what do you use? A mild-steel bucket with welded seams is all that's needed. It shouldn't be very large because temperature control is easier on a smaller vessel. Just make certain that the bucket is large enough for the parts to fit inside with enough extra space for proper circulation of the bath. You need at least three of these vessels. One is used as a blueing tank; one holds the cleaner; and the other is used for a cold rinse. In addition to the buckets, you also need some sort of parts basket to hold the pieces to be blued. The basket should be made of iron or mild steel.

Mixing the Salts

You need blueing salts and a blueing thermometer. Add salt until the water boils—usually between 275 and 310 degrees F, depending on the type of salts used. If the temperature is too high, add a little water to bring it down. If it is too low, either let some water boil away or add more salts. This more-or-less foolproof formula ensures that the proper amount of salts are added to the solution. Be careful when adding salts or water, as this causes the solution to splatter.

After the solution is properly mixed, you can either proceed with your blueing or let it cool and then store it in a loosely stoppered glass container for future use.

Preparing Your Materials

The secret to a good bath is having the metal surface absolutely clean of any rust, oils, waxes, or other substances that could interfere with the action of the salts. I suggest degreasing the items to be blued with an acetone bath or a thorough washing in trisodium phosphate (TSP). TSP can be rather nasty on your hands, so wear vinyl gloves. Gloves protect your hands from the solution and the pieces from your skin oils.

Here is the beauty of a hot-bath blue: the surface finish remains the same once it is blued. If the piece has a mirror polish "in the white" it will have a mirror polish after it's blued.

Handling the pieces in the baths is easier by wiring the larger ones together or placing the smaller ones in a parts basket. Using the parts basket lets you see what's going on at one time.

Cleaner Bath

The next step is essential in getting a good blue. While the pieces should be degreased prior to starting, the cleaner bath removes anything that was missed. This bath is a hot solution of TSP, diluted muriatic acid, or some other caustic solution that removes all of the grease, oils, or other substances that can cause spots on the final finish. The premixed commercial gunsmith's cleaners have always worked well for me.

The pieces should be set in the hot cleaner for approximately 5 to 15 minutes. Next, rinse them in a cool-water rinse to remove any clinging matter and continue with the process.

To do the actual blueing, preheat the pieces in the hot cleaner solution for 5 to 15 minutes to remove any residual oils that you may have missed. Remove the pieces from the hot bath and rinse well in cold water. All of the cleaner must be removed for the blueing to take. If not, you end up with spots, smudges, or smears.

Blueing Bath

After rinsing, place the pieces directly into the blueing salts. Be careful of the spattering when the pieces are first placed into the salts. Let the pieces remain in the bath for 15 to 30 minutes. It takes time for the salts to react properly with the steel. Keep an eye on the temperature to make certain that it remains in the proper ranges. If the temperature gets too low, the salts will not take on the steel; if it gets too hot, the blueing turns a brilliant rust red.

After approximately 20 minutes, remove a piece or two and see how the blueing is progressing. If the pieces are deep blue/black, remove and rinse. If not, return the pieces to the bath for an additional 5 to 10 minutes.

When the pieces are the proper color, remove them from the salt bath and place immediately in a cold-water rinse. They should steam a bit when first immersed. This is normal. Make certain that the pieces are completely rinsed of the salts. If not, the salts corrode the metal. Dry immediately to prevent any flash rusting. Next, oil the parts with a high-quality, water-displacing oil to prevent rust.

The hot bath blue is one of the easiest metal colorations to apply, and gives a durable, beautiful finish. It improves the rust resistance of the pieces it protects and requires no more care than a light coat of oil.

NOTE: To dispose of old or contaminated salts, never pour them down the drain. This causes all sorts of environmental problems, as well as playing hell with your plumbing. Call your local fire department to find out where they can be taken for disposal.

Common Blueing Problems

Uneven blue. This is caused by removing the pieces before getting an even blue. Simply return the pieces to the bath and continue the process.

Areas not blued. This is due to uneven cleaning and/or oils on the metal's surface. You must totally refinish and try again.

Red or plum brown color. The bath is too hot, there is some element (such as chromium) in the steel, or both. Lower the temperature approximately 15 degrees and try again. If this doesn't work, add a salt purifier or replace the salts and start again.

Charcoal (Fire) Blue

This is one of the oldest metal colorations used by man and one of the hardest to do properly. Fire blueing was used in the nineteenth century to finish cap-and-ball revolvers and other firearms. It cannot be used on some metals or for some blades. Because it is an oxidizing finish, fire blueing only works on carbon-steel alloys. The extreme heat involved (in excess of 500 degrees F) would anneal the steel to the point of making it useless on blades. As with all blueings, the metal retains the same finish after blueing.

It is simple in theory but more complicated than it looks. Preparing your materials is the key to this type of finish. Again, the metal surface has to be absolutely clean and free of all oil, wax, grease, and anything else. So clean and degrease the metal before starting the blueing process.

Traditionally, this type of blueing took place in a charcoal-heated hot box (oven), hence the name charcoal blue. You can still do it this way, but you must make a hot box and use charcoal without a thermostatic control.

The best way to charcoal blue is to place the pieces inside a jewelry burn-out kiln, turn it on, and set it to 550 degrees F. If this is not hot enough, turn the temperature up another 25 degrees and let it bake.

Getting the correct temperature is crucial to a good blue. If it is too low, the color won't be a true, deep blue; if it is too hot, the metal may scale. When the scale is removed, so is the blueing.

Let the pieces heat for an hour to an hour and a half. This allows the temperature to penetrate the steel for an even blue color. Immediately quench the pieces in a light oil to cool them. The process is now finished. Vibrant blue cannot be obtained in any other way that I know. It is a pretty finish for carbon steels.

This technique can be used for other oxidizing colors. I oxidized the trigger of a Luger pistol a straw yellow by the same basic techniques but at a lower temperature. This heat blueing is durable but not as rugged as a hot-bath blue.

ACID ETCHING

This is one of the most artistic techniques for decorating a blade. The design possibilities are limited only by the etcher's imagination and ability. The basics are simple, but the refinements can take a good deal of time and require artistic talent to do something more than simple lettering and inscriptions.

The process is simple:

1. Cover the blade with some sort of resist.
2. Cut out what you want to etch in.
3. Place the blade into the etchant and wait until it's done.
4. Remove and clean the etchant and resist.

Granted, I oversimplified things, but those are the basics. It is almost as easy to do as it is to explain. The main problem is getting the right resist, or material used to cover the area that you do not want to be chemically etched. You can use almost anything that adheres to metal, cuts cleanly, and remains unaffected by the etchant. Several different mixtures work well, but I like the following:

1 part beeswax

1 part powdered asphaltum

Both of these materials are reasonably priced and available from art-supply stores. To mix, melt the wax in a double boiler (to prevent flame-ups) and add asphaltum until they are well mixed. (Don't mix this in anything you use to cook with.)

Applying the Resist

The surface of the blade must be clean and free of all oils before applying the resist. This ensures that the resist stays on the blade and the surface below the resist is clean for the action of the etchant. Use a small brush to cover the entire surface of the slightly warmed blade (finished but unmounted so no guards, pommels, or grips get in the way) with the hot resist.

Make certain that the coat is even in the area where you will be working and pay special attention to the edges of the blade. These tend to thin out when the resist cools. It doesn't hurt to go back over the edges with another coat. The tang should be covered as well, to prevent any action there that could cause fitting problems later. When covered, set the blade aside where it can cool undisturbed.

Etching Tools

An etching tool is commonly referred to as a burin or stylus. These can be made of steel, wood, bronze, horn, or bone. Most of the commercially available burins are steel, but they can scratch the blade, which is damaging to the etching process. The resist is easy to cut, so I suggest using a softer metal for the burins. Bronze is a good choice because it is hard enough to cut the resist cleanly, yet not hard enough to scratch the blade beneath.

Your burin should have a sharp edge to cut, not tear, through the wax. The cleaner the cut, the cleaner the edges of the etching. You can shape the burins to give different types of lines from broad to extrafine.

The design or pattern you cut into the wax is what will be etched into the blade. It is the pattern at the bottom of the cut where the etchant makes contact with the blade that counts, so make certain that the area inside the cuts are clean and sharp.

To facilitate the cutting, warm the surface of the blade slightly to soften the resist. This can be done by holding it under a 100-watt bulb for a few minutes or blowing it with an electric hair dryer set on low or medium. Another trick is to use a magnifying lens to see the finer details better. You do not need much magnification—4x8 power should do it.

Practice on several pieces of hardened steel before attempting this on a finished blade. Make a few different cuts, straight lines, curves, letters, and dots. Clean round dots are hardest to cut, whereas wider lines and letters are comparatively easy.

Make certain that you cut cleanly and remove all of the material in the area where you want the etch to be. Any leftover resist prevents the etchant from purchasing a uniform bite on the steel. This will be very apparent after the resist is removed.

The shape of the cut's sides is also of great importance. The sides of the resist should be perpendicular to the blade surface. By keeping the sides vertical, you lessen the chances of lifting the resist by the etchant's action. If you feather the cuts, as in an angular cut, the etchant can get underneath the resist, causing damage to the design.

When you are happy with the pattern, go back over it to clean it up and ensure that the surfaces exposed at the bottom of the cut are totally free of resist. While you are working, make certain that you do not touch the exposed surfaces. The oils from your skin can form a "stop out" of their own, leading to an uneven or splotchy etch. With the design cut in, it is time to do the actual etch.

Etchants

Etchants can be as simple as ferric chloride or as exotic as aqua fortis. I have had good results on carbon steel by using the following formula for aqua fortis:

1 part nitric acid

3 1/2 parts distilled water

Remember, add the acid to the water to prevent splatter or an explosion. And wear adequate face/eye protection whenever you are using or handling any caustic material. This aqua fortis mixture is somewhat mild on steel, but it is dangerous when mishandled. Let this mixture set for 7 to 10 days to "age" a bit. This improves the bite of the etchant, producing a cleaner bite.

Another good etchant is ferric chloride. The same solution used for Damascus patterns works for etching as well (see Chapter 15).

Etching Container

Now that you have your etchant, you need something in which to do the etching. Some makers use glass; others porcelain. I have had great results using polyvinyl chloride (PVC) plumbing pipe with end caps to make a tube of sorts. I made a framework to hold the tube upright while the blade is being etched.

Most blades fit easily into a 1 1/2- to 2-inch round, 12-inch long pipe section. Other diameters of pipes are available at various lengths, as desired. Cut the pieces to length and cement a pipe cap on one end, and you have an etching tank. The joint between the cap and pipe must be watertight and very secure. I add a little bit more cement than necessary just to make sure. You do not want any acid or other etchant leaking out.

Doing the Etch

Etching is similar to engraving a Damascus blade, with the blade immersed in the etchant and left until the etching is complete. The

amount of time required depends on the type of steel and the etchant. If you use the above formula, you need 5 to 10 minutes to get a solid etch. Experience is the best teacher for what you are doing—another good reason to practice before trying it on a $300 knife.

While the blade is immersed, a small amount of bubbling should be expected. However, if there is extreme agitation, remove the blade immediately. The etchant is far too strong. Remember, a slower etch is a better etch.

Remove the blade and soak it in a strong solution of baking soda and water for a minute or two to neutralize the acid. This is very important because any active acid blurs or otherwise smears the etch when the resist is removed.

It takes considerably longer for a ferric acid etchant than for aqua fortis, but the results are well worth the extra time. A 30-minute etch is not unusual when using this bath. Again, experience is the final determinant.

To remove the resist, simply warm the blade and peel it off. Any still present wipes off the blade with a soft cloth and a little acetone. Next, lightly buff the blade with a soft-muslin buff and a fine (either crocus or some sort of rouge) compound to remove any stubborn resist and to highlight the blade.

You should have a smooth, evenly etched design that is exactly like the one you cut into the resist. If not, then something went wrong.

Common Problems

Blurred or smeared edges. This results from the cuts not being squared or too-strong an etchant, either of which causes the ground to be lifted or undercut by the etchant.

Broken design. This can be caused by either a rough cut or a contaminant on the metal. The cuts must be clean and free of burrs, and you should not touch the surface once the cuts are made.

Uneven etch. This can take the form of a quilt-like pattern or pits and areas of too-heavy etching. Several factors can cause this, including the bath being too hot, the blade being unevenly warmed, or, most common, the etchant being too old.

Acid etching is just now making it into the custom blade world. It is a viable alternative to engraving, as it is nearly impossible to engrave a hardened blade satisfactorily. Etching has been used for many years on commemorative firearms. It enhances the beauty of a presentation-grade blade, and, when tastefully done, it brings added beauty to everyday blades as well.

WOOD-FINISHING TECHNIQUES

Wood can be finished in a variety of ways. These range from simply applying a stain to using an acid reagent to darken the surface and enhance the wood's inner beauty.

Stains

These can enhance the color already present or change the color of the wood completely. I do not like the idea of staining grip woods, although some woods, such as ash or oak, can be improved by the judicious application of a light stain to enhance their grain and color. Other than these few exceptions, I cannot see why you would use a stain with all of the readily available exotic hardwoods. But if you must use stains, there are a few things that you need to know.

There are two types of stains: oil and water. These are simply water- or oil-based pigments. Both look good on most woods.

Oil-based stains penetrate better and produce darker finishes.

Accentuating Maple's Natural Beauty

Maple is usually finished without stains or reagents. When finished in this manner, maple has very little color and a pale figure. Yet there is a way to bring out the beautiful deep browns, golds, and reds of maple. The old black-powder gunmakers realized how beautiful this wood can be when properly finished.

There are two ways to bring out the grain in maple. The first is to use a water stain. This only brings out the grain and doesn't give the wood any coloration other than the stain's own pigment. I don't like water stains because the results aren't comparable to that of a reagent, but they are easy to do.

An acidic reagent on maple—be it hardrock, curly, bird's-eye, or fiddleback—brings out all of the color this wood possesses. I recommend the following reagent:

1 part hydrochloric acid

1/2 part nitric acid

10 parts water

Always add the *acid* to the *water* and wear eye/face protection and rubber gloves. This reagent is not all that corrosive, but it is an acid and can cause burns.

Mix the reagent and let it age for several days to stabilize the mixture. When it is ready, finish the maple to 120 grit and apply the reagent to the wood. The wood should turn a yellowish hue.

Let the reagent soak in for a minute or so and then warm the wood. This can be done in many ways, including using a gas stove, a flame spreader on a propane torch, or an industrial heat gun—my favorite. Warm the wood slowly and watch for the color change.

Remember, you do not want to scorch the wood, only to warm it enough for the reagent to react with the sugar in the wood and

Detail of an acid-etched blade by Bill Wyant (far left). Photo by Bill Wyant

caramelize it. It is the caramelization of the sugar that gives the browns, golds, and reds to maple. The wood goes through several color changes—green, gold, brown, and finally red. Different types of maple turn different colors. Curly maple, the favorite for black-powder rifle stocks, responds especially well to this treatment.

When the preferred color is reached, stop the heating. If you get the wood too dark, you can lighten it up by lightly sanding the surface with 180- to 220-grit paper. You more than likely will need to do some sanding, as the reagent sometimes raises the grain. Besides, the surface may have reacted with the reagent, causing some heavy oxidation that must be removed for a nice smooth surface and finish.

This technique should be followed by a top-quality oil finish, such as Danish, linseed, or tung oil. I haven't tried polyurethane or epoxy finishes on maple, but they should work.

Maple can be a very beautiful wood when properly treated to bring out all of its inherent figure and color.

WOOD FINISHING

Even the most beautiful of woods can be enhanced with the proper finish. Bladesmiths must choose from several types of wood finishes ranging from traditional oils—Danish, linseed, and tung—to state-of-the-art plastic varathanes and polyurethanes. Each has advantages and disadvantages.

I prefer the more traditional oil finishes. While not as durable as the modern synthetics, they are more forgiving if they become scratched. They also tend to darken the wood a bit, which can affect the figure on more exotic woods such as coco-bolo and rosewood.

Modern plastic finishes do not oxidize or darken the wood, but they are more difficult to apply and repair if they become scratched. Yet some open-grained woods, including some walnuts, do not need to be sealed when using this type of wood finish.

Both finishes preserve the wood and bring out its inner beauty. To an extent, the simpler a finish is to apply, the more apt you are to use it. Some, including tung and linseed oil, take a lot of time and effort to apply properly. This is one reason why these finishes have faded in popularity.

Preparing the Wood

Before any finish can be applied, you must prepare the wood. Usually, this means that the wood must first be seasoned (dried), fitted, shaped, and fine-sanded.

Some woods, especially the walnuts, have a tendency to whisker. Whiskering is where the grain partially lifts when a liquid is applied to a freshly sanded surface. To prevent this, rub a damp cloth over the surface of the sanded wood to moisten it enough to raise the grain. Then go over the surface with 000 or 0000 steel wool to remove the raised grain.

With the wood properly prepared and fine sanded, apply the finish. Most oil finishes can be applied by hand (linseed and tung oil), or cheesecloth can be used to apply and smooth the oil onto the surface. Most of these finishes benefit by a light buffing, using a soft, lint-free cloth to shine the surface to a nice luster. Always follow the instructions on the particular finish you are using.

Oil Finishes

These are easy to apply and look great. There are many varieties to choose from, ranging from neutral finishes to color-enhancing stains. The key to a successful oil finish is the preparation. These finishes magnify even the slightest sanding irregularity or scratch.

Most oils must be applied at a temperature above 60 degrees F. I prefer to heat the oil to approximately 85 to 90 degrees F to improve penetration into the wood. Also, the hand-rubbed finish that everyone touts works well with this type of finish.

Apply the oil to the wood with a lint-free cloth, making certain that the entire surface is well coated. To aid in penetration, I place the grip under a vacuum for approximately 3 minutes. This draws out the air, allowing the oil to penetrate deeper into the wood and, when it hardens, increasing the protection.

Drying time can vary from several minutes to a couple of days, depending on the type of oil. Some oils, including mineral oil, never harden, and they should not be used for finishing grips. When the oil has dried, vigorously wipe off any excess with a clean, soft, lint-free cloth. This buffs the surface and smooths out any sags or runs that may have occurred.

Once dried, most of the oils (at least the natural ones) leave a dull matte finish that can be brightened by the application of hard paste wax. Carnauba wax is the best wax to protect and shine hardwoods. It leaves a hard protective coating and a high-gloss shine.

Since most of the oil finishes are self-solvent, they blend a new application with the previous one. This means you can repair minor surface scratches by applying another coat of oil to the affected area and hand rubbing to penetrate into the wood and blend the finishes.

Traditional oil finishes should be standard for most woods. And when followed by a judicious coat of quality paste wax, they will last for many, many years with a minimum of care.

Plastic Finishes

Developed primarily for the firearms industry for use on the stocks of sporting arms, these finishes include polyurethane, varathane, cyanoacrylates, and the popular epoxy finishes.

On the average, you have to work harder with these to get a smooth, even coat than with the oils. Given the small size of a knife grip, this shouldn't be too hard.

Surface preparation is the first step. Dewhisker the wood and apply the finish to the wood, following the manufacturer's instructions. Use a brush and—since these are plastic—brush in one direction only to prevent trapping air bubbles in the finish.

Drying time is much longer than for oil; hence, the grip must be placed in a dustfree area and left undisturbed until it is completely dry. When dry, these plastics have a satin or high-gloss finish, depending upon what you use. Also, plastic finishes do not darken wood as do most oils; as a matter of fact, they can lighten the wood a bit.

These finishes are not self-solvent so scratches cannot be easily removed. Instead, the entire surface must be stripped and refinished. This is difficult to do when the grip is on the knife, and this is a consideration when deciding on whether to use this type of finish.

These finishes are extremely hard and durable, and require no waxing. With proper care, they last a long time. They improve the beauty of any wood, especially already beautiful ones. Another factor in favor of using a plastic finish is that, unlike oils, they are unaffected by environmental conditions, dampness, or extremes in temperatures. Actually, the finish could possibly outlast the wood it is used on!

FINISHING STAG ANTLERS

There are other materials other than metal and wood used to embellish blades that benefit from finishing. One of my favorites is stag antlers, which make beautiful blade accents—especially Indian sambar and Sitka antlers. These antlers are dense and have colors that range from blacks and browns to golds, yellows, creams, and sometimes purple. Their coloration comes from the minerals the animals absorb through their diets.

North American stag antlers, on the other hand, are light in color, mostly in the light browns, tans, and creams. While still attractive, these colors pale in comparison to the imported Indian variety.

Through the judicious application of quality leather dyes you can improve the coloration of American stag antlers. Bladesmiths have all sorts of schemes for coloring antlers, including long soaks (up to several weeks) in exotic concoctions ranging from potassium permanganate dissolved in acetone to iron oxide. While many of these work, the coloration is on the heavy side, and it can penetrate completely through the antler, making it all one color. The overall effect looks fake. You want to enhance the appearance of the stag, not change its color. If the end product doesn't look natural, you may as well stick a piece of plastic on the grip.

I use three colors to improve the antlers that I use: cordovan red, light brown, and dark brown. Of the three, a combination of any two will improve the color. To do this, you need to fine sand the grip, and then apply the darker of the two colors first. This keeps you from dyeing the lighter color when you apply the second color. Apply the darker color in a natural pattern, unevenly streaked on to resemble the patches and splotches on natural stag.

When the first color is dried, lightly sand the surface with very fine paper, and apply the second color, feathering it into the area where the first color was applied. Let this dry. Lightly sand the stag again with fine paper and polish using a soft muslin buff and a very fine compound.

At first you may simply erase the dye, but as you become more accustomed to the process and the dyes, you will start to get usable results.

NOTE: This basic technique can be used to make cattle bone look like fossil oosic. (Oosic is an Eskimo word for a walrus penis bone, and it is a legal classification of ivory as long as it is fossilized.) When properly done, this is difficult to tell from the real thing without extremely close examination. Of course, dyeing stag and bone shouldn't be done for the purposes of forgery.

Finishing has been called an art unto itself. It is a skill that every craftsman should perfect. After all, doesn't a fine piece of wood deserve a high-quality finish?

LEATHER WORKING
& SCABBARD MAKING

A sheath or scabbard provides a way to safely carry a blade. Sheaths can be simple pouches designed only to carrying a knife, or they can be as elaborate as one wishes, with all of the bells and whistles one can conceive.

Most of the sheaths in the custom market are leather, usually cowhide, with an occasional wood or exotic skin scabbard seen from time to time. Why more elaborate sheaths are so uncommon is a mystery to me. But unfortunately, most makers, including me, put a lot of time and effort into the blade and grip and then spend 15 to 20 minutes on the sheath. A good, sturdy sheath needn't be simple, crude, or plain. They can—and should—be pleasing to look at as well as functional.

Most of the leather used in sheathmaking is vegetable-tanned cowhide (oak-tanned). This leather molds easily when wet and maintains its molded shape when dried. Oil- and chrome-tanned leather, although more durable than vegetable-tanned, does not take and hold the shape required of it for scabbards. It can also cause rust and corrosion, an unacceptable condition for a carbon-steel blade.

The leather for most molded sheaths should weigh between 5 and 7 ounces. Some larger blades may require a heavier leather, while for smaller ones, a lighter weight would be best.

You should already know the basics of constructing leather sheaths, such as the welt, single-seam, and folded, molded pouch sheath. Several interesting variations on these themes exist, including wooden and leather-covered wooden sheaths.

BUTTED-SEAM CONTOURED SHEATH

The butted-seam scabbard is similar to the single-seamed version, except it has no welt extending its length. Instead, its edges are butted edge-to-edge and sewn so the the seam is relatively smooth. This is important if you are planning to make a chape and locket because there are no severe bends to deal with and forming the sheet metal is easier.

This type of sheath works best for a symmetrical blade, but it can be used for other designs. The only prerequisite is that the shape of the blade allows for an even draw, without widening or curving toward the tip.

Cutting a Pattern

The key to doing a butted-seam scabbard is getting an accurate blade pattern. There are two ways to do this. One is to make an exact pattern from wood, plastic, or some other material from which to cut the leather. The disadvantages of this method are rather obvious. The work is nerve-wracking and takes a considerable amount of time. Fortunately, there is a simpler way to cut a pattern. For this method, you form the pattern using good-quality duct tape.

First, lightly oil the blade to prevent the tape from sticking to the surface. Next, wrap the tape sticky side out so the blade does not stick to the pattern, and spiral the tape snugly up the length of the blade and over the tip. You should have a taped blade that is easy to hold onto.

On top of the first layer of tape, wrap another layer, sticky side down. This second layer prevents the pattern from sticking to anything it touches. You now have a duct-tape tube that is the same shape and size of the blade that it encases.

NOTE: This pattern works as long as the blade is symmetrical or has no other design feature that prevents it from being drawn from a form-fitting sheath. It works very well for Sheffield Bowies, double-edged daggers, and broadswords.

With the blade encased, simply slip off the tape, and you have the basic pattern. To use the pattern, draw a centerline down the length of the tape on one flat. This line should be on the back of the sheath, so blade design and carrying should be a consideration.

Cut the tube open following the line and flatten it out. Mark the top (up side) of the pattern to avoid confusion and the problems caused if the wrong side of the pattern is placed down onto the leather.

Here is where experience in leatherworking comes in. Since the tape has more flexibility than leather, the pattern must be enlarged for the sheath to fit properly. Place the pattern, top side down, onto the back side of the leather. The leather should be no heavier than 7 ounces for this type of scabbard because heavier grades are too difficult to work.

Draw your pattern on the leather around the master with an approximately 3/16- to 1/4-inch space between the edge of the pattern and the line being drawn. This space accommodates the difference in flexibility and yet still gives a snug, form-fitting sheath.

Mark the tip of the sheath (the blade tip end) on the leather and lay out the holes. Your holes must match up and be equal on both sides for the sheath to fit. Leave 1/8 inch between each hole, which gives a tight, secure stitch.

You can punch or drill the holes or simply push the needle through, although the idea of pushing a needle through such heavy leather doesn't do a thing for me (or my hands). I've had little success with using a punch, so I drill the holes using a 3/32-inch drill. This makes neat little holes, and the spacing is easy to lay out. With the holes laid out and drilled/punched, you are ready to sew the sheath.

Stitching the Sheath

You can choose from several different stitches, some of which are rather pretty while others are plain, utilitarian seams. The most effective stitch for the beginner is the baseball stitch. For this stitch, you need about 3 1/2 times the sheath's length of thread, depending upon the thickness of the leather.

Start stitching at the tip by running the thread through the first hole on each side of the tip and pulling it through evenly. Next, run the left needle through the next hole on the right side from the inside (the rough side) of the sheath. Run the right needle through the first hole of the left side of the sheath, again from inside, and pull the thread tight (similar to lacing up a boot). Alternate the sewing, left to right and right to left, each time entering from the inside of the sheath and pulling the thread tight. The edges of the sheath butt up against each other at this point. When you have reached the end of the scabbard, double back a few holes, tie the thread off, and trim as usual. You should now have, more or less, a tube.

To fit the tube to the blade, oil the blade liberally and douse the leather with a healthy dose of acetone until it is pliable. Insert the blade into the sheath with the seam running down the flat of the blade on the sheath side that will be next to your body (carrying side). It isn't necessary to position a blade into a sheath designed for a symmetrical, double-edged blade, but it is crucial for one fitted to a single-edged or asymmetrical blade.

Block or mold the sheath around the blade to give it the shape it needs. Form it as close as you can to the blade and allow it to dry thoroughly, usually overnight. Of course, drying time varies, especially with temperature.

After the sheath is dry, you can finish it by simply trimming off any excess and then dyeing it, or you can opt for a wraparound strap. But this style simply screams for metal scabbard fittings.

The sewn, fitted, single-seam butted sheath prior to making the sheath mounts and final finish. Photo by Stephen Jacobson

Making a Chape and Locket

To make a chape and locket, use silver, nickel silver, bronze, steel, or some other type of metal sheet. I prefer using 18-gauge sheet for these, which is thick enough to do the job and yet not difficult to form.

Make your original pattern out of paper (ordinary typing paper is fine), contact cement the pattern to the metal sheet, and then cut out the pieces, following the paper as a guide. To remove the paper, simply anneal the sheet, paper side down, and the paper burns off. Wipe off any residue that remains and proceed with the forming.

Before you do any forming, deburr all edges and make certain that there are no sharp protrusions or anything else that can cut, scratch, or damage the leather while forming. Before forming the pieces around the sheath, make certain that you have the blade inside the sheath to lend some support.

Bend the pieces around the sheath by hand, as any additional force may cut or damage the leather. If you do need more force, use a small, soft-rubber mallet (a rawhide mallet might dent the metal) to persuade the pieces to move. Tap lightly; it is better to use a number of small blows to move the piece than one monstrous, smashing one. You may have to anneal the pieces from time to time, as some materials work-harden faster than others. Silver is notorious for doing this, as are most of the cupro-nickel (German silver) alloys being used today.

The formed-and-roped-edge locket ready for the seat to be applied. Photo by Stephen Jacobson

Make certain that the seams come together tightly and mate exactly. This makes the soldering easier and better. This may be difficult on the chape (tip), but work slowly and anneal frequently and it should go well.

Soldering

Hard soldering, or silver soldering as it frequently called, is closely related to brazing. Used primarily for jewelry making and some industrial applications, it requires a higher temperature than the soldering done between the blade and guard. If you are not familiar with this sort of metal attachment, learn it. It takes practice, but the skill is a requirement for the more advanced craftsman.

After forming the pieces, lightly file the mating surfaces to remove any fire scale that might have formed during the annealing processes. This leaves a clean surface for the solder to adhere to, preventing pits, voids, or other unsightly things.

Flux the pieces, making certain that you get good penetration, and heat slowly. When the piece is close to the proper heat, apply the solder and continue to heat until it flows. Like the lower-temperature solders, hard solder follows the heat source and—if the surfaces are clean and properly fluxed—flows into the seam to fill it.

NOTE: These solders are available in various flowing (melting) points; make certain that you use a solder that flows below the melting point of your metal. If not, you will know it as soon as you try to try to solder the pieces together.

Let the solder cool until it solidifies and then quench the piece.

Mounting Rings

Most swords and some daggers have mounting rings attached to the locket for securing the sheath to a belt. I have discovered how to make and attach the rings easily and yet still achieve the correct period appearance.

Make the rings from the same material as the rest of the fittings. Form the rings around a mandrel (rod) of the correct size (the rod diameter will be the inner diameter [I.D.] of the ring). Swords usually have an inner diameter of 1/2 inch, while a 3/8-inch diameter works better for daggers and smaller knives. The rod may need to be annealed prior to turning, but this in no way affects the strength of the ring once it is in place.

If you are planning on forming a lot of rings, make a ring mandrel with a handle (crank-type) and a frame to hold it. Roll the rings tightly. When you have formed enough, remove them from the mandrel and cut them. Cutting the rings can be done by using diagonal cutters (wire cutters), but that leaves a burr. For this, you need a straight butt joint, so use a jeweler's saw. Make certain that your saw is vertical, or the blade may bind or break. Simply lay the roll on its side and cut into rings.

Since the rings have been cut with a saw, you must close up the gap (the width of the saw blade) so the edges touch. Squeeze the rings together slightly and then close the ring to form a tight butt joint. Next, file or grind a small flat area around the joint. This forms a seat for the ring to sit on while it's being soldered into place. The soldering will also join both ends of the ring, thereby making the ring solid at the same time.

Position the rings onto the locket and hold in position either by wiring or clamping. There is a handy little gadget called a Third Hand that is used to hold small items to be soldered, and it works perfectly to hold the ring in place while it is being soldered. Flux and solder the ring in place, using silver solder. You may have difficulty getting the pieces to the correct temperature using a larger, industrial-grade oxyacetylene torch without melting or damaging them. A smaller minitorch, used in jewelry making and other detail work, excels at this sort of soldering. It has a small, precise flame that can get into the smallest places with little danger of melting or overheating the surrounding area. Even this is hazardous, however, as even the smallest flame can cause nasty burns. Do be careful.

When soldering the rings in place, use just enough solder to do the job. Also, heat from one side of the ring/locket and apply the solder from the opposite (off) side. Let the solder flow into the joints. Remove the torch and let cool. Quench and proceed with the other rings, if any. After soldering the rings into place, you can add further ornamentation if desired or finish in any way you want.

Roped Edges

Roped edges are one of the oldest decorations used in metalwork. Traditionally, metal workers rolled the edges and then hammered/ punched the rope design into the metal roll. This takes a great degree of skill and years of practice. Yet, by using twisted wire you can get the desired effect without all of the work, time, and practice.

I have an abundant supply of twisted wire that is too short for grips, so I simply use it to form the decorative borders on some of my sheath fittings. It looks great, and it is not that difficult once you know how to silver solder.

The wire should be annealed for close fitting of the wire to the surface. Also, one side of the wire should be ground or filed flat. When doing this,

Close-up of completed roped-edge fittings made by the author. The roping effect is accomplished by soldering twisted wire to the edge of the sheath mounts prior to their attachment to the sheath. Photo by Stephen Jacobson

be certain that you do not flatten the wire all the way through. This causes the wire to come apart. Just flatten the tops of the twists for this to work. You are ready to rope the edges.

The easiest ones to do are simple, straight-edged collars without any fancy shapes, cutouts, or other projections to complicate matters. On the simple fittings, take the wire and make a ring around the outside of the fittings, along the edge where the wire will be positioned.

The flat area on the wire should be against the fitting's surface. Cut the wire slightly undersized to get a snug press fit on the mounts. This lets you hold the wire in position without difficulty.

When the wire is cut to size, hard solder the ring together and let cool.

Next, reposition the wire on the fitting and check for fit. If everything is correct, flux and soft solder. I heat from the inside of the fitting, letting the heat radiate through the wall to heat the wire from underneath.

Also, apply the solder sparingly, from the outer edge of the assembly, along the joint between the two. Pounding the solder into a thin strip lets you use a smaller amount. The solder flows when the proper temperature is reached and follows the heat around the seam. The entire seam must be soldered down to ensure that it stays in place during use.

After attaching the first rope, go on to the second one. There may be a tendency for the heat to bleed into the first seam. To prevent this, use some sort of heat sink on the first roping. There are various types of this material available, most of which look like cold oatmeal. Simply apply it around the area you wish to protect and then solder.

NOTE: Keep the heat sink material off the working area because it can prevent the solder from adhering.

When the second rope is completed, you can finish the edges. I apply the roping before I do any additional decoration, such as setting stones or applying pierce work.

Setting Stones onto Sheath Fittings

The practice of setting semiprecious or precious stones onto a sheath dates back a millennium or more. Some designers go in for a decadent, opulent look, while others prefer a more austere appearance. I prefer the latter, more subdued approach.

The presence of a single, well-cut stone on the sheath can make both the sheath and the blade look better. I like to use stones of the harder varieties, including agate, quartz, and corundum. These hard, durable stones are better suited on scabbards than the softer, more delicate stones, such as turquoise and opal. I also prefer cabochon-cut stones, most of which are oval with a slight dome on top. They are available in a variety of sizes and materials.

Seat and Bezel

The seat is a piece of thin sheet on which the stone sits. It can be made of almost anything, but I use the same material as the rest of the piece. The bezel is a narrow strip of thin-gauge material (lighter than 22-gauge) that is usually made of silver, but jeweler's bronze, copper, nickel silver, or other soft materials can be used. Again, I use the same material as the rest of the piece. The bezel should be no wider than 3/16 inch and absolutely dead soft to allow for the stone to be set and the bezel rolled.

To form the bezel, simply wrap the bezel strip around the stone, closely following the shape of the stone, and cut to length. With the bezel cut, prepare to hard solder it together. Edges and seams that are even, smooth, and perfectly mated simplify the soldering of the bezel.

You should use a mini-torch for soldering because a larger torch melts the bezel before it can be soldered. Flux well and heat slowly and evenly to prevent the bezel from melting during the process.

Apply a small amount of solder and monitor the heat. Excessive heating not only melts the bezel, it can also cause a grainy appearance on the finished surface. When the solder flows, stop heating immediately and quench the bezel.

Your stone should pass through the bezel snugly. If the bezel is correct, solder the bezel to the seat. Check the fit between the bezel edge and the seat's surface. There should be no gaps. If there are, trim the edge of the bezel until it rests evenly on the seat. To do the trimming, use a small, fine-cut file and lightly remove material until the bezel sits without gaps. Remember, this material is very thin and deforms easily, so work lightly.

After fitting the stone, you hard solder it. To do this, place the bezel down onto the seat and flux. I apply the flux to the inside of the bezel, and this is more than adequate to do the job. Apply the heat from underneath the seat and move it around under the bezel to get an even heat. Apply a small amount of solder and let it flow around the joint, filling it and leaving an even-soldered seam.

When the solder flows, remove the heat and quench. Next, trim the excess sheet from the seat and file flush to the bezel. NOTE: If you are mounting this stone on fittings with a roped edge, a nice touch is to rope the edge on the stone mounting as well. To do so, form a tight-fitting ring out of the same wire that you used for the roping and solder it in place before you trim the excess off the seat. This little extra adds a lot to the overall appearance of the piece.

With the seat completed, trim the bezel down to approximately 5/32 of an inch high. This gives enough room for packing and securing the bezel without looking ridiculous on the finished stone.

Next, attach the stone seat to the mounts by using soft solder. You may have to apply the heat sink to the previously soldered roping to prevent it from moving.

To solder the seat, take a small section of soft solder, approximately 1/8 inch long, and flatten it with a hammer. Flattening allows for a minimal amount of solder to be placed between the two, thereby reducing any excess solder.

Position the seat, flux the area on the fittings, and place the solder on the fittings. Next, flux the bottom of the seat, place that in final position on top of the solder, and secure in place. Heat slowly from the bottom using a soft flame until the solder flows. The solder joins the two into a single unit. Remove the heat and let cool until the solder is hard.

If the seat moves, reheat and reposition it while the solder is still molten. Hold the seat in place (using a small piece of bamboo or whatever) until the solder solidifies.

The fittings are now ready for cleaning and polishing. Remove any excess solder with files, extra-fine sandpaper, or a flexible shaft machine. I strongly recommend the flexible shaft, with fine or extra-fine wheels to keep final buffing to a minimum.

You also must remove any fire scale, discoloration, or other surface blemishes. These can be removed with a jeweler's pickle. These come in two types: acidic hot pickles and nonacid cold pickles. Both work, but I prefer the hot pickles because they remove almost all of the fire scale and discoloration quickly.

NOTE: You cannot use any iron, steel, or other ferric alloys when pickling. Iron poisons the pickle and causes a hard-to-remove flashing of copper to appear on everything in the bath. I use a Pyrex container and bamboo tongs to handle the pieces. Copper tongs also work. Remember to take all of the standard safety precautions advised when using acids: wear face/eye protection, rubber gloves, and an apron, and keep a box of baking soda handy in case of a spill.

Follow the instructions on the pickling container and place the pieces in the pickle so they are completely covered and do not touch. I check every 5 to 10 minutes. When the pickling is complete, the pieces should be dark with an even gray coating. This gray coating is the leached outer surface of material (after all, these are acids) that is easily removed. In fact, it usually wipes away with a soft cloth.

Rinse the pickling solution off in clean water and then neutralize with a soda bath for about a minute. Wipe the surface with a soft cloth and then polish. The polish should remove all of the scratches and shine the surface to a perfectly smooth, mirrorlike finish. Be careful not to deform the bezel; I prefer to use a flexible shaft and small muslin wheels for working in this area.

After completing the buffing, you must hand polish. Use a top-quality metal paste polish and a soft muslin cloth to do the hand polishing to really bring out the beauty of the metal, especially bronze or silver.

Setting the Stone

Stone setting is not difficult, but it can be tricky. First, you need some sort of cushion to protect the stone in the setting. The cushion helps the stone to absorb shocks and bumps that could cause it to fracture or shatter. Even the slightest bit of give is better than none at all. But, even more important is the fact that the cushion allows for adjustments in seating the stone that may be necessitated by irregularities in the shape or cut of the stone itself.

For my cushioning, I use sawdust—it doesn't matter what kind. Place

STONE, FOIL, CUSHION, ROLLING

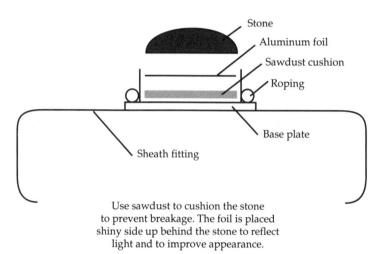

Use sawdust to cushion the stone
to prevent breakage. The foil is placed
shiny side up behind the stone to reflect
light and to improve appearance.

"Roll" the bezel over the stone so it is smooth
against the stone. Use a smooth steel burnisher
and work gently but firmly until the bezel
is rolled over evenly.

a pinch or two in the bezel and press it down. Leave room for the stone and for rolling the bezel over the stone's edge. Even out the cushion so the stone sits straight in the bezel.

If the stone you are using is translucent, you can improve its appearance by using foil backing to reflect some of the light back through the stone. I use a small piece of aluminium foil, shiny side up. This technique has been used in jewelry making for centuries to improve the looks of a stone. It is not unethical to do this; in fact, it serves the same purpose as the hole at the back of the most mountings. This hole is a major reason that faceted stones refract so much light and seem to sparkle.

Insert the stone on top of the foil. Make certain that it is even and centered in the bezel. This is the secret of a good bezel mount, keeping the stone straight and centered during the process.

Hold the stone down securely in the mounting and roll the bezel over the edge of the stone until it is flat against the dome. I use a curved burnisher (available at jeweler's supply stores) to do this. If you do not have one, a teaspoon accomplishes the same thing. Place your thumb in the spoon and use that to roll the bezel over. Polish the outside of the spoon first so you do not mar the bezel. On really stubborn bezels, a spoon lets you put more pressure on the bezel without worrying about impaling yourself with the burnisher.

You may have to go over the bezel two or three time to ensure that there are no gaps between it and the stone. As you roll the bezel, make certain that the stone remains

The finished mount has been fitted; the seat soldered, cleaned, and polished; and the stone set prior to mounting on the sheath. Photo by Stephen Jacobson

The completed wrapped sheath has been dyed and waxed, and the fittings have been mounted. The author made the silver mounts set with lapis lazuli. Photo by Stephen Jacobson

centered and straight. There should be no movement of the stone in the mount. Polish the stone by hand, using a top-quality metal paste and a soft cotton cloth.

You are now ready to mount the fittings on the scabbard. Coat the area of the leather where the fittings will rest and the inside of the fittings with contact cement. When this is dry, place the two together in the proper position. Next, place the blade inside the sheath to force the two together more securely. They should stay together for a good many years.

If you would prefer not to use cement, you can rivet the pieces to the sheath from the back, but the rivets could mar the blade if the two touch.

Metal scabbard fittings, whether plain or fancy, can vastly improve the overall appearance of both the scabbard and the blade.

WOODEN SHEATHS

Wooden sheaths are traditional for swords and larger knives. They come in many styles and variations, from simple, yet elegant lacquered Japanese sheaths to fleece-lined, leather-covered Viking scabbards. In fact, there are so many variations that to list them all would require more than a single chapter. So we will deal with the basics, and you can always pursue the topic if you wish.

Wooden sheaths can be broken down into three types: simple, lined, and lined and covered.

Simple Wooden Sheaths

Simple wooden sheaths are usually encountered with Japanese blades. They are unlined and usually finished in either a natural (shira saya) or lacquered finish. Their construction theory may sound simple, but to do one correctly takes a great degree of skill and practice.

Since these sheaths are unlined, you must give careful consideration to the type of wood used. Do not use a wood that weeps sap or other resins onto the blade surface. The Japanese use well-seasoned white magnolia. You can use any of the exotic hardwoods as long as they are properly seasoned and pitch-free. There are two ways to make this type of scabbard, the two-piece and the three-piece method.

Making a Two-Piece Sheath

The two-piece sheath requires basic woodworking skill and knowledge. You must gouge/chisel a cavity the same shape and size as one-half of the blade in each piece.

The wood stock should be large enough to allow for a 3/16-inch wall thickness, plus some error. Roughly shape the sides to size prior to tracing the blade onto the mating surfaces on each side of the sheath blank.

If you lay the blade with the grain (along the grain in the wood), tracing the inletting guide is much easier than attempting to cut across the grain. The most important step in inletting is cutting the tracing into the wood with a bench knife. A bench knife is very sharp and stout and cuts down into the wood, thereby providing a stop to the inlet and preventing overcutting.

Inletting is a very tricky process. It goes slowly at the start and gets slower as the work progresses. If you rush it, chances are you'll ruin it. Use either a sharp gouge or wood chisel. I use a chisel because it gives a smooth cut and shapes the angles properly.

Start cutting at the throat (the end that the blade will enter) and work toward the tip. You can do a rough cut, but be careful that you do not cut too deeply and remove too much wood. You want to make the cavity as close to the shape of the blade as possible for a better fit.

Using an inletting compound makes the fitting easier. Inletting compound is a pigment in a grease base. Apply the compound to the blade before placing it in the cavity. The compound rubs off onto the high spots, showing you where the wood needs to be trimmed. As the inletting progresses, the area marked by the compound will get larger and larger. You have a properly inletted sheath when the cavity is totally covered by the compound—indicating that the inletting is even and fitted—and exactly one-half of the blade protrudes above the sheath surface. Align the cavity and the edges of the sheath blanks to prevent any errors in wall thickness and shape.

To remove the inletting compound from the wood, sand the inside of the sheath with a medium-grit paper. This not only removes the compound, it also gives you a little extra room in the inletting for fitting the two halves prior to the final assembly. To do this, remove any high spots between the two halves with a sanding block and medium grit paper. When the two pieces form a perfect seam, you are ready to glue them together.

Before gluing, sand the pieces with 80- to 100-grit paper to leave just enough roughness for the glue to get a good purchase on the surfaces. The pieces should be perfectly flat so there are no gaps, visible seams, or other apparent clues as to how the sheath was put together. (You should try to match the grain on the pieces being used if the sheath is going to be finished in the wood's natural graining. If you are going to lacquer the sheath with a colored lacquer, this isn't necessary.)

Apply the glue sparingly because any excess is squeezed out and could interfere with the blade if it dries on the inside of the sheath. You can also improvise a long "Q-Tip" swab to remove the excess glue from the inside.

After the sheath is set and cured, you can shape it entirely by hand using wood rasps and sandpaper, or you can use a belt grinder to do the rough shaping and do the final shaping by hand. It is up to you, but remember not to remove too much wood or the walls and edges will be

END VIEW OF WOOD SCABBARDS

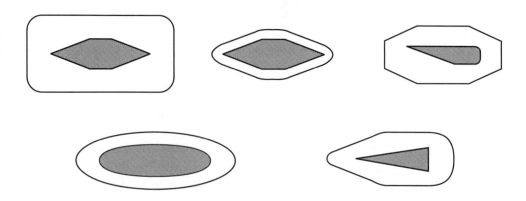

too thin. How thin is too thin? It depends on the wood. Some woods, including oak, ash, and magnolia, are stable in thin sections. Others, including coco-bolo, ebony, ironwood, and most of the so-called tropical woods, are prone to checking.

Unless you like a squared-off rectangle, you should shape the scabbard. You can select from many different variations. An end view as shown above gives you an idea of how they can be shaped. Apply a final finish after final shaping

Two-piece sheaths are quite beautiful in their simplicity. As with most simple things, their beauty secrets lie in raw materials, the lines and execution of the design, and the sophistication of the shaping, fitting, and finishing.

Making the Three-Piece Sheath

To make this type of sheath, form two sides and a spacer. Match the grain closely so the sheath looks its best. (If you are going to cover the blade, this is not necessary.)

To make the spacer, simply take a piece of wood the same thickness as the blade and the same width as the sheath you are making. Next, position the blade on the spacer and trace around the outside of the blade to give you the cutting lines. You are now ready to cut the cavity where the blade lies inside the sheath.

You can use a coping, jig, or band saw to do the cutting. To make cutting the tip easier, drill a small diameter hole at the tip (3/16 inch or so is fine). This makes it easier to end the cut without cracking or breaking the wood.

When you are cutting the tracing, cut on the inside of the line and then remove any excess with a hand rasp, file, or sandpaper. Make certain that you check the fit occasionally so you do not overdo the filling. Do a dry run on the fit using rubber bands and when everything checks out,

LINED CONSTRUCTION

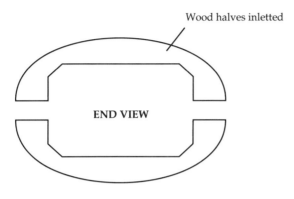

END VIEW

Wood halves inletted

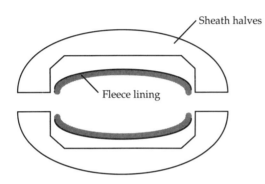

Sheath halves

Fleece lining

With the sheath halves inletted, place the lining inside the halves and try the fit prior to cementing the lining into final position.

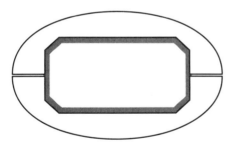

When the fit is correct, cement the lining into place and then cement the scabbard halves together.

do the final assembly.

For the final assembly, apply a light coat of a quality glue, such as carpenter's glue (the yellow, not the white glue), to the pieces prior to assembling and clamping. After the glue is cured, shape and finish the sheath in any way you desire.

The three-piece method is in some ways a lot easier than the two-piece, but it requires a lot more wood. If the sheath is to be covered, you can use almost anything that is stable enough to make a sheath, with little concern for color or grain.

Lined Sheath

Lined sheaths are the next step up from simple sheaths. They are usually lined in leather, felt, or fleece to protect the blade. While a little more complicated than the simple sheath, they are still simple to construct. The outside is usually finished naturally, but you can lacquer, stain, or paint it if you choose.

Choosing a Lining

Keeping a blade in a lined sheath is one of the best ways to preserve it. The right lining can keep a blade in near-perfect condition. Using the wrong lining, however, can damage it severely. Traditionally, scabbards have been lined with close-shorn sheepskin. Its natural lanolin preserves the blade and prevents rusting.

The lining of these sheaths makes them bulky, but the added size does not mean that they can't be graceful and beautiful. Getting the lining the right thickness is important in determining how the sheath looks. If it is too thick, the sheath will look too big for the blade.

Although sheepskin was the material of choice in the past, its availability has become severely limited in most areas. It is still available, but it takes time, effort, and money to find a good supply. If you can obtain it, choose skin whose nap (or fleece) is no longer than 1/8 to 3/16 inch long. This reduces the bulk of the sheath so it will not look like a log on the end of a sword grip.

For those who don't choose to use sheepskin, any top-quality vegetable-tanned leather (undyed is best) in the 2-ounce range will do.

Constructing the Sheath

The lining touches the blade on the flats but not on the edges, as this will result in a cut lining. If the lining gets cut, it can pull away from the wood covering, causing it to bunch up in the bottom of the sheath. This can prevent the blade from being inserted or withdrawn, which could be embarrassing at best or fatal at worst.

The cavity isn't fitted to the blade. Rather, it is rectangular, with the lining filling the spaces created by the blade's cross section. You can fit the wood to the blade/lining, but it's far more work than it's worth. It makes no difference in the finished scabbard's looks or function. It is best to fit the sheaths around the lining.

The wood does not need to be as thick as on the unlined scabbards, but it must be thick enough in the walls and edges to support the lining and to last. With most woods, a wall thickness of 1/8 inch works well.

Making this sheath is basically the same as the simple sheath described above, but you must place the blade and both strips of the lining in the sheath halves before fitting. The fit should be snug the entire length but not too tight. If it is too tight, you can't easily insert or withdraw the blade. If you force a blade into too tight of a sheath, you may split the wood or the seams. A too loose sheath may allow the blade to snag the lining and tear it free of the scabbard walls. A snug fit is needed to maintain the lining's position within the sheath's housing.

Cut the sheath lining the same basic size and shape as the blade profile, and then trim it to the exact dimensions when the time comes to do the final assembly. Check the size and fit prior to the final assembly. The inside surfaces should be smooth but not finely sanded so the cement can adhere. A surface of 80- to 100-grit (the same as for gluing the seams) provides a more-or-less smooth surface with enough purchase to allow for the lining to be held securely.

Fitting the linings seems tricky at first, and it requires a great deal of practice and patience. The first few may appear clunky, but as you acquire the skills, you'll turn out sheaths that complement your blades.

After fitting the lining, you must cement it to the wood. This part is somewhat tricky. You have to glue the lining into the sheath halves without getting any glue onto the lining. Work carefully, slowly, and sparingly as far as the amount of glue is concerned. You may wish to cut the lining slightly undersized to prevent any glue from getting into the lining, hardening, and causing scratches on the blade.

When the lining has dried, try a final fit before gluing the two halves together. Clamp the two halves together and let the glue harden. At this point, you need to make a plug to seal the throat and prevent any dust, grit, dirt, or other contaminants from entering and causing all sorts of problems later. I use tissue paper (the drawing type, not the "personal" variety) and duct tape to form the basic shape and then wedge this in the sheath tightly to seal it.

With the plug in place, you can shape the outside of the sheath. Follow the basic shape of the blade. As you are shaping, make certain that the plug remains in place to keep out contaminants. Finish the wood to your personal preference, and, after everything is dried, remove the plug.

When the outside of the sheath is completed, "charge" the lining. Charging is simply applying oil or some other rust preventative to the interior of the sheath to help protect the blade. If your lining is sheepskin, use lanolin, which is found naturally in the hide and is effective in preventing rust.

To get the oils into the lining, simply apply a heavy coat of oil to the blade and then place it into the sheath. Do this every time the blade is drawn for the first five to seven drawings, and the lining should be fully charged. Thereafter, apply occasional coatings to keep the lining charged. The process is the same for any petroleum-based oil. Do not use any vegetable or organic oils because these deteriorate or turn rancid, which can corrode the blade.

Although lined sheaths are thicker than simple ones, they are not that ungainly. They can be graceful and beautiful.

LINED AND FULLY COVERED SHEATH

The most difficult of the three styles is the lined and fully covered sheath. This sheath is usually lined with close-shorn fleece, and its outer surface is covered with lightweight leather. This style is the most appropriate for Viking-style swords and period blades.

This sheath is made exactly like the lined one—except you do not need an exotic or expensive wood for its body, which will be covered. I have used 1/4-inch plywood and even laminated doorskins (Luan mahogany), and they work great. Who cares if they are uglier than sin? They're going to be covered anyway. Using laminated "wood" lets you make the walls thinner than is possible with nonlaminated wood, which translates into a lighter, stronger, and better-proportioned scabbard.

Follow the directions for fabricating, lining, and shaping this sheath given in the section on the lined sheath, except allow for the leather covering. Since the leather is thin (garment weight), undersize just slightly.

Sand the outer surface smooth but rough enough for the glue. Your surface should be free from dips, waves, rough areas, or any other imperfections that would be visible after the leather covering is in place. Sand the surface to 80- to 100-grit. If you sand through the top veneer of the plywood into the center-core laminations, you have to fill in the depressions. Use wood putty to plug the holes and sand it smooth. The putty does not interfere with the cement that holds the covering in place.

Since the sheath is rigid, make the covering along the lines of a butted-seam wrapped scabbard—except do not sew the leather until it is on the sheath body. I have tried all sorts of different tannages, types, and weights of leather, and I believe garment weights work best. They are soft and stretchable enough to give a snug, smooth fit. Snakeskin is also excellent for this. But whatever you use, remember it needs to be durable and stretchy.

Cement the top side of the sheath and leather together, then glue the edges and both flaps of the leather on the underside, leaving the edges uncemented. You want about one-third of the total amount left loose to allow for sewing. Use the baseball stitch described in the section on simple sheaths. You should have to stretch the leather slightly to make the edges meet. This pulls the leather down close to the sheath and allows for a tight stitch. As you sew, cement the leather down. This keeps your covering from moving in the slightest. When the sewing is completed, trim off any excess, and finish as desired.

You can attach metal fittings, leather straps, or anything you desire. You can overlay leather cutwork in a contrasting color, use exotic leathers, even install pierced metalwork fittings. And you can vary your tooling, dyeing, or leatherworking techniques for new and unique designs.

A sheath is the only way to carry and protect a high-quality blade. And a handmade blade deserves a handmade sheath, especially when you consider that it's the sheath that people usually see when you're carrying a blade. So the sheath should be pleasing to look at as well as functional. Sheaths made by the techniques described in this chapter last for a long time.

SWORDMAKING:
THE ROMANCE
OF THE SWORD

The term "sword" stirs the imagination. Legends of great powers and magic are interwoven around swords of myth and history. King Arthur, wielding the sword Excalibur, carved out the magical kingdom of Camelot and left his name in man's memory. But what causes this infatuation with the sword to be so strong? I cannot answer.

There is something that lives inside a piece of well-forged steel that compels most of us to pick it up, feel its spirit, and admire its sheer strength and beauty. This is especially true of the sword. I have felt the power that dwells within this majestic blade many times. I am not talking about some occult or supernatural phenomenon. Sooner or later, every bladesmith feels this yearning, this need, that can only be fulfilled by forging a sword.

Swordmaking is the most demanding, difficult, and rewarding aspect of bladesmithing. The talent, patience, skills, and knowledge required to forge a sword are far greater than those needed to make a knife or dagger. The differences between a 3-foot sword and a 1-foot knife are far more than the 2-foot difference in length.

First, one must understand the function of a sword. It is not a big knife. The function of the sword is not to cut but to chop and cleave through muscle, bone, and light armor. While the functions seem similar, they are fundamentally different.

A knife is expected to cut and hold a fine, sharp edge for the longest possible time. In normal use, there are few, if any, vibrations or shocks that a knife has to endure. That is not the case with a sword.

Swords swing and impact either on human targets, metal shields, or other impediments, including another sword. Swords have to be tougher and more durable than knives, or, after a few encounters, you find yourself holding a nice hilt with about six inches of blade.

Because swords are designed to withstand these powerful impacts, the first difference between them and knives is the steel. Just because a certain steel makes a good knife does not mean that it makes a functional sword. Most "knife" steels get too hard and brittle for swords. And if tempered to an acceptable toughness, they become too soft to withstand the beating expected of swords.

SELECTING A STEEL

The best steel to forge into a sword has a carbon content between 60 and 75 points. That is enough carbon to harden sufficiently without becoming brittle. I recommend the alloys 1060, 1070, and especially 5160. Of course, you can use 1095/1084 or other simple alloys, but the richer alloys are not acceptable (with the exception of the S series and L-6, which are designed for high-impact use).

Some bladesmiths—and stock-removal makers as well—do use high-tech steels. To compensate for the brittleness, they make the blades much thicker than required with a simpler, more appropriate steel. They end up with an extremely heavy sword that is difficult and tiring to use.

SWORD WEIGHT

Weight must be considered when selecting a steel to make a sword. Keep the weight as light as possible, without sacrificing strength for lightness. Fighting swords were lighter than most people think. For some reason, most people think that medieval broadswords weighed between 10 and 20 pounds. A blade that heavy would be far too difficult to lift, much less swing in earnest. Most period swords had blades 3/16 to 1/4 inch thick and weighed around 4 pounds.

The 4-pound range seems ideal. Most men can swing 4 pounds for hours with little training, but handling 6 pounds is a task. Most bladesmiths use a 3-pound hammer; some use a 4-pounder with little effort; but very few wield a 6-pound hammer for the majority of forge work because it is just too tiring. Even a small difference in weight makes a big difference when swinging a sword.

CONSTRUCTION CONSIDERATIONS

The construction methods for swords are entirely different than for knives. Although knives can be put together in just about any fashion, the design and construction of swords are much more critical.

Form Follows Function

The basic design should be able to withstand the vibrations and shocks that a sword encounters. These can be severe, but if the design is sound and the materials and craftsmanship are up to standard, there should be no problem with this aspect.

Form should follow function: the design should not conflict with the basic use of the sword. There should be no weak spots in the design or execution, such as square corners, faulty tempering, or underbuilt tangs.

Flexibility

A sword must be flexible as well as strong. While swords should be stiff enough to thrust effectively, they should have a small degree of flexibility to absorb some of the strains and vibrations of combat. No sword can withstand a powerful blow delivered with the flat of the blade, but a properly tempered sword can withstand a blow delivered to the blade's flat.

Hilt

Another construction decision is the type of grip. You can use almost any material for a knife grip, but sword grips require special consideration. They must be tough and resilient enough to withstand tremendous vibrations.

Classic Broadsword Design

Many different sword designs have been used through the ages, but we will concentrate on the classic medieval broadsword used from the fall of Rome in the sixth century through the early Renaissance period, the sixteenth century. Even within this relatively short period of time (1,000 years), the broadsword evolved into its finest forms, and it is these forms that people think of when they hear the word sword.

Everyone has his or her own ideas about what a sword is supposed to look like. Some of these ideas are right on target in terms of design and function, while others edge on the fantastic, with form being more important than function. But a quick look back in history shows us what types of swords were used and why. Swords were weapons, and the designs that prevailed did so for just one reason: *they worked.*

I am not discounting the modern designs being produced by some contemporary swordmakers. Most of these are works of art; they are not weapon quality in design or function. We're not going to deal with the sword as an art form, so we'll look at the classic broadsword, a double-edged blade used to fight.

The broadsword was designed to enable its holder to do one thing: terminate an unfriendly encounter in the shortest possible time. The earliest swords had blades that were wide and relatively flat. They usually didn't encounter much in the way of armor, so their blades were

SWORD CROSS SECTIONS

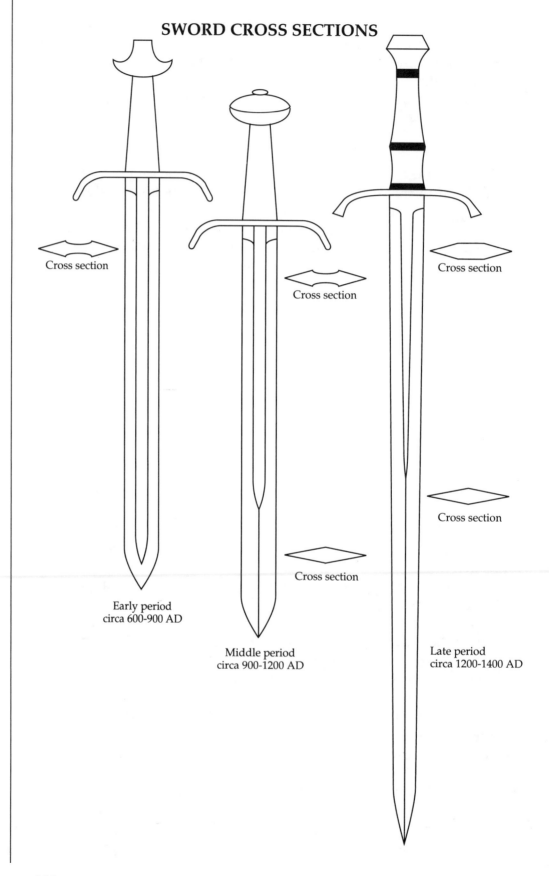

Cross section

Cross section

Cross section

Cross section

Cross section

Early period
circa 600-900 AD

Middle period
circa 900-1200 AD

Late period
circa 1200-1400 AD

designed to slice and cut rather than chop and cleave. (For a more complete discussion of these blades, read R. Ewart Oakeshott's *Sword in the Age of Chivalry*, Arms and Armour Press, London, 1964.)

Blade lengths ran from 26 to 36 inches, with widths being in the 1 3/4- to 2-inch range. The grips were 4 to 4 1/2 inches in length. These short grips limited the swordsman to sweeping motions using the entire arm rather than the more comfortable chopping action controlled by wrist movements.

With time, the use of the sword changed from the more cumbersome arm-only movement that the short grip required into a more effective combination of arm, wrist, and hand. This meant that the sword grips had to be longer to accommodate the movement this fighting style demanded. So the sword evolved into a more tapered blade, with a usable point for thrusting attacks. Blade cross sections remained either flattened diamonds or were fullered with a deep hollow grind to maintain stiffness.

The points themselves were sometimes thicker to remain intact during heavy thrusts. The blade's center section was heavier, and later blades commonly had central ribs.

Overcoming Problems of Length

The blade is what makes a sword. But at what length does a knife become a sword? Any blade over 18 inches, in my opinion, becomes a sword.

The length itself can cause some problems. Not all forges can accommodate a sword-length piece all at once. This is not a problem in the actual forging, but it can be a great drawback when it comes to hardening/tempering. During forging, sectional heating is actually preferable to heating the entire length, since one can only work a small section at a time before the metal drops below forging temperatures. The unworked portions risk the possibility of grain growth.

You can overcome the length problem by building or purchasing a long gas- or coal-fired forge for heat treating. Although a coal fire has some advantages when it comes to welding and localized heats, a gas-fired forge (like the one illustrated on page 166) can facilitate forging and tempering a long blade and reduce heat-treating time on most other blades because fire maintenance is nil.

This isn't the easiest forge to build, but it does work. By using the proper refractories and carefully monitoring the heat, you can maintain a welding heat, which helps in forging a pattern-welded sword.

Another problem associated with the sword's length is how to harden the blade. Most commercial heat-treating firms can handle lengths to 24 inches, but how do you harden/temper a 36-inch piece of steel?

I commissioned a custom tempering tank that measures 14 x 14 x 48 inches and has a removable lid. It is made from 16-gauge galvanized steel, but any nonflammable material can be used.

A quick and easy tank can be made from 10-inch diameter steel pipe

LPG SWORD FORGE

Use same burner assembly as in Chapter 1.
Position burners every 6". Plumb the burners
in 2 sections, i.e. 1 - 3 burner assembly
and 1 - 2 burner assembly.

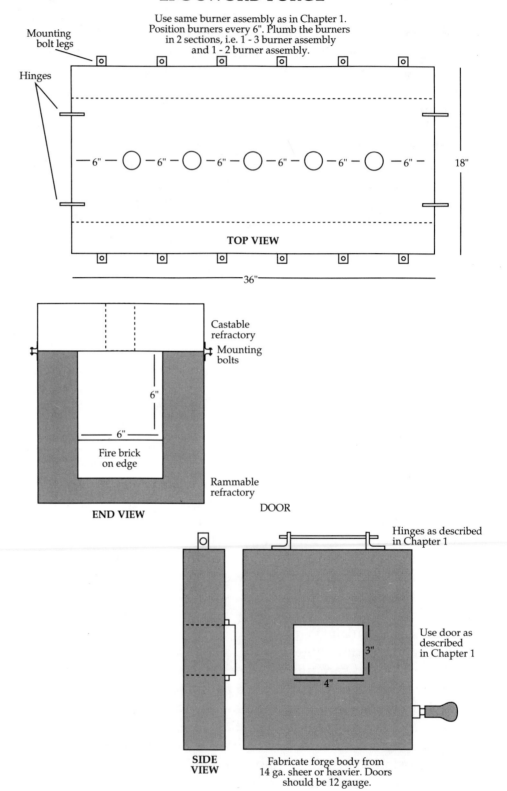

Mounting bolt legs

Hinges

18"

TOP VIEW

— 6" — ○ — 6" — ○ — 6" — ○ — 6" — ○ — 6" — ○ — 6" —

36"

Castable refractory

Mounting bolts

6"

6"

Fire brick on edge

Rammable refractory

DOOR

END VIEW

Hinges as described in Chapter 1

Use door as described in Chapter 1

3"

4"

SIDE VIEW

Fabricate forge body from
14 ga. sheer or heavier. Doors
should be 12 gauge.

166

with a 1/8-inch steel plate welded/brazed onto one end to form a watertight seal. Make certain that you have at least 2 to 2 1/2 inches of additional depth over the length of the longest blade you intend to make. For example, if the quenching tank is 32 inches deep, then the longest blade you can handle is 30 inches.

If you are going to have a custom sheet-metal tank fabricated, be sure to place a piece of weighted lumber at least 1 inch thick on the bottom to prevent any punctures if you drop a blade. Also use at least 16-gauge steel because the weight of the quenching medium can get heavy, and lighter metals may bow out quite a ways.

Cutting the Steel

The steel stretches out quite a bit during the actual forging, so cut the steel slightly shorter than you want the finished blade. The difference depends on the blade's design, whether it is fullered or not, and the forger's skill and ability.

Forging the Tang

After cutting the steel, the next step is forging the tang. This can be done by hand or by using anvil top/bottom tools or a power hammer with a double round fuller to separate the ricasso/tang sections.

Start the tang about 2 1/2 to 3 inches from the end of the bar, depending upon the width/thickness of the material and the desired length of the tang. Do not overheat the steel at any time during the process. This weakens the grain structure and can cause the steel to fail.

The sword's tang is perhaps the most neglected area when it comes to design versus function. It is also one of the more structurally sensitive areas in terms of stresses and vibration. So if not properly constructed, it can break easily.

How does one decide how big a tang to leave when making the separation? This answer is simple: as big as possible. This is easier on some blades than others. A good rule to follow is this: the tang's width should be no less than one-half the width of the blade at its widest. For example, a 1 1/2-inch blade should have a tang that is at least 3/4-inch wide, and 7/8 inch or 1 inch is even better.

Getting the right tang thickness is another factor in preventing breakage. Leave as much thickness as possible in the tang. The more material there is, the more stress the tang can withstand.

The main reason the sword breaks at the ricasso/tang junction is the stress localized by square corners at the junction. Steel under stress hates square corners. Any abrupt or radical change in cross sections produces a stress "riser" that can cause cracking or fracturing when placed under a stress load.

This problem can be prevented by properly radiusing the tang/ricasso shoulders. This allows the quillion (hand guard) to align flush against the ricasso, while the ricasso makes a smooth transition into the tang. This smoothness in metal distributes the stress and vibration more evenly into the tang from the blade.

Draw the tang out, tapering evenly from the top to the end. The finished length should be in the 6-inch range, with the last 2 to 2 1/2 inches being 3/8-inch diameter round. Refine the round section with a tenon tool of the appropriate size. Do not file the corners of the ricasso/tang junction at this point in the process.

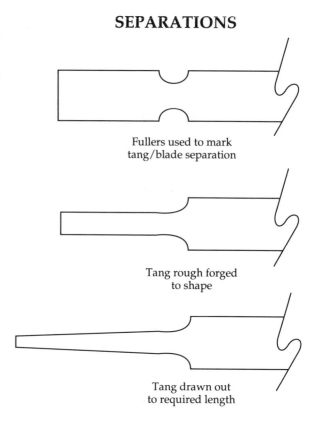

SEPARATIONS

Fullers used to mark
tang/blade separation

Tang rough forged
to shape

Tang drawn out
to required length

Forging the Blade

Forging a sword blade is similar to forging a long dagger with bigger dimensions—except the steel is less cooperative. If you are going to taper the blade, do so at this time. Remember that the steel stretches as it is worked, lengthening the blade in proportion to the amount of taper. Also, as you taper the width of the steel, you also put in a distal taper to aid in the overall balance and function of the blade.

Start the taper at the point of the blade and work back down its length toward the ricasso, keeping the taper as even as possible.

Begin each successive series of hammering in the same basic manner but stop slightly short of the ending point of the prior series. This puts the basic taper in the blade. Also, the steel thickens somewhat as the blade is drawn down, so correct this as you work. Start to forge in the distal taper on the thickness of the blade.

Fullering

If you are going to fuller the blade and if the fuller is to terminate at the ricasso, the entire blade from where the ricasso ends and the

CORRECTION RADII/INCORRECT SQUARED CORNERS

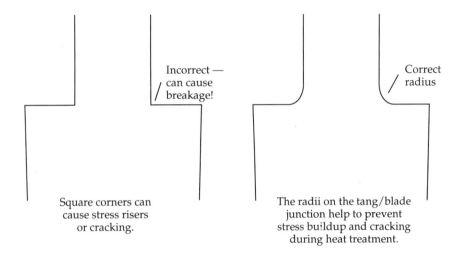

Incorrect — can cause breakage!

Correct radius

Square corners can cause stress risers or cracking.

The radii on the tang/blade junction help to prevent stress buildup and cracking during heat treatment.

choil/fuller starts must be forged narrower than normal to compensate for the expansion of the fullering. Make certain that the ricasso area is full-sized. The blade widens as the fuller deepens, spreading out until it is full width (or slightly wider).

Also, do not put a heavy distal taper on a fullered blade. A heavy distal taper prevents the fuller from being forged to the proper depth toward the point because the blade is too thin to allow it. To reduce the chances of error, it is better to grind in the taper after forging.

Fuller the sword with a top/bottom fuller at high heat. A high heat is necessary because of the amount of steel to be moved. The fullering tools can be used manually or with a power hammer, but the basic techniques and results are much the same.

Just as in the forging and hardening processes, some problems can arise when fullering sword-length pieces. The biggest problem is aligning the blade during the fullering. To make this easier, draw a centerline with a soapstone marker to guide you. Of course, draw this line on a cold blade, prior to the first heat. The soapstone disappears as scale forms, but this isn't a problem. You'll heat the blade in sections and forge in a light tracing prior to the heavier fullering.

To trace in the line, strike light blows on the fullering tool, while holding the blade between the dies in line with the mark. The marks are only a guide to be followed when the blade is fullered, so they do not need to be deep.

After completing the tracing, start the actual fullering at the ricasso and work in sections toward the tip, overlapping the sections to keep the fuller from becoming "chop marked."

The bottom thickness should be at least 100 thousandths (.0001) of an inch at the ricasso, and that should be tapered down to 65 to 80

FULLERING PROCESS

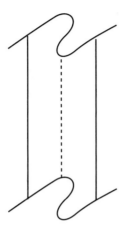

Trace fuller position
into blade blank.

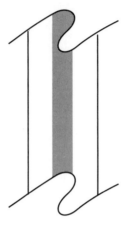

Lightly forge fuller
into blade blank to
show position on blade.

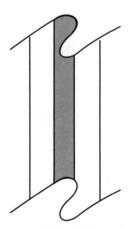

Forge fuller full depth
once proper position is
established.

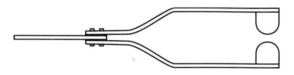

Using a top and bottom tool
will make the fullering
easier than forging fullers
one at a time.

thousandths (.0065 to .0085) of an inch at the tip. This leaves enough steel to clean up small imperfections without worrying about cutting through the bottom of the fuller.

The bottom thickness can be checked with a tubing wall micrometer. This instrument is difficult to find, but most machine shop suppliers should be able to order one for you. Make certain that you get the one with the jaws, not the cylinder. In my opinion, it is required to do this process properly.

As the fuller nears the tip, strike heavier blows to forge deeper. This reduces the cross section and weight slightly, improving the balance and handling of the sword. It also widens the blade tip, so you should have compensated for this in the prior forging. After completing the fullering, check for straightness and correct if required.

Beveling the Edges

The next step is forging in the edge bevels. Be carefuk while doing this because misplaced hammer blows can ruin the fullering and the blade.

This step is similar to forging a fullered dagger but a little trickier.

Forge the bevels at a medium heat, working in sections from ricasso to tip and alternating edges and sides as you work each section. A forging plate may make this easier, depending upon blade design. Forge in the edge bevels on all four surfaces and then "true up" the blade so that it is, for the most part, forged to its final shape.

After the truing, go over the fuller once more with the top/bottom tool to correct any small errors that may have occurred during the edge forging. Straighten, stress relieve, and anneal overnight in a hot box. Next, profile and rough-grind the cooled blade.

Common Fullering Problems

Problem	Cause	Solution
Fuller running off to one side	Improper alignment of the blade	Hold the blade straight and secure between the dies
Fullers offset from one side to another	Dies out of alignment with each other	Check for proper mating of working surfaces and correct as needed
Chop marks in the fullering	Overlap too short between worked sections	If not too severe, can be corrected by careful reworking. To prevent, overlap work areas by 1/2 to 3/4 inch or more as needed
Blade twisting while being worked	Fullering tool out of alignment	Exact mating between top- and bottom-die surfaces

Grinding the Blade

Grinding a sword is difficult for a novice, but practice makes the task easier. The two most popular methods to grind a blade are flat grinding and hollow grinding.

Period blades were usually flat-ground, but hollow grinding was also used, especially during the later periods. You can use either method. Flat grinding is a little stronger, although I doubt you can tell the difference. In a nonfullered blade, flat grinding results in a cross section like the one

UNFULLERED FLAT-GROUND CROSS SECTION

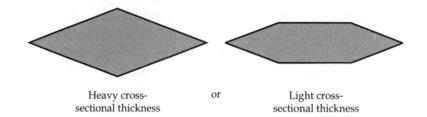

Heavy cross-
sectional thickness   or   Light cross-
sectional thickness

FULLERED FLAT-GROUND CROSS SECTIONS

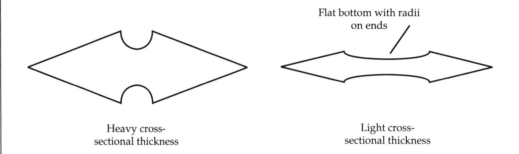

Flat bottom with radii
on ends

Heavy cross-
sectional thickness

Light cross-
sectional thickness

illustrated above (top). This is the classic flattened-diamond cross section commonly seen in medieval pieces.

In a fullered blade (a single fuller on each side), the cross section looks like the ones above (bottom).

As you can see from the illustrations, there is still sufficient steel to support the cutting edge. The hollow-ground edge, while still appropriate to period blades, is easier to grind and control than the heavier flat-ground blade.

The cross section of a unfullered hollow-ground blade is illustrated on the facing page (top). As you can see, there is a strong resemblance to the flat-ground flattened-diamond cross section. The bottom figures on the facing page show a fullered blade with a hollow-ground cross section.

A hollow-ground blade has a slightly thinner cutting edge surface, which produces a keener edge. Also, hollowing out a blade reduces its weight, making it lighter and more controllable. How light is too light? I have yet to encounter this difficulty in a broadsword. I forge most of my blades from 1/4-inch flat bar in various widths, and none have been too light to use.

Flat Grinding

In flat grinding a sword, maintaining the angle of the grind is crucial but difficult because of length. Failure to maintain the same angle throughout the length of the edge bevel will result in flaws and breaks in the grind lines that ruin an otherwise serviceable blade. You can keep a consistent angle by working slowly and in sections of 4 to 6 inches in length, blending in newly ground sections with those previously ground. Blending results in a smooth, uninterrupted surface on the edge bevel.

Hollow Grinding

Hollow grinding is easier than flat grinding, but it still presents some problems. The most commonly encountered problem is what I call "wheel scoring." These are marks that appear on the blade at increments equal to the width of your contact wheel, i.e., every 2 inches if you use a 2-inch wheel.

These marks result from uneven pressure/contact on the wheel, and they can be hell to remove if not caught early on in the process. To prevent these, work in sections 4 to 6 inches long and blend the sections into one even edge bevel.

UNFULLERED HOLLOW-GROUND CROSS SECTION

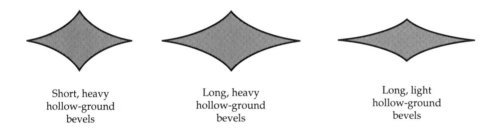

Short, heavy
hollow-ground
bevels

Long, heavy
hollow-ground
bevels

Long, light
hollow-ground
bevels

FULLERED HOLLOW-GROUND CROSS SECTION

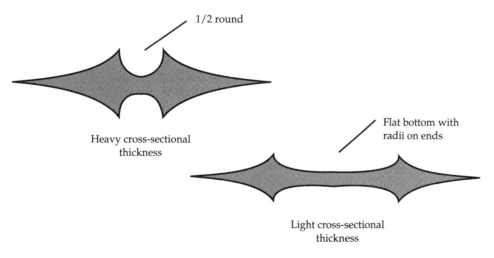

1/2 round

Heavy cross-sectional
thickness

Flat bottom with
radii on ends

Light cross-sectional
thickness

Note the different shape of the fullers
in the two different cross-sectional thicknesses.

With both flat- and hollow-ground blades, leave a rough-ground edge thickness of at least 60 thousandths (.0060) to 70 thousandths (.0070) inch to prevent warpage. The excess disappears in the final grind. Also, with both grinding methods, you should fully rough-grind the blade before heat treating/tempering, making certain that it is straight and even throughout its length to prevent stress from building up.

Also, make certain that the grind marks from the profile grind are running parallel to the edge, not across it. Any heavy grind marks running across the edge can cause cracking during heat treating.

Heat-Treating Swords

Any carbon or alloy steel must be hardened and tempered to function properly. Although most swords made today are either too hard or too soft, you can achieve a happy medium that is hard enough to hold a decent edge yet tough enough to withstand combat.

Granted, much of your success depends on the type of steel and the size and shape of the sword. The more exotic the shape, the greater the chances of problems, ranging from simple warpage to stress cracking. As mentioned at the beginning of the chapter, square angles or drastic changes in cross sections guarantee problems.

To harden, I use a dull cherry red for most simple alloys, such as 5160 or the 10XX series, and quench in a medium-weight oil until the blade reaches the bath temperature. On the rich alloys, I harden at a full cherry red and quench in oil.

The evenness of heat is of utmost importance. Uneven heating results in uneven hardening, which causes warping, internal stressing, or—in the worst case—cracking. You can move the blade in the forge to even your heating. Because of the blade's length and the risk of grain growth occurring, remove the blade as soon as the steel is evenly heated and quench quickly.

Quenching

Quench the blade point down (vertically) into the bath to help prevent warpage and other problems. An oil quench has a considerable amount of oil flare-up, so be careful. Keep a fire extinguisher handy in case the flame gets out of hand. In all likelihood, the flare-ups will die once the blade is totally immersed in the bath.

Tempering

I have tried different degrees of temper, varying from full hard to nearly dead soft. I have found that a full brown temper is useful for most sword blades. This should give an Rc hardness of approximately 53-55 C. I consider this the maximum hardness for a working sword. While you can go for a harder temper, you run the risk of its breaking under use—

and that could be embarrassing or dangerous. A softer temper toughens the blade but reduces its cutting and edge-holding ability.

I am not saying that blades tempered at 53-55 degrees C are indestructible. What was made by man can be destroyed by man. The best blades break when abused, but the proper temper can mean the difference between a broken blade and a sword when a minor error in judgment occurs.

I wouldn't temper a broadsword any softer than magenta, while a spring temper is better for more flexible blades such as the rapier. I triple temper these blades to ensure even tempering.

You can send your pieces out to be tempered or do your own in an oven (if you have one large enough) or over a forge. I do my own in a forge because I think it gives a better temper and I can see what is going on. It all comes down to personal control. The smith who does his own hardening has the advantage over the grinder jockey who sends his blades out to someone else to harden. After all, whose name is on it, yours or the heat treater's?

Straightening

The blade can be straightened when it is being tempered if the straightening isn't too severe. Slight warpages happen from time to time no matter how careful you are.

Straightening a blade takes know-how and experience. When the blade is at the proper tempering color, quench it for a few seconds. This short quench halts further tempering, yet leaves enough heat for minor straightening. Place the blade in a vise at the point of warpage and strong-arm it straight.

The degree of straightening possible depends on the blade's length, temperature, thickness, and cross section. If you overdo it, you may break the blade. Unfortunately, only experience can teach you what you can and cannot do with this method. If you are concerned about doing it this way, you can take small local heats with the oxyacetylene/gas torch to straighten. Actually, I suggest that you do so until you get some swordmaking experience.

Final Grinding

Final grinding should refine the profile and the grind bevels/lines. Again, you face the problem of how far to grind down and what edge thickness to leave for a sword.

On most chopper-type blades, the slightest use either rolls over or otherwise damages a sword blade of knife-edge thickness. I suggest an edge thickness before sharpening of no less than .0025 (25 thousandths) to .0030 (30 thousandths) inch. This thickness won't take a super edge, but it gives enough of an edge to do the job with plenty of steel to support the edge during use.

When grinding, make certain that you maintain the same grinding angle on the edge bevels to prevent flaws in the grind.

NOTE: If the blade is fullered, clean up the fuller with an appropriate contact wheel on your grinder's small wheel adapter. This is by far the easiest way to do so. Also, polish and buff the fuller prior to final grinding of the edge bevels to keep the grind lines sharp.

After grinding, do any necessary final polishing and fitting.

Hilting the Sword

Attaching the hilt is one of the major difficulties in swordmaking. It is the part that people see most, so it should be attractive as well as comfortable and secure to hold.

A sword hilt can be as plain or as fancy as one wishes. This sword has a blued-steel mount and a wire-wrapped grip in a snakeskin sheath with bronze fittings set with carnelian. The author made both the sword and sheath. Photo by Stephen Jacobson

The Grip

Since this is the part of the hilt that your hand makes contact with, it should feel comfortable and provide a secure grip on the weapon. There are many techniques to ensure this.

A look at some historical blades shows how ancient swordmakers did it. The blades of long ago had grips of wood, horn, smooth leather, spiral leather, wire wraps, ivory, or just about any other material at the disposal of swordmakers.

You can always use a sturdy wood for a sword grip, but why not explore some other materials that can dress up the appearance and provide a sound hold on the blade. Of course, the grip material has to withstand the shocks and vibrations of use as well.

How does one fashion a proper period grip? One must first decide what type of grip to use. In the case of wire and leather wraps, a wood core can be fashioned from one or two pieces of resilient hardwood such as ash, oak, or hickory. Since it is not going to be seen, the wood does not need to have a fancy grain or other aesthetic appeal. The most important attributes are stability and toughness—it is the core that has to absorb the shocks and vibrations.

You can also use some of the man-made materials, including the various micartas and pressure-laminated woods, if the grip doesn't require any soldering. But I have found that none of the artificial products outperform hardwood in terms of beauty, ease of construction, and durability. Although the synthetics won't rot, crack, or otherwise deteriorate, neither will wood that is properly prepared and cared for.

Period blades had two different methods by which their hilts were attached. The laminated method entailed hollowing two pieces of wood so the tang could pass through the hollowed area, resulting in a tight fit between the pieces. This method was used for leather-wrapped grips and some other types of hafting as well.

After the wood is fitted to the tang, the two pieces are glued together with hide glue, and the rest of the shaping is done. The covering is then applied, followed by final assembly.

(Interestingly, most Japanese blades incorporate a similar method of grip making on swords and knives.)

The second method, which I prefer, is the burn-on method that you should already be familiar with. (For those who aren't, see my earlier volume, *The Complete Bladesmith*.) Drill a block of wood through lengthwise and open up one end with a wood chisel to accept the top of the tang. Hold the sword in a vise with the tang exposed and heat to a very dull red. Slip the wood block over the tang, burning it into the block.

Remove the block and reheat the tang until the block slides all the way to the top. NOTE: Wear safety gloves to prevent burns or other injuries. Also, this process generates a lot of smoke that can be irritating or somewhat toxic, so wear a respirator and do this step outdoors.

When the wood is burned on, dip the core in water to prevent further smoldering and check the tang for alignment. Straighten if required and air-cool slowly. Do not quench the tang. This may cause hardening and/or stress to occur in the steel.

When the core is fire-fitted, go on to the quillion and pommel.

The Quillion (Hand Guard)

These must be made from a tough and sturdy material that is able to withstand the abuses of combat. They can be of various designs, some of which are shown on the following page.

Attach as you would any standard blade/guard attachment as long as the method is sturdy enough to withstand use. Solder the guard securely in place, unless you are planning on using a blued iron/steel guard. The fluxes used in soldering remove the blue.

To get around this problem, I solder a thin bronze spacer to the blade and then do a press fit on the guard. This seals the gap between the blade and guard, and since the spacer and the guard are tightly butted together, there is no gap there either. Consequently, no flux touches the guard, and the blueing is unaffected. You have to compensate for the use of the spacer in the length of the tang. The tang must be lengthened the same amount as the thickness of the spacer.

The Pommel

The pommel serves two purposes in a sword: as a butt cap to keep the sword from slipping out of your grip and as a counterbalance to the blade. Pommels can be made out of most materials, although with the softer ones you may have some problems keeping it tight and secure.

Pommels can be of just about any design or shape. The pommel should be shaped to prevent sharp edges from coming in contact with the hand, or its tang should be long enough to prevent the pommel from touching the hand. This gives a more comfortable grip.

Pommels do not need to be overly large. After all, a doorknob on the end of an otherwise fine sword would look rather odd and out of place. To attach to the grip, run the tang all the way through the pommel and

QUILLION DESIGNS

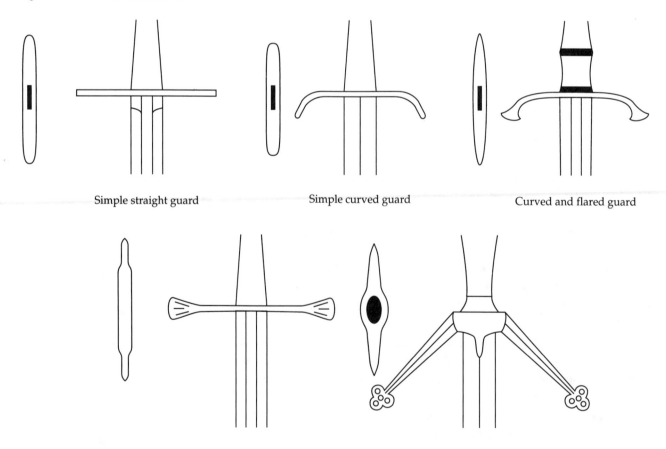

Simple straight guard

Simple curved guard

Curved and flared guard

Early Irish guard

Scottish Claymore guard

178

secure it by peening it over a washer or using a cap nut. This works, but over time it can loosen. The loosening is easily corrected.

On the other hand, you can always thread the end of the tang and then screw on the pommel. This can present some problems as well, mostly with durability. You can overcome this by using a large, healthy thread of no smaller than 3/8 inch x 16 inches—and 1/2 inch x 13 inches is better. Both methods make a serviceable sword, but the former is more correct than the other.

POMMELS

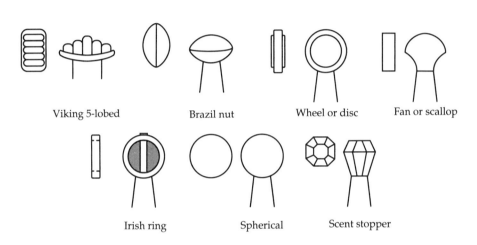

Viking 5-lobed   Brazil nut   Wheel or disc   Fan or scallop

Irish ring   Spherical   Scent stopper

PEENING AND NUT CAP

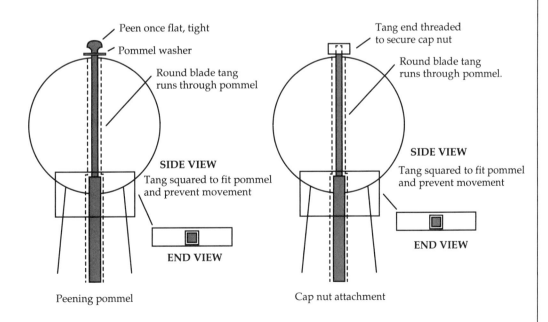

Peen once flat, tight
Pommel washer
Round blade tang runs through pommel

SIDE VIEW
Tang squared to fit pommel and prevent movement

END VIEW

Peening pommel

Tang end threaded to secure cap nut
Round blade tang runs through pommel.

SIDE VIEW
Tang squared to fit pommel and prevent movement

END VIEW

Cap nut attachment

Finishing the Grip

With all of the metal work finished, go back and finish the grip. As mentioned before, there are numerous ways to do this. The most common grips are made of wood, horn, bone, or the composite grips of wire-wrap, leather-wrap, or a combination of both.

If you use a plain, noncomposite grip, proceed as the material dictates. If you are making a composite grip, the steps are discussed in Chapter 7.

Final finish depends on the design and type of the blade and the inclination of the maker. The assembly should be as sturdy as possible. I pack the grip with a slow-set epoxy that fills gaps, seals the grip, and holds the grip tightly in place. With the sword completed, you can begin on the sheath and other accessories.

Making a sword is different from making other blades, but the techniques are basically the same. A sword gives one a sense of chivalry, glory, and times past. It is a fulfilling yet humbling experience that every bladesmith should have at least once in his career.

THE SPEAR:
THE ANCIENT
WEAPON OF CHOICE

The spear is another weapon that has made its place in history. Its great advantage is that it gives the average man-at-arms the luxury of being able to reach his opponent while keeping out of range.

Throughout history, man has used the spear with great success on the battlefield and to hunt wild boar, bear, and even big cats. In spite of their enduring popularity, however, few quality spears are being made today. They are far less difficult to fashion than I first imagined, yet few smiths even make an attempt to forge this versatile weapon.

THRUSTING VERSUS THROWING SPEARS

Spears can be classified into two families: thrusting and throwing. Thrusting spears include the Viking spear, European boar spear, Zulu *assagai*, Japanese *yari*, European knight's lance, and others too numerous to mention.

Thrusting spears are built stout to withstand the vigors of repeated thrust impacts. The head is broad and heavy, usually double-edged, with flattened-diamond or raised-center-rib cross sections. The sturdy haft is made of a tough, resilient, straight-grained hardwood such as ash or hickory. Rattan has been used in certain parts of the world for lance shafts. Haft lengths run from 5 feet to more than 12 feet for some longer pikes. The average length is 6 to 7 feet.

Throwing spears include the classic Greco-Roman javelin, Roman *pilum*, Frankish *angon*, Arabic *jarid*, and others. Primarily projectile weapons, these spears can be used for thrusting if the need ever presents itself. They are lighter in design and construction than their thrusting counterparts, with narrower heads and slimmer hafts. They are also shorter and, therefore, more manageable and easier to throw. Spear makers usually fashion hafts from resilient wood, and some

THRUSTING SPEAR HEADS

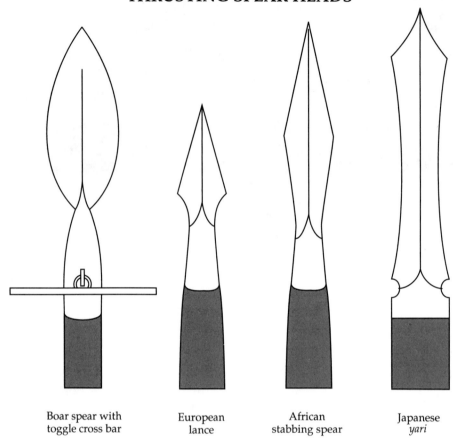

Boar spear with
toggle cross bar

European
lance

African
stabbing spear

Japanese
yari

THROWING SPEARS

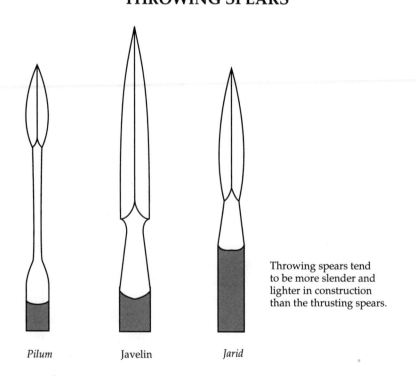

Throwing spears tend
to be more slender and
lighter in construction
than the thrusting spears.

Pilum

Javelin

Jarid

spears bend or otherwise destroy themselves on impact, making them useless to one's opponent.

SPEAR HEADS

The basic construction remains the same for both types of spears. The first part to consider is the spear head. There are three types of heads to choose from: the tanged one-piece, socketed one-piece, and socketed two-piece. All make good, sturdy heads.

The most important consideration for the head is choosing the right steel. Spear heads have to withstand a great deal of impact, shock, and other abuse, and toughness is the primary attribute you're looking for in a steel. I have had good results with 1045 for throwing spears and 5160 for thrusting spears. Both steels are extremely tough, and the somewhat softer 1045 is ideal for the more abusive throwing use.

Some makers prefer a higher-carbon steel, but I advise against using any steel with more than 60 points of carbon. The amount of leverage applied to a spear head, even unintentionally, can be severe enough to cause even a slightly brittle steel to snap.

Tanged One-Piece Head

This is the simplest form of spear, but it can also be one of the most graceful. The Japanese *yari* and several of the Balinese spears serve as fine examples of this.

With this type, you forge the head after making the tang. I make mine from 1045 round stock in 3/4- or 1 1/4-inch diameter and use the tenon tool to reduce the steel to a usable dimension for the tang. I prefer 7/16- and 1/2-inch square tangs because this leaves enough room for the wood hafting but is still not the diameter of a small tree. The square section prevents the head from rotating once it is on the haft. Of course, you can use a round-sectioned tang, but you may have some difficulty in pinning it through the ferrule, tang, and haft to secure it in place after final assembly.

It is important that you put in a very slight taper from the end of the

TANGED CONSTRUCTION

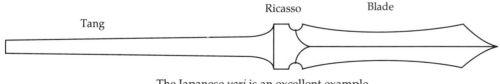

The Japanese *yari* is an excellent example
of the tanged spear head.

SPEAR TANG CONSTRUCTION

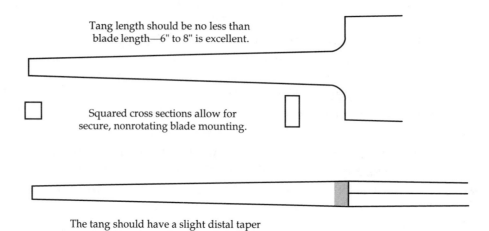

Tang length should be no less than
blade length—6" to 8" is excellent.

Squared cross sections allow for
secure, nonrotating blade mounting.

The tang should have a slight distal taper
to allow for easier mounting.

tang to where the blade begins. The taper lets you drive the head into the haft, and the straight, untapered section gives a snug, secure fit.

For tang length, anything longer than 6 to 8 inches is more difficult to mount, and the shaft requires drilling, tapering, and ferruling for the length of the tang. It is hard to drill straight into most hardwoods over 8 inches. After forming the tang, anneal and stress relieve it to keep it soft and prevent any fracturing at this point.

Forging the Blade

Forging the spear blade is basically the same as doing any other blade. However, working the blade/tang junction (the "neck") is fairly difficult without a tenon tool or some other device. You can do it with just a hammer, but you leave a rougher surface with more unsightly hammer marks that have to be cleaned up later if you don't use a top/bottom tool of some sort.

Mark the transition area from the blade to the tang and form it with a round 1/2-inch tenon tool. The transition should be only 1/2 to 3/4 inch, as any longer would not look correct. The tenon tools you have may be too wide, so you may have to make one for this purpose. When forging the neck, remember to keep rotating the work in the tool as the neck is forged to ensure an even round section.

Forming the neck before working on the blade is infinitely easier than trying to form it after the blade is forged.

I flatten the steel into a rectangular cross section of 1 1/4 x 3/16 inch wide (approximately) and however long it is at the time. I work back from the tip toward the neck, using localized heats and working in

FORMED NECK AND UNWORKED AREA

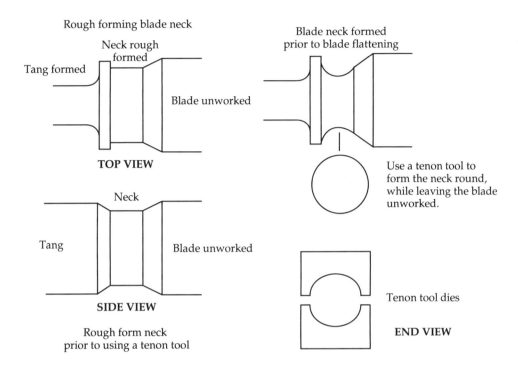

Rough forming blade neck

Neck rough formed

Tang formed

Blade unworked

TOP VIEW

Neck

Tang

Blade unworked

SIDE VIEW

Rough form neck
prior to using a tenon tool

Blade neck formed
prior to blade flattening

Use a tenon tool to
form the neck round,
while leaving the blade
unworked.

Tenon tool dies

END VIEW

BLADE FLATTENING AFTER NECK FORMING

TOP VIEW   **SIDE VIEW**

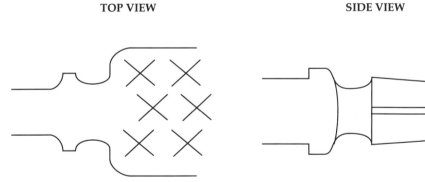

Flatten blade as shown,
leaving the neck untouched
and the blade thick enough to
allow for proper blade forming.

Blade flattening should taper
from neck to point as shown.

SPEAR TOOL #1

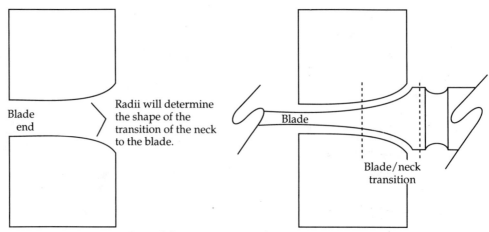

Blade
end

Radii will determine
the shape of the
transition of the neck
to the blade.

Blade

Blade/neck
transition

The neck/blade transition is formed
by this tool. Remember the tool die's
shape dictates the shape of the transition
between blade and neck.

SIMPLE TAPERED SPEAR POINT

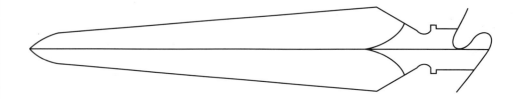

sections to prevent grain growth.

After forming the blade, you are ready to refine the transition between the blade and the neck by using the forming tool shown above. The spear tool smooths out the area between the blade and the neck. Place the blade (flat down) between the top/bottom section with the radii of the tooling over the unworked heated section of the blade/neck junction. Holding the blade straight and level between the dies, forge this area until the radius forms a smooth transition from neck to blade. This may take two or more heats. If any distortions occur during the forming, use the tenon tool to smooth them out.

Blade shapes vary, and specific styles are discussed later in this chapter. For our purposes here, we will concentrate on a simple, straight-tapered blade as illustrated above.

Forge the blade much like you do a double-edged dagger, but leave the point somewhat blunt. A sharp knife taper on a spear is not rugged or serviceable enough. Tanged spear heads are subjected to a great deal of impact and torque, both of which can be sudden death to an improperly made blade.

After forging the blade to its final shape, refine the entire head and make certain that the tang/blade alignment is straight. Anneal, stress relieve, and place the blade in a hot box to cool. Grind to final profile and heat-treat.

Clean up the tang shape by using a file or grinder. Some smiths rough grind before heat-treating, depending on the spear style and steel thickness. I prefer to grind after hardening because it lessens warping and cracking.

Socketed One-Piece Head

The next spear head, in terms of difficulty, is the one-piece socketed design. This is the most common head on ancient spears. The blade and the socket are forged from a single piece of iron/steel, and the socket is formed around a mandrel. The seam could be welded or left open, depending on the weapon's use and the weight of material employed.

This method may produce the strongest heads, but it has a small drawback. It is almost impossible to align the head and socket perfectly. The method of construction makes the blade slightly off-center. To make the one-piece socketed head, you need a triangular piece of steel 3/16 to 1/4 inch thick, long enough to make the head and socket, and wide enough to form the socket and base of the head.

How do you know what size to make the head? Make paper patterns of the socket and the blade, tape them together, and make a metal template to work from as described below. To arrive at the correct size of socket, you must make a socket mandrel. These mandrels can be used for both the one- and two-piece construction techniques.

BASIC SPEAR SHAPE

The basic shape for forming
a one-piece socketed spear point.

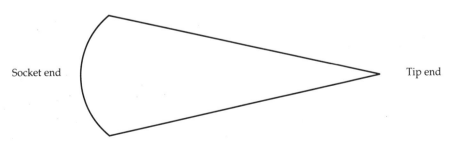

Socket end   Tip end

This long triangular shape allows for shaping
the socket and point from a single piece of steel.

Making a Template

After making your paper pattern, transfer it to a metal template. I used 18-gauge aluminum sheet for my patterns, and they have lasted for more years than I care to mention. Plastic is undesirable because it melts or burns at the slightest heat, whereas metal only gets a little hot.

There are two basic ways of transferring the design. The first one is to trace it onto the metal and cut it out. To do this, use machinist's layout blue and a scribe. Hold the pattern steady so it doesn't shift or move during the trace, or you may have difficulties later on.

The second and best way to transfer a pattern is to lightly coat the paper and the template sheet with rubber cement and place them together. With this method, you don't have to worry about the pattern slipping while the design is being transferred. Simply cut around the paper to duplicate it in a metal template.

Forming and Sizing Mandrels

To make a mandrel, use a piece of round stock of the same diameter as the finished inside diameter (I.D.) of the socket. This I.D. should match the diameter of the hafting to ease the transition from haft to head and make the head look like it was made to fit rather than simply slipped over the end. I suggest using 1045 or 1060 steel. Either makes a tough, serviceable tool that should last a lifetime with careful use.

The length of the socket should match its intended use. For most points, I use an 8-inch socket. Slimmer throwing heads work and look better with a shorter socket of 5 to 6 inches, while heavy-duty boar spears need a heavy-walled socket 10 to 12 inches long to withstand the torque to which these spears are subjected.

Construction techniques are the same for all sizes. Cut a 12-inch piece of 1 3/4-inch diameter round stock. There are two ways to make this tool. The simplest is to forge or grind down the end to a taper, then put the

SQUARED END OF MANDREL

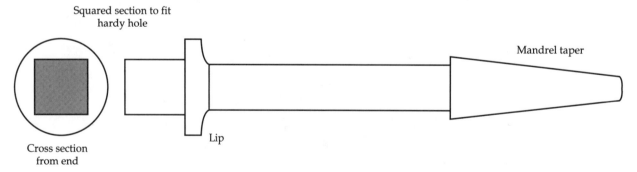

Spear socket mandrel is formed from medium carbon steel prior to bending.

mandrel in a vise and use it that way. Though simple, this method is not very professional, and it places undue wear and tear on the vise. The best method is to forge one end to fit into your hardy hole. Leave enough lip on the steel to prevent wobbling or driving the mandrel into the hardy hole during use. The squared section should be at least 2 1/2 inches long. This is enough length to penetrate into the hole and prevent any tipping and also to be tapped out from the bottom if it ever gets jammed.

Forge the section into a square on the anvil at a full cherry red heat. Work one side at a time, then rotate one-quarter turn (90 degrees) and work the steel down again. Be careful that you do not form a parallelogram; you need a perfect square. Check the size of the section by placing it in the hardy hole. Slightly round the end for easier insertion into the hole and then form the taper.

To make forming the lip easier, work the squared section on the edge of the face, holding the unworked area off the anvil. You form the lip as you forge the section into a square. The section must be properly aligned so the lip is even.

To form the taper on the other end, draw the bar out to the length of the socket desired, maintaining the round cross section. Don't bring the mandrel to a sharp point; rather reduce the mandrel to about 1/2 inch in diameter and round the end. This leaves enough of an opening in the socket end to insert the finished point when you are making two-piece spear heads. You can reduce the 1/2-inch diameter to a more graceful 3/8 inch if you want.

After forging the taper, forge down the center section between the start of the taper and what will be the lip of the squared section. Forge this down to about 7/8- to 1-inch diameter round. This stretches the steel somewhat and allows for easier bending when the time comes. After the center is forged, allow the piece to cool slowly to room temperature and then do the final shaping of the taper.

This final shaping can be done with hand files or a belt grinder. The taper must be smooth, even, and well centered. If not, the socket is uneven or, in the worst case, misformed and unusable. An even taper facilitates the easy removal of the finished socket.

With the taper smooth and even, heat the center of the piece and prepare to bend the section into a 90-degree curve. Heat the section to a full cherry red heat, place the mandrel into the hardy hole, and bend the piece into an even curve. You can use round-jawed tongs, or you can use a brass-headed hammer on the taper to force the center to bend. Bend the piece until the taper is parallel with the surface of the anvil. It is easier to form the socket when the mandrel is horizontal. Take another heat, this time to a medium cherry red and harden in oil. When quenched, use a full spring temper (blue) to ensure that the piece will maintain its shape during use.

The mandrel should be polished, but the degree of polish isn't as important as the evenness of the surface. Polish to 220/240 grit and lightly buff to prevent rust.

As with any tool, the tool is only as good as the man who made it, and the ability to use it is learned. Put the same care into fashioning your tools as you do into making your blades. The ability to make your own tools is the major difference between a good smith and a mediocre one. A wise man once said: "It's amazing that when you haven't enough time to do the job right in the first place, there's always enough time to do it over." A rush job is a bad job.

Completed socket mandrel. Photo by Stephen Jacobson

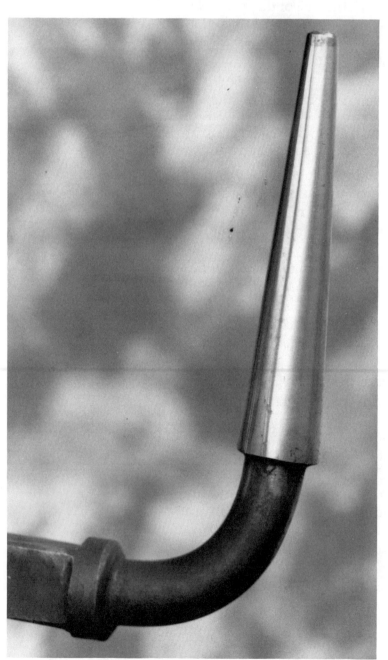

Forming a one-piece head is a lot of work. First, you must forge the neck portion of the blade between what will be the socket and the blade areas. The metal tends to fold and thicken considerably at this point, and it must be forged down to a workable thickness (about 3/16 to 1/4 inch).

As you forge, draw out the socket area until it is approximately 1/8 inch thick. When making the patterns, you have to factor in this drawing out. Several attempts may be needed to get the pattern correct.

When you have drawn out and shaped the socket area, anneal it and then do a final profile. Next, form the socket on the mandrel. Most of these have open seams because the wall thickness adequately supports the head. But you can weld the seam either by forge or gas/arc. I think welded seams look better on the finished head.

With the socket formed, start on the blade. You can do any design or style of blade that the volume of your material allows. This type of construction is most prominent on the classic arrowhead points, but other shapes can also be used.

When the blade is approximately 80 percent formed, use the spear-necking tool to smooth the transition between the blade and socket. Finish forging the blade, anneal, and profile. Complete the blade by grinding, hardening/tempering, and final finishing.

FORMED, PROFILED, FINISHED SOCKET

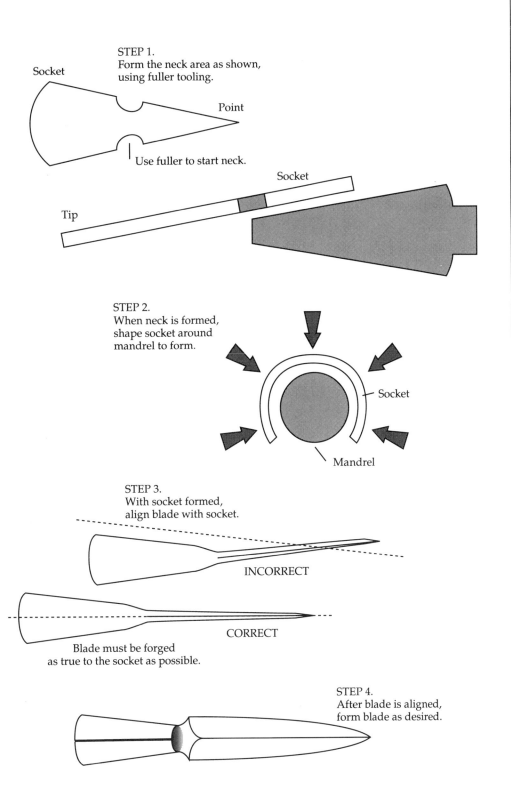

STEP 1.
Form the neck area as shown,
using fuller tooling.

Socket

Point

Use fuller to start neck.

Socket

Tip

STEP 2.
When neck is formed,
shape socket around
mandrel to form.

Socket

Mandrel

STEP 3.
With socket formed,
align blade with socket.

INCORRECT

CORRECT

Blade must be forged
as true to the socket as possible.

STEP 4.
After blade is aligned,
form blade as desired.

Socketed Two-Piece Head

Technically, the most difficult spear head to make is the socketed two-piece. You forge the head separately from the socket and weld the two together. Bladesmiths usually form the socket from heavy sheet and weld the seams. The advantage of two-piece construction is that the head is centered exactly between the socket and the shaft, which is almost impossible with one-piece construction.

Making the Socket

The two-piece method is by far the easiest way of making a socket. The forging is minimal because the socket and head are forged from separate pieces. The difficulty with this method lies in welding the blade to the socket. We shall start with the socket.

To make the socket, you simply form the precut sheet into a cone on the mandrel and cut the steel to the exact size. To size the piece correctly, make a paper pattern and then a metal one—as you did with the other two heads. Since you use the same mandrel to form the paper pattern and the metal socket, make the paper pattern by wrapping it around the mandrel and cutting to shape. This gives you the dimensions for the metal template used to cut the sheet stock.

A word about sheet stock is in order. The thicker the sheet metal, the better it turns out. Anything lighter (thinner) than 12-gauge steel has a tendency to twist and ripple while being worked. I get excellent results using mild-steel (1018/20) plate that is 3/32-inch thick for the sockets. I

TWO-PIECE CONSTRUCTION

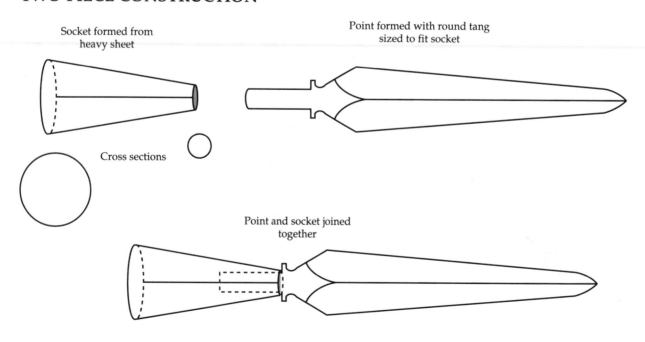

Socket formed from heavy sheet

Point formed with round tang sized to fit socket

Cross sections

Point and socket joined together

use a bench shear to cut the steel shear.

Forming the socket is the easiest part of making this type of point. Simply take a heat and form the sheet around the mandrel. Try to keep the seam straight and make the socket as even as possible. The better job you do here, the better the results later on. Also, make certain that the opening on the ends is round—no ovals. You will form the openings further by drifting after you have welded the seam.

Welding the seam improves the looks and strength of the spearhead. It you are good at forge welding, weld the socket in the forge, which is the old way of doing it. If not, the seam can be gas/arc welded. Both welding methods work.

"Drift" the shank opening to the final size and shape. A drift is a dull punch that you lightly hammer into the opening, causing the hole to take a desired shape or size, in this case round. The drift has to be the same shape as the head's shaft but slightly smaller to allow for the expansion of the socket when it is heated. If it is too large, the shank/socket will not stay together during welding, which complicates an already tricky process.

To drift the hole, simply take a heat on the shank hole area, place the large end of the socket down on the anvil, lightly tap the drift into the hole, and then remove. Do this quickly so the socket does not cool and contract with the drift inside the hole, which could make its removal difficult. Withdrawal can be eased by using a slightly tapered drift, as shown on the following page.

With the socket formed, the seam welded, and the shank opening drifted to size, you are ready to form the blade.

Forming the Blade

There are two ways to form a blade. The first one is to form the blade entirely before the socket is attached, and the other is to attach the socket and then forge the blade to shape.

On throwing spears, which have narrower heads, I prefer to form the blades completely before joining them with the sockets. I get a better point this way. On spears with heavier heads, I join the pieces before the blades are formed. You have to try both ways and see for yourself which works best for the particular type of point you are making.

If you form the point before welding on the socket, do so at this time. Make certain that the shank is the same size as the hole in the socket.

If you plan on forging the blade after attaching the socket, forge the shank on the blade section and then weld. Regardless of the order of the forging, the welding sequence is the same.

Welding the Blade and Socket

The difference in the size (volume) of the blade shank and socket means you have to take some steps to get the both at the right

This spear point features two-piece construction with center-ribbed blade. The author used 1060 for the blade and 1018 for the socket. Photo by Stephen Jacobson

DRIFTS

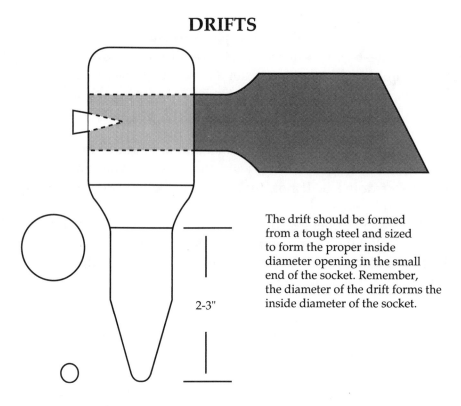

The drift should be formed from a tough steel and sized to form the proper inside diameter opening in the small end of the socket. Remember, the diameter of the drift forms the inside diameter of the socket.

2-3"

temperature at the same time. Heat the shank first and then the socket. Also, remove the blade before you remove the socket from the fire because the socket cools faster.

After removing both, place them in position on the way to the anvil and lightly strike the two together. This takes practice because timing is so critical. The temperature must be correct, or the weld will not take.

Forging the Blade (Prior to Welding)

Socketed heads tend to have wider and thicker blades than those on tanged points. The tanged head cannot support beefier blades, but the socket's added strength easily handles the increased weight and stress of a bigger blade.

I draw down the shank first and then work the blade from the shank toward the tip. Make certain that you leave enough shank to weld the socket—3/4 to 1 inch should be sufficient for the heavier thrusting spears. The longer the welding area, the more secure the welding.

The same basic principles and techniques used for forging a tanged head apply with the socketed head, with only minor variations. The major difference is that instead of forming a tang, you form a round shank for inserting into the socket.

SPEAR BLADE DESIGNS

In addition to the designs discussed at the beginning of the chapter, there are other blades worthy of mention, ranging from the slender awl spear to wide-bladed partisans. These blades are easily formed by hand or by using top/bottom tooling. Most of the earlier-period spears featured median ribs, but some had heavy, flattened-diamond cross sections.

Leaf shapes were a favorite of early spear makers, as were stout broad-headed blades. The broader heads topped hunting spears, not fighting spears, as they didn't do well against most armor.

Blade lengths ranged from a few inches to well over a foot. In making these heads, make certain that you leave enough center spine to withstand the torque and shock they have to absorb.

Winged Spear

An interesting variation on the socketed spear is what is known as a winged spear, which saw a lot of action in medieval Europe. About the only apparent difference between the winged spear and more common types is the inclusion of wings on the socket, and much controversy exists as to why these wings were added. Some bladesmiths believe they prevented the spear from completely pene-trating the target, while others argue they were only orna-mental. Regardless of their purpose, they are quite beautiful.

Attaching the wings can be done in several ways. They can be welded on, brazed on, or simply passed through the socket and haft and pinned to hold in place.

Forge welding the wings can be tricky, requiring considerable patience and skill. The secret to doing this is to bend a little foot on the base of each wing as shown on the following page.

After forming the wings, weld them to the socket. Placing the head on the mandrel to do this prevents the socket from collapsing. The quick-and-easy way of doing this is to braze (an authentic period technique, by the way) the wings on or weld with an oxy/gas or arc weld. The brazing is more correct, but the welding works as well.

Remember that these heads need to be sturdy enough to withstand use, and this must be considered when making the points.

A trio of spear points made by the author. Left: Japanese yari. Middle: welded cable. Right: Viking-style.

Grinding Spear Points

Grinding a spear point is slightly different from other grinding. The cross section should be heavy and the tip left as thick as possible. Most of the medieval spear points were flat-ground with flattened-diamond cross sections, but some had center ribs. Modern improvements in steel technology have made hollow-ground blades acceptable, but flat-ground blades still deliver more strength.

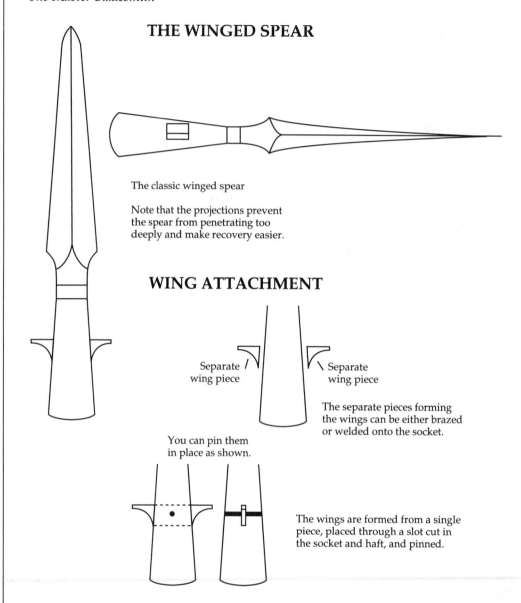

THE WINGED SPEAR

The classic winged spear

Note that the projections prevent
the spear from penetrating too
deeply and make recovery easier.

WING ATTACHMENT

Separate
wing piece

Separate
wing piece

The separate pieces forming
the wings can be either brazed
or welded onto the socket.

You can pin them
in place as shown.

The wings are formed from a single
piece, placed through a slot cut in
the socket and haft, and pinned.

Heat Treating and Tempering

A spear head is heat-treated much like most other blades. The exact quenching medium depends on the steel. Most alloys appropriate for spears respond well to an oil quench. Some makers claim decent results with air-hardening steels, but I cannot recommend these alloys for spears.

Since grain growth can decrease both strength and impact resistance, bring the blade up to critical temperature and hold it no longer than absolutely necessary for an even heat. On 1045 to 1060 steel, I heat to a dull red and then quench. Some alloys may require a higher heat.

Do not heat the tang on tanged-head spears because the tang must remain soft. On socketed-head spears, the socket should remain unheated

FOOT

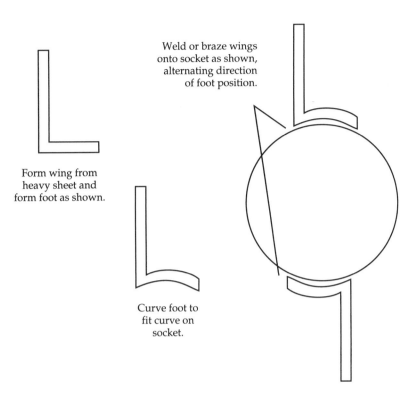

Weld or braze wings onto socket as shown, alternating direction of foot position.

Form wing from heavy sheet and form foot as shown.

Curve foot to fit curve on socket.

both on the one- and two-piece versions.

A light oil quench or commercial-grade tempering oils work well for quenching oil-hardening steels. Quench straight (point) down and hold in the bath until the blade reaches the temperature of the bath. Remove and prepare to temper.

At this point, you must make some trade-offs. Do you want a tough blade that doesn't hold a keen edge for long or a blade that takes and holds a sharp edge but is not very tough? Spears shouldn't be thought of in same terms that apply to knives. Serviceability should be the rule. You want a spear with a blade that holds an edge for a given period of time but also withstands hard impacts.

For the 1045/60 steels, a softer temper of brown to magenta for the main body of the blade and a softer temper of blue for the point (a full spring temper) serve quite well. Of course, you can always temper harder, but you run the risk of making the blade brittle.

You should draw a higher temper on the tang or socket to remove any residual hardness before proceeding. This way, there is little chance of encountering hard spots when you drill the mounting pins.

As with any edged tool, tempering is what makes or breaks the spear blade. After tempering, do the final grinding and polishing.

The Hafting

Mounting the head on the haft can be frustrating and time consuming if not done properly. First, you must choose the right materials. Any hardwood is a good choice as long as it is tough, resilient, straight-grained, and somewhat flexible. Of the four characteristics, straight grain is the most important, followed closely by resiliency. If you are making a spear to look at, you can use any wood you like. For a working spear, function should be placed above aesthetics.

The best wood for spear shafts is either ash or hickory. Both woods are tough and flexible and lend themselves to staining or flame graining. Also, both are becoming harder to find, but they are still available.

Oak, while handsome and quite sturdy, is a bit brittle, and it is difficult to get a straight-grained piece. But if you insist on using oak, Japanese red oak has a straighter grain and is considerably tougher than white or black oak. And, while scarce in some areas, it is generally available in most sizes and lengths.

Rattan may be the best material for spear shafts. A member of the bamboo family, rattan is fibrous, tough, and quite light—characteristics that make it ideal for furniture and spears. While not a traditional choice for European-style spears, it has been used in the Orient for many years. I have several Indo-Persian pieces with rattan hafts in my collection, and even after more than 200 years, the hafts have retained a remarkable degree of flexibility.

If anything, rattan can be a little too flexible for spear shafts. Sometimes just the weight of the head causes the haft to bend. But the old Persian armorers solved this problem rather ingeniously by hot-warping the hafts to compensate for the weight. They bent the haft into an even curve, so when the spear or lance was held level—with the concave side of the curve up—the weight of the head straightened out the haft.

Mounting the Head

The best way to mount socketed spear heads is with the socket flush with the haft, not simply over it. This requires the haft to be the same diameter as the wide end of the socket. For this, you must first taper the end to match the inside taper of the socket. Finish the taper in a straight section where the socket abuts the shaft.

Getting a solid mount requires a good deal of fitting. The taper length should be as long as possible since it is this end of the haft that secures the head to the shaft. The longer the taper, the less chance of the head being ripped off the shaft.

Coating the inside of the socket with inletting compound (as described in Chapter 9) simplifies the mounting. If you do not have inletting compound, use any cheap red lipstick, which is about the same thing.

Coat the inside of the socket, place it on the haft, and twist it around a bit. The compound marks any high spots, which can then be rasped or sanded away. The last fitting should show contact (or red lipstick) over the entire surface of the tapered area. You must remove the lipstick or compound because the epoxy binds only to clean, grease-free surfaces. Use acetone or denatured alcohol to wipe away the lipstick or compound.

When the socket and shaft are dry, try a final fitting to make certain that everything mates perfectly. Finish the haft as desired, let dry, and mount the head for final assembly.

For the final assembly, place the head on the haft and check alignment. Next, remove the head, coat both the inside of the socket and the tapered area of the haft with epoxy, and place the two together. Remove any excess epoxy that may squeeze out with a rag and a bit of light oil. Let set until the epoxy cures.

When cured, drill a 3/16-inch hole through the socket and haft. Slightly countersink the hole on each side for pin expansion during peening. (You can use about any diameter pin, but I have found that 3/16 inch is ideal for most spears.) Place a piece of 3/16-inch round stock into the hole and grind to length for peening. Peen the pin over on each side so the peening fills the countersunk area. When completed, file or grind the peen flush with the socket, as in the tanged construction. Properly done, no pins should be visible. Polish to finish.

Mounting Tanged Heads

Mounting a tanged head is more complicated than mounting a socketed one. After making the head, ream out the end of the shaft with a

INLETTED MOUNTING

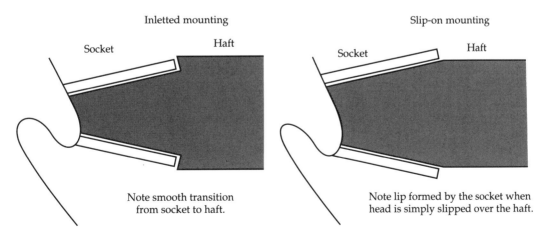

Inletted mounting	Slip-on mounting
Socket Haft	Socket Haft
Note smooth transition from socket to haft.	Note lip formed by the socket when head is simply slipped over the haft.

While it takes more skill, the inletted mounting method results in a smoother joint and one that is more pleasing to the eye than the simpler slip-over method.

SOCKET/SHAFT JUNCTION

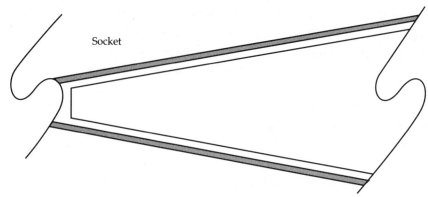

Socket

The haft must be tapered to match the inside of the socket
as closely as possible. This makes for a more secure
and "wobble-free" mounting.

drill the same size as the untapered section of the square tang. This gives a snug press fit without using glue or other adhesive.

The length of the hole should equal the length of the tang plus 1/4 inch. This extra length gives you a small margin for error in driving in the point. If you get overzealous, your chances of splitting the shaft are greatly reduced.

Next, you must taper the shaft to fit the ferrule. Do this the same way as you did with the socketed heads. When this is done, prepare to mount the head and ferrule. Place the ferrule on the shaft and glue it on to prevent the ferrule from shifting around when driving the head into the shaft.

After securing the ferrule, place the end of the tang into the hole and push it in by hand as far as it will go. Next comes the fun part. Place the spear point down onto a block of hardwood and drive the shaft down onto the point by striking the butt of the spear with a rubber or rawhide mallet. This task is easier if you position the spear blade so it cuts across (perpendicular to) the grain and not with it (parallel). This keeps the blade from entering the wood and splitting it.

Drive the shaft down until the top of the tang (where blade and tang meet) enters the ferrule. When that is done, pin and peen the head, making certain that you center the pins through the tang. Since the pins are the only things holding the head together, use at least two, if not three, of them.

NOTE: On some Oriental spears, the hafts were bound with cane work or, in some instances, wire or textiles for a more decorative look. I doubt the suitability of the textile wrapping, but the cane should hold up quite nicely. You might wish to explore this option if you are fashioning a Japanese spear.

MOUNTING THE TANGED SPEAR POINT

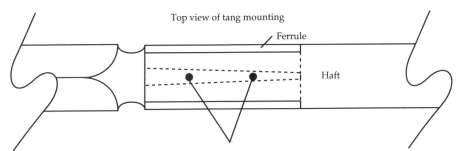

Top view of tang mounting

Two pins should be the minimum for most points.
Diameter should be at least 3/16".

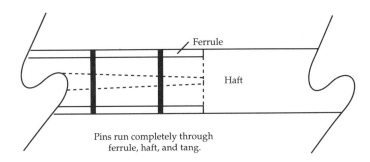

Pins run completely through
ferrule, haft, and tang.

SPEAR/TANG HOLE POSITION AND GRAIN

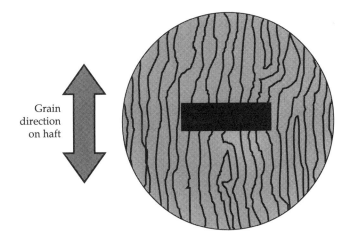

Grain
direction
on haft

Tang hole should be across
the grain of the haft for 2 reasons:
1. It will help prevent splitting.
2. It aligns the edge across the grain allowing for a stiffer haft.

Finishing the Shaft

As with most woods, the shaft should be finished to improve its looks and protect its wood. On a practical note, the wood must be smooth to prevent any splinters from getting under your skin. Most woods respond well to 180- to 220-grit dry sanding. Some, including walnut and other open-grained woods, must be moistened prior to final sanding (called "whiskering") for a smooth finish.

The next step is to seal the open-grained wood so its surface is smooth. The easiest way to do this with oak or other open-grained wood without fancy figures is by applying high-quality varnish. Apply a light coat, let dry, then lightly sand to remove the varnish from the surface, but not enough to get down into the grain. Finish as desired. Of course, you can leave the varnish, but I like a fine, hand-rubbed oil finish. Any good oil works, but I prefer old-fashioned linseed oil, hand-rubbed and applied in several coats, followed by a healthy hard-paste wax to really bring out the beauty of the wood.

Finishing rattan is another matter entirely. Rattan is available in two different grades: skin-on and skin-off. Skin-off rattan has the hard, smooth, protective bark removed, exposing the fibrous material underneath. This doesn't look that good, and it doesn't seal well because of rattan's spongelike nature. To deal with this, do as the old armorers did: leave it alone or paint it.

Unskinned rattan finishes nicely with oil, or it can be lacquered much like bamboo pieces. The nodes (the joints between sections) may be a little rough, but they smooth out with a light sanding. If you lacquer, apply light coats and follow directions exactly.

Some of you may wonder what to do with the butt end of the spear. Do you leave it plain or what? You can always leave it as is, but it is better to put a butt cap of some kind on it to protect it and prevent splitting.

Making a butt cap is simple. Make another ferrule along the lines of a spear socket and then either weld or braze another piece on the small end to close it.

Finish, inlet, and mount like a spear head. The pins do not need to be as heavy as those used on the point, but they should be heavy enough to form a solid, durable connection. If you do not want to go to the trouble of tapering and closing the end, you can slip a small length of seamless tubing over the end and pin it on. Although this is usable, it is tacky.

Spears are among the oldest weapons made by man. Whether it was a simple, fire-hardened stick or a pattern-welded boar spear, this weapon has served man from the beginning of time, bringing down game and foes alike. There is something about a well-made spear that evokes thoughts of long-ago days, when life was simpler and man was—for lack of a better term—younger.

Spears can be delicate and swift or massive and devastating. All of them should be made to look attractive and serve their purpose admirably. Making spears is part of our collective history, and this craft shouldn't be lost.

Along with the spear, the ax is one of the earliest and most versatile weapons made by man. There are many examples of both that have survived from ancient times to illustrate their widespread use.

At one time axes were more common than swords and maybe even knives. Today, however, few bladesmiths would even consider making a custom ax, and it is hard to find axes at any custom knife show. I don't understand why. They are simple in design and easy to make. But they are so different from the established blades that bladesmiths have no interest in forging them.

The ax cuts, chops, trims, and digs to a certain degree. In my opinion, a well-made ax can outperform any survival knife ever made. An ax can accomplish the same duties as a knife and then some.

Aside from being a handy tool, the ax is also a devastating weapon capable of massive destruction. Throughout time, the ax has been a favorite weapon of noble and peasant alike. It could penetrate armor that was invincible to swords or knives.

What makes the ax so powerful? The ax's mass—although no greater than an average sword's—is concentrated at the end of a haft, which increases the impact of blows on the target. Deadly, beautiful, but deceptively delicate, an ax in the right hands is a thing to be feared.

PARTS OF THE AX

All axes, regardless of design, have the same basic features. These are:
- *The edge.* This is the working area of the ax. It can be narrow or wide, straight or curved, thick or thin.
- *The body.* This is the area between the cutting edge and the eye. Length, thickness, and width vary depending upon the particular ax.
- *The eye* (also known as the *poll*). On a hafted ax, this is where the ax

AX PARTS

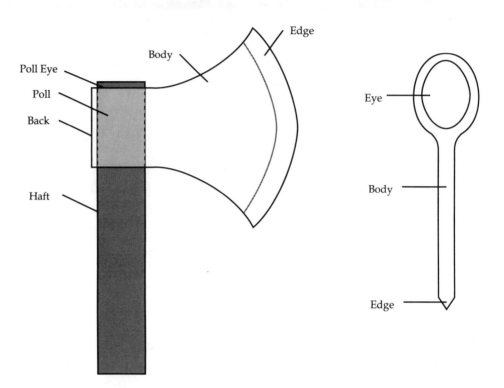

handle pierces the head, allowing the user to grip the ax. The eye is usually oval, although round or even square polls are not unusual.

• *The handle.* This can be a separate piece or forged in one piece with the head. On most axes, the handle is fashioned from hardwood and attached through the ax eye. Lengths and shapes vary. Some axes, especially those from the Orient, have an iron extension forged with the head by which the grip sides are attached.

The illustration above shows the basic design of most axes. Some improved versions incorporate various other features, including a hammer face on the back of the eye, thrusting spikes, nail pullers, and so on. But regardless of the extras, the techniques for forging and using axes remain the same.

TOOLING

There are some tools that help you make a better ax with less time and trouble: the eye mandrel and the eye drift. You can fashion these tools from a medium-carbon steel (60 to 80 points) and temper them on the soft side (to a blue) to absorb the shocks and strains to which an ax is subjected.

Eye Mandrel

The mandrel is simply a bar of steel that takes the basic shape of the inside of the eye. This can be whatever shape you desire as long as it facilitates withdrawal of the mandrel from the eye after the steel is forged around it.

I have mandrels in various sizes to use depending on the size of ax and the eye. They should be as heavy and massive as possible because they have to be able to absorb a lot of heat and withstand the stress to which they are subjected while the eye is being formed. They must be cooled often during the process to prevent the temper from being damaged. The mandrel's surface should be smooth, but it doesn't need a polished finish.

Mandrels can be either a loose tool, where it simply is an iron bar used as a guide in forming, or a tool to be inserted into the anvil's hardy hole to provide a secure working surface. I use the hardy tooling for the primary forming and the loose tooling for the final shaping.

Eye Drift

Because the eye receives its final shape from this tool, it should be the same shape as the inside of the eye. The eye drill is usually handled like a hammer. I suggest a slight taper of 1 to 5 degrees to ease insertion and extraction from the work after the forming is completed. The taper also gives a slight flair to the eye's top that accommodates expansion when driving the wedges into the handle. This expansion locks the head and handle together, providing a secure hold between the two.

MANDREL

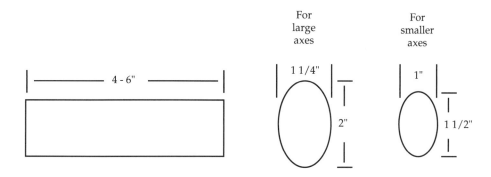

The eye mandrel should be an oval cross section to
properly form the inside of the poll eye.

EYE DRIFT

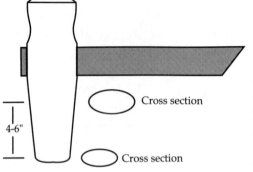

Cross section

4-6"

Cross section

The diameter of the oval
cross section should taper
from top to bottom with
the top being 1/8" larger
than the bottom so the head
will be secure and free from
movement.

SET HAMMER

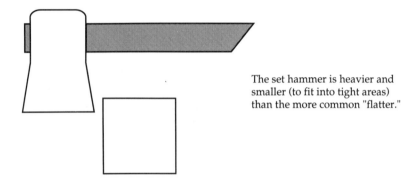

The set hammer is heavier and
smaller (to fit into tight areas)
than the more common "flatter."

Set Hammer

The set hammer is used for smoothing out and sharpening the line between the blade and the eye. Although it is not necessary, this step does make the ax look better.

The ax has evolved from a simple chopper into one of the more specialized tools used by various tradesmen. The basic ax can be modified into a more sophisticated designs while still allowing the smith a great deal of artistic license. As with most other forged blades, an ax can be as simple or as complex as the maker desires.

FORGING THE AX

There are several ways to forge an ax. Some of them make fine tools/weapons, while others make only passable arms.

The best way to learn how to make an ax is to look back at how they have been made in the past. A glance at history shows that the availability of materials was the principal factor in construction techniques. Steel and even simpler-to-smelt iron were highly valuable commodities for centuries. For this reason, most of the better axes were constructed from two or more grades of iron/steel.

Choosing a Steel

There are many grades of steel appropriate for making axes. The style of the ax, to a certain degree, determines what steel is best. After all, there is a difference between making what I call a "composite" ax (built from two or more materials) and a "self" ax (made from one material).

Self Versus Composite Axes

All of the mass-produced modern self axes are fashioned from a single piece of tool steel. A self ax is easier to make, but it lacks the feel of a composite ax. In other words, they may look somewhat the same, but when compared to a properly made composite ax, a self ax doesn't look or feel right. You must use a good grade of carbon steel. Any medium grade of the 10XX or the S series can be used, but the best steel for a self ax is L-6. Unfortunately, this is scarce in the required sizes.

Higher-carbon, richer tool steels aren't ideal, but if you are intent on using one, I recommend an air-hardening steel such as D-2. This steel is tougher and more capable of withstanding shocks than most of the other, richer oil-hardening steels.

Composite axes were originally fashioned from soft-iron bodies with a steel edge either welded to, around, or between the sides of the blade to form the cutting edge. Wrought iron has become almost impossible to obtain, so I substitute 1018/20 to 1045 steel for the ax body. While it isn't the same as fine wrought iron, it does suit this purpose.

For the edge, almost any carbon steel works. I am fond of using sections of old leaf springs (this is about all they are good for anyway) or some other medium-carbon steel. Files with all their teeth ground off also can be used. I haven't tried any of the richer alloys, although I cannot see why they wouldn't work as long as you leave enough of the softer material sheathing the edge to support the harder steel.

Forging Techniques

You will use the techniques of drawing out, widening, thinning, bending, forge welding, and differential tempering. Forging can be done at the start or end of the process, depending upon the type of construction and design. On the simpler self axes, forge the blade prior to forming the eye. On most of the other designs, form the blade after welding the eye.

To form a basic blade, start out by widening the steel, using the peen of either a cross- or straight-peen hammer. Deliver the blows with the peen in line (parallel) to the sides of the steel. When this is done, flatten the surface of the blade until it is smooth and even. A flatter works well for this. This smoothing widens the steel and thins the edge into a sharpenable thickness.

At this point, you may also need to lengthen the neck of the piece if it is overly thick or short. Simply draw this area out as required.

Continue to forge the piece until you get the shape you need. Fabricating a curved-bladed chisel in the appropriate size and shape can simplify making the hook section at the bottom of the ax. These chisels are similar to a woodworker's gouge, except that they are heavier in construction. I made mine from 1060 round stock that was forged flat on one end, then curved (rolled) into shape. I attached a handle made from 1/2-inch round stock and hardened the cutting, leaving the top soft so it would not chip or damage a hammer face.

To use, take a strong full cherry red heat on the ax head, place the head on a cutting plate, and position the chisel where you wish the cutout to be. Strike the chisel as you would in any hot cutting operation.

NOTE: There is a strong tendency for the cutout piece to fly off with the final blow. A large piece of red-hot steel flying around on its own can be hazardous. To prevent, lighten the blows as the cut nears completion.

Ax Construction

The simplest, quickest, and also poorest method of making an ax is simply to forge the blade and eye from a single piece of iron. Forge in the shape of the blade and an iron tail that is long enough to be folded over a mandrel to form the eye. This tail is not welded or attached in any way to the blade. It simply abuts the blade.

CURVED CHISEL

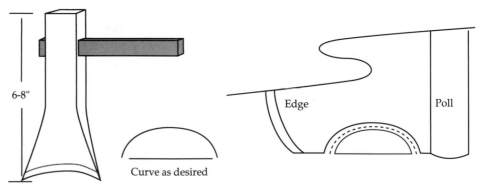

6-8"

Curve as desired

Edge   Poll

The curved chisel makes forming the "hook" at the
bottom of the ax head easier. This hook lightens
the blade without sacrificing strength.

SIMPLE BUTTED CONSTRUCTION

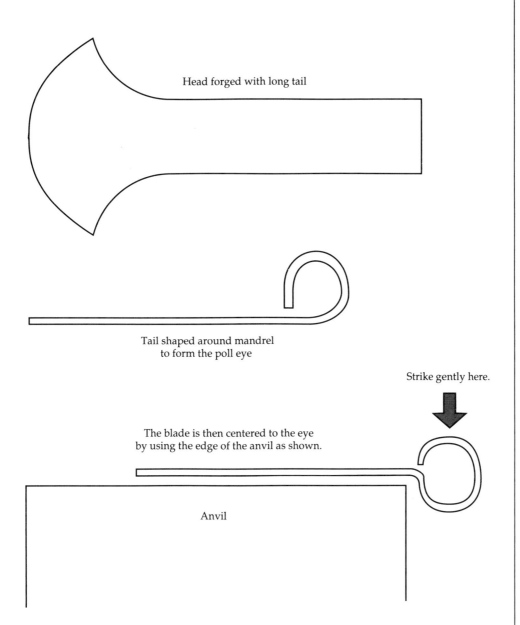

Head forged with long tail

Tail shaped around mandrel
to form the poll eye

Strike gently here.

The blade is then centered to the eye
by using the edge of the anvil as shown.

Anvil

Most of the axes built in this way are throwaway tools or weapons. If you are making throwing axes, where you do not want a brittle edge, or some type of disposable weapon, this is the easiest way to go. By using this technique with good-quality steel and properly tempering the edge/body, you may get a decent ax, but I have found the more sophisticated construction techniques to be more suited to axes of heavier use.

Improved Butted Ax Construction
Start with the same basic construction as above, except make the tail a

SET HAMMER USED TO REFINE LINES

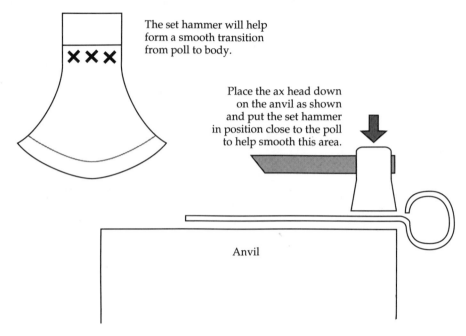

The set hammer will help form a smooth transition from poll to body.

Place the ax head down on the anvil as shown and put the set hammer in position close to the poll to help smooth this area.

Anvil

little longer than normal. Overlap the end of the tail along the blade and weld together. Next, insert the eye drift and hammer it into the eye. This forms the eye into its final shape.

The drift may become jammed into the eye. You can prevent this by coating the drift with fine coal dust before putting it into the eye. This may smoke and smolder a bit, but it lubricates the drift and helps to ease it in and out of the eye.

You may want to take an additional heat, place a mandrel into the eye, and then refine the transition area from blade to eye with a set hammer. To do this, place the ax head onto the face of the anvil with the eye over the edge so that the eye is tight against the anvil edge. Place the set hammer on top of the ax head and hammer the set to refine the line between the blade and the eye.

Steeled-Edge Construction

These next two techniques give better results than those described above, but there is still room for improvement. Both involve "steeling" the edge of a softer, mild-steel ax body.

The first technique is the least desirable. Essentially, it involves jump-welding a section of medium-carbon steel along the edge. To do this, make a butted or improved butted blade and a piece of tool steel in the same shape as the outer edge of the ax blade. Wire the two pieces together as shown at right, leaving one end free to start the weld.

To weld, place the unwired area of the ax into the forge and bring up to a cherry heat. Flux with anhydrous borax or other simple flux. Bring

WIRING OF PIECES

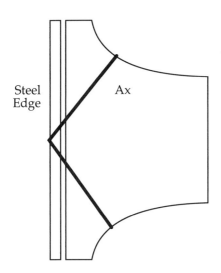

Steel Edge

Ax

up slowly to a welding heat, being careful not to burn the steel.

When at welding heat, place the ax edge up, resting on the poll, and strike the steel firmly to set the weld. When this is done, unwire and proceed until the edge is securely welded to the ax body.

NOTE: There may be a tendency for the steel to slide around and peel away from the ax body during the welding, so correct this as needed.

V-Edge Construction

This is similar to, but better than, the jump-welding method described above, although it still isn't top quality. In doing V construction, you need a V swage and a V fuller to fit it. These can be easily made from 1/4-inch-thick angle iron forged into a "V." I made mine from 1/4- x 1-inch angle iron forged into a "V" with a 45- (rather than the customary 90-) degree angle. I designed my sets to fit in my top/bottom tooling, described in Chapter 3.

You can easily fashion the V fuller from a piece of medium-carbon steel bar stock either ground or forged to fit. To check the fit, place a piece of yellow-hot scrap mild steel (of the same thickness as the piece you will be working on) in the V swage, place the fuller on top, and drive it into the swage to form it. When the fuller and the swage form the steel into the proper shape, the fuller is correct for that thickness of steel. Mine are set for 1/8-inch stock, but you can use any thickness less than 3/16 inch. Mine are 8 inches long since this is the longest piece that I use. Your tooling should be made with your longest requirements in mind. You can use the tooling for shorter pieces, but not for pieces longer than the ones for which it was designed.

Forge the body of the ax but do not put a curve in the edge. Rather, leave this part straight and bevel the last 1/2 to 3/4 inch of the edge to allow for the steeling. Next, form the steel edge in the swage and lightly flux the edge of the ax body at a cherry red heat. When fluxed, heat both the edging and the ax to a cherry red, insert the ax body into the edging, and lightly hammer closed.

Preheating provides an even heat while welding. This is vital because the steel has a tendency to burn before the milder steel inside heats up. Weld the pieces together, starting at one end and working toward the other. After this is completed, forge the edge to its final shape.

Both the steel-edged and V-edged construction methods produce a serviceable but low-quality ax. Mainly, these techniques were used to

SWAGE

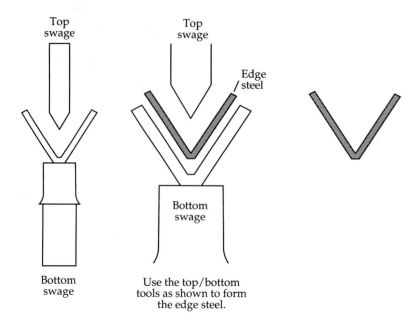

Top
swage

Top
swage

Edge
steel

Bottom
swage

Bottom
swage

Use the top/bottom
tools as shown to form
the edge steel.

The "V" swage for forming ax edges

V EDGE CONSTRUCTION

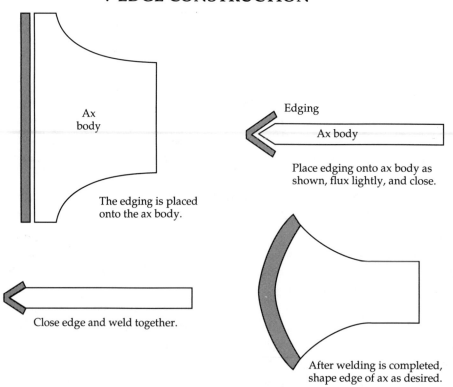

Ax
body

The edging is placed
onto the ax body.

Edging

Ax body

Place edging onto ax body as
shown, flux lightly, and close.

Close edge and weld together.

After welding is completed,
shape edge of ax as desired.

repair or resteel edges of worn or damaged axes during times that iron and steel were difficult to obtain.

Center-Cored Construction

This is the traditional method of making axes, and some respect must be given to tradition. I prefer this method of making an ax. It gives a keen edge with the softer ax body providing support for the harder, brittler-edged steel.

It involves sandwiching a mild-steel (or iron) body around an edge steel. There are several ways to do this, all of which have their advantages and disadvantages. In the basic ax, a bow-tie piece of iron is cut/forged to form the ax body. To do this, I suggest using 1/8- or 3/16-inch iron plate. Make certain that you leave enough of a center section to form the eye properly.

Taper the ends of the piece so the material can be doubled and the edge of the steel can be inserted as well. This tapering does not need to be severe. You are just reducing the blade's thickness to a more reasonable dimension, not forming the blade. The "outside wrappers" must match as closely as possible for the best results in positioning and welding the core. Also, the inside mating surfaces must be flat and blemish-free so the weld takes and holds.

You must decide on the shape and type of edge to insert. I use sections of leaf springs that have been feathered (tapered) away from the body. In other words, the insert's thicker side forms the edge, while the tapered section is toward the eye. This provides a more-or-less even thickness throughout the ax body, instead of a sudden massive cross section where the edge insert starts.

I use a section that is as long as the body is wide and that is wide

BOW-TIE CONSTRUCTION

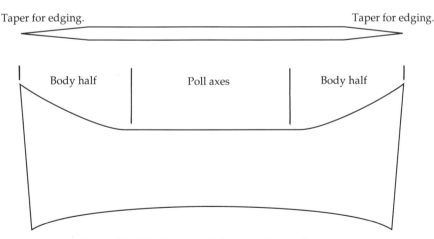

Form a blank in the general shape, as shown above,
to form the poll and body and to allow for insertion of the edge steel.

SECTION TO BE WELDED

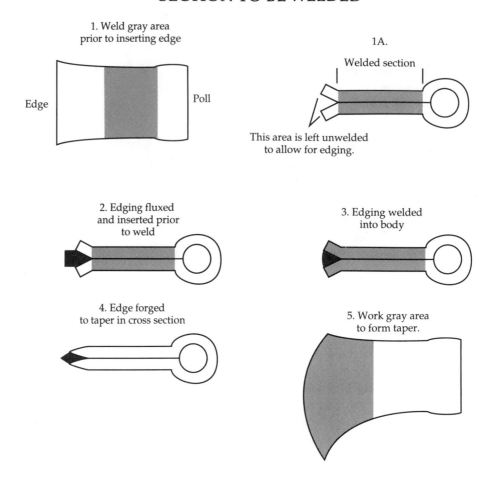

1. Weld gray area
prior to inserting edge

Edge

Poll

1A.

Welded section

This area is left unwelded
to allow for edging.

2. Edging fluxed
and inserted prior
to weld

3. Edging welded
into body

4. Edge forged
to taper in cross section

5. Work gray area
to form taper.

enough to extend at least one-third of the way into the ax body. Almost any thickness from 3/32 to 1/4 inch can be used, but I generally use either 1/8 or 3/16 inch. Some ax makers get good results from tool-steel shim stock, but it is difficult to keep the thin steel insert aligned down the cutting edge when you are forging the blade.

After forming the body and matching the halves, fold the eye section around a mandrel and weld a small section of the body next to the eye. You must insert the edge steel before the body is completely welded. The smaller welded section stabilizes the insert during the final welding, and the eye provides a good hold when working.

To weld, preheat the area, flux at a full cherry red with anhydrous borax, and bring up to a welding heat. The temperature must be higher for mild steel than for higher-carbon steel. The welding temperature should be in the orange range.

When heated, remove from the fire and strike the area next to the eye to set the weld. Reheat and continue welding until you have completed the entire section to be welded prior to the insertion of the edge. Before inserting the steel edging, return the body to the fire and place the steel in the forge to preheat. This brings both pieces up to an even welding temperature. Remove the insert from the forge when it reaches cherry red and lightly flux the insert, again with anhydrous borax.

With the insert fluxed, remove the ax body and spread the unwelded section of the halves enough to accept the insert. Clean the inside with a wire brush to remove clinkers or excess scale and prevent any inclusions from forming. Return the pieces to the fire and reheat until the insert and the ax body are the same temperature, a full medium red. Remove both pieces from the fire, place the insert—tapered edge first—into the ax body, close the halves securely over the insert, and return to the fire. This must be done quickly to prevent any heat loss. The more heat the piece retains when it's returned to the fire, the easier it is to bring it up to a deep, even welding temperature.

Bring the piece up to a welding heat slowly and check on the progress often. Since you are welding a piece of higher-carbon steel to a piece of milder steel, the welding heat is somewhat lower—in the full cherry ranges, depending on the exact steels. Remove the piece from the fire when it reaches the proper temperature and place it on the anvil with the the eye toward you and the insert away. Positioning the insert away from you protects you from the heavy and exceedingly hot flux/scale spray that occurs when you strike the welding blows. This must be done quickly because the welding heat does not last long.

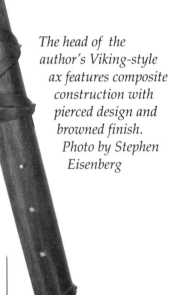

The head of the author's Viking-style ax features composite construction with pierced design and browned finish. Photo by Stephen Eisenberg

Strike rapid, controlled blows, starting at the bottom of the insert and working your way up to the edge. This forces out flux, scale, or any other impurities that may be present and allows a secure weld to take. The welding may take one or more heats depending upon the size of the piece. But work carefully so the steel insert doesn't overheat and burn.

After completing the welding, forge the body until it is in its final form and refine the eye. Make certain that the steel edging remains centered in the blade. If it ends up off-centered, the steel won't form a cutting edge, and it is useless. To ensure that this doesn't happen, flip the ax over and work both sides.

It is up to you to decide on the final shape of the ax. There are too many possible designs to list them all here.

Hardening and Tempering

Most of grunt work has now been done, but the blade still needs to be hardened and tempered. Hardening an ax is easy—only the edge should be done. The body remains soft to absorb impact.

Before the hardening, anneal and stress relieve the whole ax. Heat to a dull cherry red and place it into a hot box to cool slowly. Remove when cool and begin the hardening.

Take a cherry red heat (or the recommended heat for your alloy) and quench in the proper medium. Again, heat only the cutting edge to eliminate excessive hardness in the ax body. Submerge the entire head under the quenching medium to prevent stress cracks. Remove from the bath and temper. Since the blade is used to chop, heat to a full spring temper. This is a soft temper, but the ax edge is harder than annealed steel or most of the things it is called upon to cut.

I suggest that you heat the ax body and let it bleed into the edges. When at a full blue heat, quench quickly, and let cool completely in the bath. (If you want a harder edge, you can temper it to brown or straw, but the steel may be too brittle for an ax.) Remove and finish.

Since the blade was forged, you should have to do little grinding of the edge. A hollow-ground edge is not needed for an ax. Flat grinding is serviceable, but a cannel-ground edge (also known as an apple-seed edge) is best for serious work. The cross section and the amount of steel left to reinforce the edges make the edges tough and durable.

Finish and Hafting

You can finish the ax in a number of ways. For a rustic look, you can leave it as is, with a forge finish. Or you can smooth and polish the head to a high luster, but that can take more time than it did to make the ax. My favorite ax finish is a slow rust brown, similar to the rust browning used on black powder firearms.

The traditional formula for this was a liberal application of strong horse urine, followed by drying period of 8 to 10 hours; another application of urine, another drying period; and so on until the desired finish; was obtained. Needless to say, this method presents some problems. Most people are unwilling to use horse urine, for obvious reasons. But how else can you get that deep, beautiful brown that the old rifles had?

Forget the professional brown finishes available. Some are the quick-and-easy, one-application liquids that, no matter how hard you try, simply can't be put on evenly. On the other end of the spectrum are the hard-core gunsmith preparations that require several weeks of daily applications to work.

I have come up with the following formula that I have used successfully for the last few years.

1 part nitric acid
1 part hydrochloric acid
12 parts distilled water

NOTE: This acid should be used with great care. Always wear eye protection, a face shield, and rubber, acidproof gloves when using this formula. And remember: always add *acid* to *water*, not water to acid.

To use, clean all metal surfaces of scale, grease, and other contaminants. The metal should be bright, with a 50- or 120-grit finish. The coarser the surface, the better this works.

Apply the finish with a cotton ball in a clothespin. Use it freely, making certain that all the surfaces are covered. The metal turns dark in a few minutes. I do mine in batches of five or more and hang them out on an iron bar where they can dry undisturbed.

After several hours, apply the second application of reagent and let set until the next day. The axes will start to develop a nice rust brown. Reapply the reagent two to three times a day until the ax has a heavy coat of rust. This takes 7 to 10 days to accomplish. With a soft, fine wire brush, slough off the loose rust, rinse in warm water, and reapply more reagent for another 3 days. Leave the axes in an area where they can "rust in piece" until the finish reaches the desired depth.

Next, mix one box of baking soda in 1 1/2 to 2 gallons of very hot water until the soda dissolves. Immerse the axes in the water and let sit for an hour or two. As the soda water neutralizes the acid, a few bubbles rise from the axes' surface. After rendering the acid safe, remove the axes from the water, lightly brush off any loose rust, and let the heads air dry. When dry, apply a light coat of quality oil. The finish should be a deep, rich russet brown, with a slight roughness to its surface.

After the heads are finished, mount them on a haft (handle). Depending on the ax design, you may want to mount the ax temporarily before applying the finish. Remove, finish, and permanently attach.

Ax handles should be made from a tough, resilient wood such as hickory or ash. Actually, any wood can be used, as long as you remember the type of wood and its characteristics when using the ax. For presentation pieces, the more exotic woods are fine. For a working ax, I strongly recommend a straight-grained ash or hickory handle.

The mounting of an ax has a direct effect on the design of the ax haft itself. The major difference is whether the ax slips over the length of the handle or, like a hammer head, slips over the end and is held in place with wedges.

I prefer the former method of attachment for my smaller throwing axes or other designs that have a strong tendency for the handles to split or break. The tapered slip-ons are faster and easier to replace when needed, but they do not allow you to get a solid grip because of their smaller size and taper.

The most important thing to keep in mind when using the slip-on handle is that the haft and the ax's eye must fit very closely, or the ax will either be off-center or come loose during use. Also, leave a heavy lip on the business end of the handle to prevent the wood from splitting or breaking away during use.

The hammer-handle haft is a different matter entirely. Since the ax head is simply slipped on the end and held by wedges, there is no need to have a spindly, narrow haft below the head. What is needed is a snug fit between the head and the handle, as the wedges expand the wood to fit into the ax eye. The rest of the haft can be almost any shape or design you desire, as long as it works.

Before attaching the ax handle, split the end that goes into the head with a saw so that the split goes between the growth rings of the wood grain. This should allow the wood to expand more readily, with little chance of the handle breaking. The split should be three-fourths of the way into the area that the ax head covers.

Wedging is easy. You can do it in several different ways, but the best way is to use two wedges, wood and metal. The wood wedge should be as wide as the handle, about 3/16-inch thick, with a gentle taper. After the head is in place, drive the wood wedge as far into the slot as it will go and trim flush with the top of the ax.

Next, place the metal wedge diagonally to the wood one and drive it in as well. The two-wedge method tightens itself and prevents the wedges from becoming loose.

For both haft types, the grain of the wood should be parallel to the cutting edge, which imparts the most strength and durability to the handle. To finish the wood, I soak my ax for 7 to 10 days in a tempering bath to temper the wood and make the ax even tougher.

A well-made ax is a beautiful tool and weapon. Forging of this versatile and deadly blade is well within the scope of most smiths. Over time, the ax evolves into more sophisticated forms in your hands.

JAPANESE
NONFERROUS ALLOYS
& THEIR COLORATION

There has been a revival of sorts in the traditional Japanese techniques of nonferrous alloying and its patination (coloring). But there are few sources, if any, to tell you what the alloys are and how they are treated to get the colors for which the Japanese artisans are famous. Below are a few of the more common alloys and the secrets of their extraordinary coloring.

SAFETY NOTE: While handling molten metals, always wear both a full face shield and safety glasses to protect your eyes and face, along with a heavy leather apron, long-sleeved cotton shirt, leather boots with cotton pants on the outside, and leather gloves. Serious burns can result from mishandling molten metal.

Any of the crucibles used in casting can also be used for alloying these materials. But remember: once you use a crucible for a particular alloy, it can be used *only* for that alloy. This keeps your melt from being contaminated from a previous melt. Also, the first time you use a new crucible, melt a small amount (about 2 tablespoons) of anhydrous borax in it and glaze the interior to prevent any excess melt from adhering to the crucible's interior.

ALLOYING METALS

Charge the crucible with the higher melting point first (in this case, copper) until fully molten. Then add the gold and stir with a carbon or silica rod (available from a jeweler's supply firm) to keep the metals from separating. To prevent excessive oxidation, cover the melt with powdered charcoal, which forms a barrier between the metal surface and the outside air.

Cast into an ingot mold and allow to cool. Work the material according to its characteristics.

• *Shakudo (or shakudo gold) for blues and black.* This material oxidizes either dark blue or blue/black depending on the time in the solution.

100 parts pure copper

3 to 6 parts (by volume, not weight) pure gold

Alloy and cast into ingots, work like copper, anneal frequently while working.

• *Shakudo (or shakudo gold) for purple.*

100 parts copper

10 to 20 parts pure gold (by volume)

Work like copper and anneal frequently.

Shakudo is ductile, but when overworked it becomes brittle and prone to cracking and breaking. Treat it like copper and anneal frequently.

It can be worked cold or hot (forged) to some extent. Since it is a copper-based alloy, its working range is narrow and its forging temperature low, in the 1500 degree F range. Copper gets a little red short at higher temperatures.

The impurities in a coal/coke fire make it undesirable to work shakudo. I strongly suggest that you use a gas forge/furnace to prevent the metal from absorbing sulphur or any other contaminants in the fire.

Shakudo can be beaten into sheets (the traditional Japanese method) or rolled in a jeweler's mill. Jeweler's mills come in all sizes and prices. They run from a few hundred up to several thousand dollars. You can select from manual or electric models that roll various sizes and thicknesses of sheet and, on some models, wire as well. You should seriously consider getting one if you do a lot of sheet work.

COLORATION

Coloration or patination brings out the beauty of the materials. It is a chemical process that forms different oxides, producing the colors that you see. The chemicals can be highly toxic, so a filtering respirator must be used when boiling the mixtures to avoid inhaling the fumes.

Since coloration is a chemical process, you have to choose the containers carefully. Certain materials react adversely to the chemicals you'll be using. Do not use any steel, iron, or aluminum vessels during this process. Copper pots, as well as ceramics, glass, china, or unchipped enamelware can be used without any adverse reaction. The same rule applies to the tongs or other utensils that come into direct contact with the solution or the pieces being colored. Bamboo or copper tongs made especially for coloration are available from jeweler's supply firms.

Support the pieces with a copper screen or wire while they are in the solution. All work surfaces must be absolutely clean. Just the smallest amount of oil, wax, or grease prevents the solution from making proper contact with the surfaces, resulting in unsatisfactory patination.

How to Get Specific Colors

- *Blue/black shakudo*. Must be used with the blue/black alloy
  for desired results.
  Verdigris (copper acetate): 1 dram (1/8 ounce)
  Copper sulfate: 1 scruple, 1 dram (1/7 ounce)
  Distilled water: 4 fluid ounces

Grind the verdigris and copper sulfate finely, mix well, and boil in water. Place the pieces into the mixture, keeping them moving constantly. Depending on the desired color, use this solution hot or cold. The coloration process takes from 5 to 30 minutes, depending on the temperature and the color desired.

- *Purple shakudo*. Must be used with the purple alloy for best results.
  Copper sulfate: 1 dram (1/8 ounce)
  Common salt: 1 scruple (1/24 ounce)
  Distilled water: 4 fluid ounces
  Use the same as for blue/blue black.
- *Dark blue on silver*.
  Quicklime: 2 ounces
  Sulphur: 1/4 ounce
  Distilled water: 4 fluid ounces

Heat the solution and immerse the pieces, which must be 100 percent chemically clean. The warmer the solution, the quicker the action. When the desired color is reached, remove from the pickle and rinse well in warm water.

These recipes were translated from the original Japanese recipes and may or may not be totally accurate, but they do work. As with all chemicals used in metal treatments, these can be highly toxic. Follow all safety procedures for handling toxic/corrosive liquids to prevent serious injury or death.

MAKING MOKUME GANE: THE ART OF PATTERN-BRAZING

Mokume gane is a laminated material made up of two or more different metals. Traditionally, mokume gane was composed of pure silver, copper, and gold sheets soldered together into a sandwich, similar to pattern-welded steel. In Japan it was used for sword furniture and other ornamental work. In the West, this process is used extensively for jewelry, with the different metals combining to form exquisite patterning that is in itself quite beautiful.

There are two ways to go about making mokume gane. The first I call the traditional jewelry technique, and the second is the fusion method. Both methods result in the same basic patterns, but the fusion method is better suited to forging, while the the jewelry technique is superior for cold working.

Traditional Jewelry Technique

The traditional way of making mokume gane in the West is by silver soldering various layers of gold, silver, and copper together in a sandwich and then rolling the sheet into thinner, longer pieces.

Using gold and silver can be expensive, especially when you are experimenting with a technique. So you can use nickel silver (German silver) and copper and/or bronze/brass and get the same basic effect.

Cutting the Metal

The first step is cutting the material. Use sheet that is between .028 to .035 thick. All materials must be totally clean to be joined, without any oxidation or oils, greases, or waxes present on the surfaces. If not, the solder joints will not hold. The cleaning can be done by using a jewelry pickle. The pickle can be used for cleaning other nonferrous materials as well. Follow the directions carefully.

When clean, make certain that the pieces are handled by the edges only and wear clean, cotton gloves. This way you do not contaminate the pieces that are already cleaned.

Fluxing and Soldering

Since you are soldering the pieces together, you have to flux them and apply solder between the layers. There are various hard solders with different melting points from which to choose. I recommend using a solder with a medium melting point of approximately 1300 degrees F. This solder, when heated to 1350 to 1400 degrees F, flows and solders the pieces together.

To flux, use a top-quality, hard-soldering flux (the flux you use to soft-solder guards to blades will not work) and apply it to the pieces with an acid brush. I start with the nickel silver for the bottom and top layers. The copper has a tendency to melt down faster if you use a torch as a heat source. You alternate the layers of materials, one nickel silver, one copper, one nickel silver, one copper, and so forth.

Starting with the first layer, flux the sheet and apply enough solder to flow between the first and second layers. There are two ways to apply the solder. The first is to place a very thin (.001) sheet of solder between the sheet; the second is to file it into a fine powder and dust it onto the sheet. I prefer the dusting method, but both work.

After applying the solder, flux the second sheet on both sides and place squarely on the first sheet. Apply more solder on top of the stack and continue until all of the desired material is used.

NOTE: If you use a torch for a heat source, I strongly recommend that the stacks be no thicker than 3/16 to 1/4 inch. Thick stacks can present difficulties in getting an even heat throughout the thickness, ruining the soldering and leaving voids and gaps in the finished work.

There are two methods of applying heat to melt the solder. The most common is an oxyacetylene torch with a large soft flame and a charcoal block. Place the stack upon the charcoal block and "play" the torch over the stack until the solder flows and the layers are soldered together.

There are some serious drawbacks to doing it this way. The outside layers can melt away before the inside layers reach the proper temperature, or the layers can shift in the heating process or when the solder starts to flow. But this is one of the traditional ways of melting solder, so I guess it must work.

A better way of soldering is by using a jeweler's burn-out kiln (the same kiln used for lost-wax casting) and what I call a pressure plate.

The pressure plate is made from 1/8- to 1/4-inch mild-steel plate. It can be of any shape that fits inside the kiln. I have found that square or small rectangular plates work best. *Do not use any iron/steel that has been galvanized, tinned, or otherwise plated or treated.* Drill 17/64-inch diameter holes in each corner so the stack and the plates can be bolted together.

To use the pressure plate, you must cut the stack to a size that allows the bolts to secure the plate without touching the edges of the stack. If the edges touch the bolts, the bolts could become soldered to the stack, which can be a serious problem.

PRESSURE PLATE

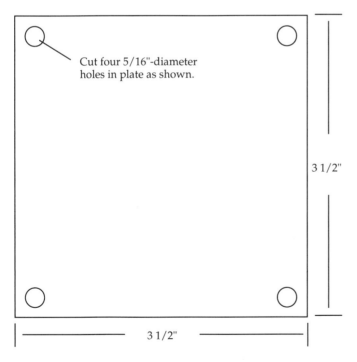

Cut four 5/16"-diameter holes in plate as shown.

3 1/2"

3 1/2"

Build the pressure plate from unplated, heavy, mild steel plate.

To prevent this, coat the plates with an antiflux, preferably ochre powder. It is available at most jeweler's supply stores. Ochre powder chemically prevents any sort of bond from forming between the solder and the iron.

To assemble, make the stack to your preference (since a "gentler" heat source is going to be used, the stacks can be somewhat thicker, up to 3/8 to 1/2 inch), making certain that the flux and the solder are properly applied.

To prepare the

plates, mix the ochre powder and water until it is the consistency of light cream and then apply to one side. When the ochre powder dries, it should stay where it was applied as long as you handle the plates gently. The plates should be prepared last to prevent any possible contamination of the stack.

When the plates are dry, place a single thickness of newsprint between the stack and the plates on both sides. This helps to prevent the plates and the stack from sweating together.

With this done, bolt the plates together using 1/4-inch bolts. Again, there should be no plating, galvanizing, or other treatment on the bolts. Any such treatment on either the plates or the bolts could poison the kiln with zinc, cadmium, or other fumes that could damage the process and injure you. There is no need for lock washers.

After assembling the components into a single unit, place it into the burn-out kiln. Place a section of kiln tile or kiln shelf underneath the plates to catch any leakage in case of a mishap.

Close the kiln and set the thermostat approximately 100 degrees F *above the melting point of the solder*. The solder should be able to flow throughout all of the surface layers, soldering them soundly together. *Caution*: At no time should the temperature exceed that of the melting point of any material inside the kiln. This could cause a partial or complete meltdown, sending molten metal all over the bottom of the kiln and possibly destroying it in the process.

The kiln temperature rises, and in about 30 to 45 minutes, it should reach the desired setting. Once the kiln is at the proper temperature, the work should be allowed to remain inside the kiln until it is evenly heated. This can take from 45 minutes to 1 1/2 hours, depending upon the individual kiln and the thickness of the stack and the materials used. You can, of course, check on the progress from time to time, but be certain that you are wearing leather gloves, a face shield, and safety glasses to protect you from the heat.

When properly soldered—the sides of the stack should look wet and shiny—close the door and allow an additional 10 minutes for the kiln to reheat and fill in any voids just to ensure that all the layers received enough heat to melt the solder.

Turn the kiln off and allow to cool to 900 degrees F. Remove the stack and place it in a bucket of water. The slow initial cooling solidifies the solder, and the more rapid water cooling helps to loosen the stack from the plates.

When cool, undo the bolts, and the plates should simply fall apart. There may be some slight sticking, but a gentle pry or a light rap on one of the plates should free the entire assembly. When the stack and the plates are separated, you should have a piece of laminated material.

If by chance you have a soldered mass, something went awry. More than likely there wasn't enough ochre powder between the stack and the plates, and/or the temperature was too high, causing an excess flow of solder.

Loosening soldered plates is a task in itself. I suggest grinding off the iron plates with a flat platen on a belt grinder. Of course, you could try to cold-chisel the plates off, but then you run the risk of loosening the layers and causing delamination. (But these rather severe methods will more than likely never be needed.)

The advantages of using a kiln over a torch are that a thicker piece can be made and the layers do not shift. The drawbacks are that it takes longer and the setup costs more.

Regardless of the method used to laminate Damascus steel, it has to be worked cold with frequent annealing to assure proper working and no fracturing. To anneal, simply heat with a torch until it glows a very dull red, quench in cool water, and continue to work.

When laminated, this material can be run through rolling mills, hammered into sheets, or put through any other processes that the component materials can endure.

Trying to forge Damascus steel (or to work it hot) melts the solder joints, causing the layers to fall apart on the anvil. This results in a great deal of mess and cursing.

Pattern Making

To get better patterns, reduce the thickness of the stacks and cut and relaminate several times along the lines of a pattern-welded billet to get the layer count up. This allows for more possible patterns.

Most pattern-welded techniques that result from surface manipulation, such as the ladder pattern and some of the the "bird's-eye" patterns, work well with soldered materials. This is not the case with the material manipulation patterns, including the various twists and most of the more sophisticated patterns used in the Damascus blade.

To get good results with these patterns, you use the "fusion method" of mokume gane.

Fusion Method

This process results in a forgeable material that can be worked hot but not cold. The process is similar to the above-mentioned soldering and stacking, but you use no solders. Instead the materials are fused together at a higher, near-melting temperature and then cooled quickly to solidify the stacked plates into (hopefully) a solid piece.

Clean the copper and nickel silver plates by pickling, the same process used prior to soldering except place no fluxes or solders between them. Instead, the plates must be totally clean of any oxides or surface impurities before they are stacked together.

To do this, sand away at the surfaces of the plates until you see fresh metal surfaces. This eliminates any possibility of surface impurities contaminating the metals once they are clamped tightly together between the plates.

Remove the pickled surface by using wet/dry sandpaper finer than 220 grit until the shiny surface is seen. The reason that the finer grit is required is that the surface is smoother and less prone to oxidation and, hence, more likely to form a tight and secure bond between the layers.

While sanding you will need to wear clean cotton gloves to prevent skin oils from contaminating the surfaces while you are cleaning the pieces.

When all of the pieces are pickled and sanded clean, alternate the layers into a stack and set aside while you prepare the pressure plates.

Since the pressure plates will be subjected to a higher degree of heat in this process than in the soldering techniques, they will have to be heavier than those used for soldering. Do not use any material thinner than 1/4 inch for the pressure plates. Also, there should be no plating or any other processes done on either the plates themselves or the connecting bolts.

Because of the heat involved (excess of 1600 degrees F) there may be a tendency for the stack to braze itself to the pressure plates, thereby securely adhering to the plates and resulting in one stubborn, massive piece of iron, copper, and nickel silver. To prevent this from occurring, you should use a parting agent that forms a barrier between the stack and the plates to prevent the two from adhering. This parting agent is simply fire clay and newspaper.

To apply the agent, simply mix a small amount of fire clay with enough water to make a slurry (paste) with the consistency of thick cream. Then coat the inside of one plate with the mixture. The ochre powder described above will not work because it is formulated to prevent soldering, not brazing, from taking place. Next, place a double thickness of damp, not wet, newspaper on top of the clay and repeat the process on the other plate.

What does this do? The newspaper holds the fire clay in place and prevents it from becoming smeared when the stack is inserted between the plates, possibly causing some adhesion to the exposed areas. Of course, the newspaper burns off almost instantly when inserted into the fire, but the fire clay is fired onto the plates, forming a ceramic skin that prevents the iron and the stack from sticking together.

When both plates are covered, place the prepared stack of plates between them and bolt the assembly securely together.

When bolting together, take care that the plates remain parallel and the pressure exerted is distributed evenly on the stack. This prevents any gaps from occurring in the stack.

To do this, secure the stack finger-tight while it is on the tabletop. Next tighten the bolts in the following order. I suggest that one-half turn of the bolt be used at a time until the sequence is completed.

After assembling, you are ready to fuse the mass together.

To fire the plates, I strongly recommend using a gas forge, although there are some smiths who get good results using a coal forge. To me, this is asking for trouble. Even with the cleanest coal/coke fire, there is always some impurity, no matter how minute, present that may cause some sort of problem. To prevent any impurity problems, a gas forge with a neutral atmosphere should be employed as your heat source.

As the piece is heated, the newspaper should burn away in a matter of seconds, and the fire clay becomes fired onto the plates. The plates' edges and top of the stack heat faster than the main body. To help even out the temperature, turn over and rotate the stack on a regular basis. If not, there may be sections of the stack that do not fuse properly, resulting in voids, delaminations, or, worse, no lamination at all.

As the pieces heat, the color runs the gamut from dull red to a full orange. The fire looks hotter than it is, but a high heat is required to make certain that a proper fusion takes place. You are sweating the metals together, and it is this that holds the pieces into a single mass.

As the temperature starts to reach the correct point, the copper starts to slowly liquefy. You can tell when this happens because beads of copper appear on the surface of the exposed edges, like beads of sweat.

NOTE: Wear didymium or other I.R./U.V. absorbing glasses and a full face shield to protect yourself when looking inside the forge.

Continue to rotate the work at regular intervals to assure that the stack is evenly heated and that fusion takes place throughout the stack. The center of the inner layers may not fuse if this isn't done. It is hard to tell exactly when all the layers are fused, but from experience you can learn how to tell quite effectively.

To tell if the stack is fused, you should see copper beads on all sides of the stack. Do not worry if there is some copper flow on one or two of the sides where the copper partially melted. If there is an excessive amount of copper flow or if the

BOLTING ORDER

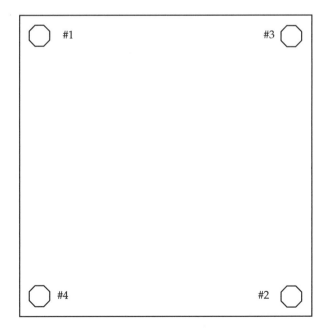

Finger tighten all the bolts in the above sequence before final tightening. To final tighten the bolts, use the same sequence to make certain that the stack is under even pressure, thus ensuring proper bonding of the sheets.

other metals melted as well, you have serious problems.

If this occurred, you do not have a fusion, you have a partial meltdown of the layers. This is caused by your heat being too high and the stack not being heated evenly. If you were to attempt to use such a piece, you would find that the laminations would not be distinct and that the piece would be riddled with small pits that simply will not disappear.

To prevent this from happening, simply keep a careful watch on the process and rotate the stack repeatedly.

What you are attempting to do is cause a fusion between the surfaces of the stacked plates. The color should be in the orange ranges, and I know that this looks like a good deal of heat, but that is what's required. You have to bring the material almost to the melting/flow point for the process to work. Do not overheat.

After the pieces are fused, remove the stack from the furnace and place it on the anvil. Lightly strike the plates to make certain that the layers fused. Do not strike the plates heavily, or you will have an excessive splatter of molten copper! Needless to say, you must wear adequate face/eye protection, leather footwear (boots are great), and long-sleeved cotton shirts when doing this.

Once the plates are hammered together, let them cool down to a dull red and then place the whole assembly into a bucket of warm water. Use a metal bucket (unless you like having a lot of water all over the floor) and stand away from it. There will be a good deal of steaming and hot water splattering when you drop the plates in.

There are two reasons why you are cooling these down so quickly. First, it anneals the piece of mokume, and second, the shock of the sudden cooling tends to blast the pressure plates apart from the billet, allowing for easy removal of the piece from the plates.

When cooled, remove the plates from the bucket and take the pressure plates apart. If all went as planned, the three pieces should simply fall apart in your hands, and all of the layers should be fused together into a solid mass.

You now need to surface grind the edges of the laminate to clean up the piece. This allows you to view the layering more easily. You should have a piece that looks like a laminated Damascus bar.

The fusion method of mokume gane cannot be worked cold. It can be forged hot in the bright red ranges, depending on the type of material you laminated. The best results are from copper and nickel silver (gold and silver can be forged, but the cost is prohibitive for the novice). Brass is so touchy and works so mushily that I recommend it not be used except for nonworked laminations (pieces that will be fused once and then worked into shapes on a grinder or with files).

When forging this material, you must carefully control the temperature. You can easily ruin a piece if it gets too hot or too cold. If the piece is too cold, the laminations come apart, and usually by the time this happens, it's too late to save the piece. If the piece gets too hot, you get molten copper splatter and, worse yet, grain separation of the material. If this happens, trying to save the piece is usually a lost cause. The best way of dealing with these problems is prevention.

Work the piece slowly and carefully in the full cherry red to light orange range. This material does not withstand heavy changes in cross section or radical changes in shape all at once. Keep the work in the full cherry/light orange range and you should be all right.

If you decide to relaminate forged-out pieces, you have to reclean all of the mating surfaces as you did when first starting out. You also have to shim the pieces with pure copper sheeting for best results. Remember, it is the copper that is fusing with the other materials, so you have to provide the copper between the pieces in order for the fusion to work.

The copper doesn't have to be very thick. I use 24-gauge sheet for the shim stock. Assemble the pieces as described above and then fire, using the same guidelines as described above.

When completed, the billet can be worked like pattern-welded steel. Although I haven't had good results with the twisted pattern, I have had a decent amount of success with the simpler patterns, such as the pool and eye and ladder.

I do not wish to discourage you from experimenting with various patterns. What may not work for me may work well for you. You may be delightfully surprised with the results.

This material was used for a variety of purposes, ranging from sword furniture and jewelry to small boxes and other items. I have found it to be a natural for butt caps and guards. As a matter of fact, the more dips, cutouts, and curves the better. Anything that reveals the laminations enhances the beauty of the metal.

To further enhance the metal's hidden beauty, you can use some of the commercially available silver/copper antiquing liquids, which work well, but the best results come from exposing the pieces to vinegar vapor.

The best way to do this is to simply suspend the pieces in a tightly closed jar that contains a small amount of common household vinegar (use full strength). The piece should not make contact with the vinegar, as this can have a negative result on the metal. Simply suspend the pieces by a light-gauge wire and set the jar in a warm place overnight.

The pieces should have a nice patina in a matter of hours, with the copper getting darker and deeper in color while the nickel silver stays pretty much unchanged. The longer the pieces remain in the jar, the deeper the color on the copper.

Of course, since this is a surface treatment, polishing removes the coloration. To protect the finish, lacquer the pieces after the coloration is completed. Or you can simply let the pieces age without polishing to keep the coloration intact.

Mokume gane improves with age and handling, with a slight etching process taking place over time. All of this translates into additional beauty that cannot be achieved by any other means.

Mokume gane is a very old process that is being rediscovered in the custom-knife industry. It is relatively unknown to the general public, and most people do not realize the work and trouble that go into making this laminated metal. But when Damascus steel hit the custom community, the story was much the same—and we all know how well the pattern-welded blade has been accepted. Mokume gane enhances the value of a custom blade, both materially and aesthetically. It is a difficult process to truly master, but once conquered, it is a true complement to a well-forged blade.

DAMASCUS STEEL: THE PATTERN-WELDED BLADE

Damascus steel has taken the custom cutlery world by storm. At one time in the not-so-recent past, only top bladesmiths had mastered the ability to make a pattern-welded blade. But today this has changed. There are more makers welding top-quality blades than ever before. And, while it takes time and practice to learn this skill, it is not as difficult as some would have you believe.

Damascus steel is what pattern-welded blades (and, to a certain extent, dreams) are made of. It is surrounded by legends of extraordinary cutting ability, unbelievable beauty, unsurpassed flexibility, and other virtues not ordinarily encountered in a blade. While some of these claims are more or less true, most of them have been exaggerated beyond belief.

Fact: a well-made pattern-welded blade is beautiful and cuts most things very well and some not so well. A pattern-welded blade derives its cutting ability from its laminations. Traditionally, bladesmiths forge-welded higher-carbon steel to lower-carbon steel or iron, resulting in a layered blade with a saw-toothed effect along the cutting edge. While Damascus steel makes excellent blades to cut anything with a fibrous nature, including rope, vegetable matter, and meat, it is not the best material from which to make precision-cutting tools for wood or wax carving. The saw-toothed edge does not leave a clean cut. But for most other cutting jobs, Damascus blades perform nicely.

Damascus blades reigned as the top cutters for a good many years, although that is not the case today. Most makers may take exception to what I am about to say, but I stand behind my words 100 percent. Damascus steel does not cut as well as some of the state-of-the-art alloys. Some of the powder-metallurgy steels and high-tech, ultrahigh-carbon industrial alloys make blades that cut damn near forever.

But to compare a blade made from these alloys with one from Damascus steel, with its inherent beauty, is like comparing apples and oranges. Compared to most carbon-steel alloys, a pattern-welded blade outcuts most blades two to one. Besides, the beauty of Damascus steel is almost enough in itself to warrant going to the trouble to make a pattern-welded blade.

Fact: Damascus blades are more flexible and less prone to breaking because of their makeup. The presence of low-carbon steel in the traditional layering method makes these blades extremely tough. Low-carbon steel does not take the same degree of hardness that the higher-carbon steel does. This is true even with an appreciable amount of carbon migration. I am not talking about the so-called high-density Damascus being touted by some makers. This is simply going too far. By the time you get 15,000 layers in 1/4 or 3/16 of an inch, you are dealing with laminations no thicker than 0.0000015 (15 millionths) of an inch. This is ridiculous. All that you are doing is making a 1050 or 1060 steel. You can't see layers that thin.

Making a patterned blade gives a smith the opportunity to express himself creatively, something rather uncommon in today's rush-and-hustle world. Many people believe that each blade has a soul. Maybe it's true, for I can see things in a well-patterned blade that transcend the beauty of the steel. Look for yourself. You may see them too.

All three of the author's Damascus khanjars have recurved, double-edged blades. The bottom and middle khanjars have buffalo horn mounts; the top mount is fossil ivory. Photo by Stephen Jacobson

234

FORGE-WELDING DAMASCUS STEEL

The basis of Damascus steel is the forge weld. The traditional method of welding it uses a coal- or charcoal-fired forge, but the availability of good-quality soft coal has made this more difficult. It seems the utility companies are buying up the best coal, leaving only the lower-quality coal for everyone else.

Pattern welding requires a clean, even heat throughout the entire welding and forging process. So if you cannot obtain top-quality coal, switch to an LPG-fired forge. A coal-fired forge gives a smith better control than a gas forge. It allows for localized heat and a higher-heat range, but nevertheless, gas forges can be used for pattern-welding.

Gas forges weld more cleanly than coal-fired ones. However, the steel may oxidize (scale) if the proper air/gas mixture is not used. This situation can be easily overcome by making the air/gas mix a little richer and increasing the gas pressure until the forge temperature rises to a welding heat.

Welding in a gas forge is basically the same as in a coal forge, but there are a few differences. The major difference is knowing when the steel reaches the correct temperature. This is achieved by raising the gas pressure until the desired temperature is reached. This can range from 10 to 12 pounds for smaller pieces, up to 17 to 20 pounds for larger pieces. *Warning: Never exceed 25 pounds or you run the risk of serious injury and/or death.*

You should know how to obtain the best atmosphere inside the forge for welding. While it can be best described as a neutral atmosphere, it is actually a slightly reducing atmosphere, one that is a little rich. This slightly rich burn helps to consume the ambient oxygen inside the forge, thereby lessening scale formation and excessive burning of the steel.

A word to the wise: *too much fuel lowers the temperature and endangers the operator.* So be very careful when it comes to welding in a gas forge. And, of course, adequate ventilation is required for operating any forge, but especially gas.

Heat-up time varies, but at my altitude (about 1,700 feet above sea level) I reach a welding heat in less than 10 minutes. This translates into a temperature range of 2250 to 2400 degrees F, well into the welding ranges for most carbon-steel alloys.

Getting the entire billet evenly heated from layer to layer is the most common difficulty encountered in gas-forge welding. While the outside of the metal may be at a welding temperature, the inside may still be too cool. You don't have this problem when using a coal fire because you can raise the heat by increasing the air blast. With a gas fire, you don't have this luxury. Rather, you must soak the piece until all of the layers are at an even welding heat.

Heating the Steel

When the forge is at an even heat (when the entire interior is glowing red/orange), place the billet inside the chamber and bring up to heat. For most of the time, leave the billet edge down so the laminates heat evenly on three sides. However, you should rotate from time to time to allow a more even heat on the down edges.

As the piece heats up, it starts to change colors, beginning with the outside layers. When the entire piece is an even cherry red, flux it and replace it in the forge.

Forging with a gas fire, as well as coal, requires a flux. There are commercial fluxes available for gas forges, but they are more expensive and, to tell the truth, less effective than anhydrous borax, the flux used in coal forges.

It doesn't take much flux because the atmosphere inside the forge minimizes scale. Don't drown the piece in flux; rather, sprinkle the flux lightly but thoroughly to coat the piece completely. The flux melts and seals the piece in an airtight coating that prevents oxidation and helps to clean the weld surfaces. This also tells you when the piece is ready to weld.

NOTE: The flux is a corrosive material that eats into the forge refractory at an alarming rate. To prevent any damage to the forge bottom, place a piece of kiln shelf inside the forge to act as a drip pan to catch any dripping or misplaced fluxes before they reach the forge bottom.

After fluxing, the piece comes up to heat quickly, so watch what is going on. The bar's surface becomes shiny as it is coated with the semi-liquid flux, and as the piece nears welding heat, the flux melts, taking on the appearance of hot honey. This indicates that the surface of the bar is at the proper temperature, but do not remove the billet yet. Wait until the flux starts to bubble and then remove it. This assures you that the center layers are at the proper heat and will weld.

Remove the billet, set the weld, and return to the fire. Do not be overly alarmed if the center of the billet doesn't weld at the first strikes. This is not uncommon with a gas forge during the first weld. Place the piece back into the forge, bring it up to another welding heat, and reweld. The piece should stick this time.

This separation in the weld is caused by the layers not reaching the proper heat during the process. It is not detrimental as long as the pieces are not overheated or burned. This problem usually corrects itself when you get more experience in welding in a gas forge. If it continues to occur, I suggest that you reduce the number of starting layers by two on all subsequent billets until the separation no longer happens.

I have had great results with billets in the 11- to 15-layer range, using pure nickel sheet and 1/8-inch-thick tool steel. But if you are using 1/8- to 1/4-inch-thick stock in your billet, I suggest that you go no thicker than 1 1/4 to 1 1/2 inch for your billets. At this thickness, you can maintain a good soak at a welding heat with little difficulty. At a thicker size, you may have trouble maintaining a welding temperature all the way through the first weld course.

With this piece welded, complete the weld series and do another course of welds to make certain.

NOTE: The flux is very hot and it does spatter, so be careful. Make certain that you wear adequate eye/face protection. Whenever you are operating a gas forge, or any heat source for that matter, make certain that you are wearing infrared/ultraviolet-absorbing glasses (didymium) so you will not damage your eyes. I cannot overstress these safety rules.

Forging

Since the operating temperature of these forges tops out in the welding range, I start to forge in the welding range and continue until the steel cools to the full cherry ranges. If not done correctly, this can cause grain (crystalline) growth, but I have had no difficulty with this. And you have even less to worry about if you use a power hammer. Even the smallest power hammer generates enough force and pressure to fracture the grain structure into smaller, stronger, more durable crystals. After all, that is what forging is all about—getting a small, tough, durable crystalline structure.

If you are hand forging, you should still work in the higher ranges, as long as the material you are using allows it. You should be more careful with your forging techniques, however, since the pressure from a hand hammer (unless you use a very heavy sledge and a striker) is less than that from a power hammer.

Gas-welding/forging and welding processes are identical to those for a coal forge because the only real difference is the heat source. Even with the limits imposed by a gas forge (limited heating ranges and no localized heats), it can still do most of the work almost as well as—and in the case of exotic materials, better than—a coal fire. If you can weld successfully in a coal fire, you should have no problem welding in a gas forge once you get used to it. It actually is easier to use in most cases.

I will never give up my coal forge because it is the traditional forge of the bladesmith. There is something about a coal fire, the smell of the coke, the glowing coals, and the nostalgia of knowing that you are doing it the same way it was done "way back when" that has me hooked. As soon as I find a steady supply of quality coal, I will be back using it. I have several tons on hand that I am saving for my special projects.

Material Preparation Prior to Welding

Most steel as it comes from the mill is covered with a heavy, black-scale coating. You can buy precision-ground bar stock, but this is usually very expensive. Besides, for welding you don't need the degree of flatness that makes these bars so expensive.

Grinding Off Scale

You can grind off the scale using a coarse belt, with the grind lines running across the bar, not down the center. Grinding removes the scale and increases the capillary action that draws the flux into the spaces between the layers.

You should grind prior to every weld. Although you lose a small amount of material in the grinding, this loss is more than acceptable when you consider how much easier the bars weld when the surfaces are clean.

There is another reason for grinding off the scale in addition to making welding easier. It also makes for a cleaner weld. If you do not grind off the scale, then you weld the scale together. While fluxing helps to remove some of the coating, there is a small amount left behind that gets trapped between the layers. Although the weld will still be sound, there will be a small dark line where the scale was welded together. This line appears as a smudged or a dirty layer in an otherwise clean pattern. While some makers simply accept this as a fact of life, I cannot.

Since this line is so simple to avoid, it should be. Taking the time and effort to do the extra grinding is what makes custom cutlery so much better than the mass-produced blades being made by the thousands every day.

Grinding the Edges

Another step in preparing to weld is grinding the edges flush. This is not very involved when you use standard bar stock, but it is still required for best results. Doing so gives you a solid bite when securing the stacked bars prior to welding. Also, since the edges of most carbon-steel bar stock are rounded and those of most mild-steel stock aren't, the grinding helps to even out the edges, which prevents any "mushrooming over" of the carbon steel. This mushrooming can cause cold-lapping problems, and it can hide any delaminations occurring during the forging process.

To help in getting everything right, clamp the layered stock in a vise and then use "C" clamps to help hold things in place. Remove and grind the ends and the one edge first, and then place the assembly back into the vise, move the clamps, and then grind the remaining edge flush and even. You may also wish to radius the corners of the bar to prevent any "splaying" of this section. This radius does not need to be heavy; only a mild breaking of the corners is necessary.

To hold things together after the grinding, some makers get good results by tack-welding either an arc- or gas-weld bead on the ends to hold things together. I personally do not like this idea, as you cannot easily tell if the welding has taken if the whole assembly is welded together. Then you have to remove the "filler" used in the welding. I wire everything together using a heavy-gauge steel wire. Baling wire is excellent for this purpose. Use two or three turns of wire in two or more places.

Make certain that one end is free to start the welding. If the welding takes, remove the wire as the welding proceeds down the bar.

Using Exotic Materials

There are more materials that can be used for pattern welding than the traditional high-carbon/low-carbon steels. Some of these produce a vibrant pattern while others yield a more subtle pattern, but all will outcut most anything else.

Pure Nickel Sheet

In *The Complete Bladesmith*, I described using pure nickel and tool-steel mixtures. From my extensive work with pure nickel, I believe that you must use it for a vibrant pattern. Pure nickel is expensive, but the resulting patterns are worth the extra cost. It is temperamental in terms of welding and working ranges, so it is tricky for novices. But once you get the hang of it, I doubt you will want to use anything else.

Working pure nickel laminate is much the same as working any other material, except the number of layers in the completed billet is lower than normal because the nickel tends to alloy with the steel. I suggest using no more than 175 to 250 layers in 3/16 to 1/4 of an inch. This allows you to see the pattern, make the pattern interesting, and maintain increased cutting ability without worrying about driving out the steel.

Nickel has a tendency to delaminate if worked at a lower temperature, so most of the forging should be done at a higher-than-normal temperature. Therefore, you must laminate this material to a steel that withstands higher heat. I recommend using 1070 to 1095, as these are a bit more forgiving than a higher-alloy steel. Most of the richer alloys tend to be red short and can develop cracks or crumble if they get overheated. This should also be a consideration when choosing the steel to which you weld pure nickel.

Unlike coal forges, gas forges run no risks of the sulphur contaminating the nickel. But the nickel may oxidize, so watch the atmosphere inside the forge to prevent this.

I prefer 1095 to most anything else because I can work this material at a near welding heat under a power hammer, assuring me of solid welds and no weld shearing or delamination.

For pattern manipulation, work at a near-welding or full-welding heat, especially when doing twist patterns. Since the working properties and stretching rates of nickel and tool steels are so different, you need the higher temperatures.

Heat-treat pure nickel as you do the steel laminate. Heat treating has little effect on nickel because it does not form carbides, so carbon migration is not a problem.

AS 203 D/E

AS 203 D/E is a viable alternative to pure nickel. This alloy is considered a mild steel and is used in pressure vessels. It contains approximately 3.25 percent nickel, enough to resist most etchants but not enough to cause problems in working the billet. A typical melt contains less than 20 points of carbon, so there may be some carbon migration in higher-layer densities.

AS 203 D/E is only available in 1/4-inch plate, and you must cut your own bar stock from the plate. It welds like most other laminates and works like other mild steels. It tends to be forgiving in working temperatures and reacts like 1095 while being drawn out under the hammer.

I don't recommend laminating AS 203 D/E with O-1 because the watering is not as vibrant. The best patterns come from welding it to a simpler high-carbon steel, such as the 10XX series, W-1/2, or WHC.

Layer density can go well into the high hundreds with little difficulty, but I recommend 300 to 550. You can use it for any pattern that can be made with high- or low-carbon steel laminations. To reduce carbon migration, I suggest fewer layers, but it is up to you.

O-1

O-1 has been used for many years for pattern-welded steel, and while it contains enough chrome to resist etchants, it doesn't contain enough to cause a serious red-hard problem. By laminating with a simpler alloy, such as a medium-to-high carbon 10XX series, you eliminate carbon migration.

It does tend to be red short, so I recommend keeping the working ranges lower than with the simpler alloys. I don't like to use this material, but countless blades made with O-1 are around, so some smiths do prefer it.

M-2

M-2 is a high-speed tool steel that is somewhat red hard. Because it was designed to maintain a degree of hardness under heat, it is more difficult to work under the hammer. But it does make a decent blade.

D-2

I do not like to laminate with an air-hardening steel because of inherent heat-treating difficulties. It too has a tendency to be a bit red hard and red short. It can be used, however.

All-Tool-Steel Damascus

This alloy can be a mixture of O-1/1095, M-2/1095, M-2/O-1, or any other similar steel alloys. These steels produce a superior cutting Damascus steel blade without any carbon migration because both materials are tool steel. Watering ranges from subtle to very good with most of the patterns, depending on alloy differences.

Vasco Wear

Vasco Wear is a special formula alloy developed by Vasco-Pacific. It is highly wear-resistant and makes an excellent laminated blade. Working unhardened Vasco Wear is easy. Hardened and tempered, it is a monster to grind or work because of its extremely high wear-resistance.

Common Pattern-Welding Problems

Problems can sometimes arise that complicate pattern-welding or, in the worst cases, ruin all of the time and effort you put into a piece. Most errors occur in welding, but some are a simple matter of temperature control. Most are easily prevented, and some are correctable if caught early enough in the process.

Carbon Migration

Carbon migration can be a serious problem. It is the result of high temperature and time. When the steel reaches its welding temperature, the carbon starts to migrate into the lower carbon steel layers. Although this usually is not much of a problem in lower-layered billets, it can start to occur with as few as 100 layers. Once you get above 600 layers, migration can be a serious problem.

You can eliminate carbon migration by using two high-carbon steels (such as O-1 and 1095) or a material that does not form carbides, such as pure nickel sheet.

Cold Shuts

This problem is caused by welding temperatures being too low. Cold shuts are little black or silver lines, depending on the materials being welded. They are usually correctable if caught early on in the cycle. If the blade has been forged to shape, they can be welded shut. Once the blade has been ground, hardened, and/or tempered, there is little that can be done. To prevent them, make certain that the steel is at a full-welding heat and the billet is well soaked (heated all the way through).

Delamination

Similar to weld shearing, delamination occurs when the laminations separate during forging. This can be caused by several factors, but the most common one is an unsound weld. Other factors include extreme differences in the materials being worked and a working heat that is too low. To correct this, simply reweld and work at a slightly higher temperature. Also, make certain that the laminating materials have similar working properties when forged in the same temperature ranges.

Inclusions

Inclusions are foreign matter trapped between the layers during welding. They appear as pits or black sections of impurities in the blade. Once present, there is little that can be done, but they can be prevented by making certain that the welding surfaces are clean and free of excess scale, flux, or other nasty impurities clinging to the surface.

Lapping

This annoying problem occurs when the edges of the bar peen over. Lapping can prevent you from noticing various conditions early in the process that, if left undetected, can ruin composite twisted patterns. It can be prevented by checking the condition of the bar's edges and, if needed, grinding away excessive oxidation or erosion of the layers.

Red Short

Red short is the condition that causes the material to crumble under the hammer. It is quite common with O-1, A-2, D-2, and most other rich alloy steels. Working above the steel's recommended temperature produces excessive grain growth in the steel, which then starts to crumble and burn. There is nothing to be done once this occurs, but it can be avoided by working within the recommended temperature range.

Spider-Web Cracking

This, too, is caused by a temperature that is too high. It is the lesser variety of red short. It looks much like the name implies—fine little spider-web cracks that appear inside the bar. They are caused by the steel's breaking down as it starts to burn. It is a common problem with some of the richer, more temperature-sensitive alloys such as O-1.

Weld Separation

Similar to delamination and weld shearing, weld separation is usually encountered when forging multiple-cored twisted patterns such as the Persian ribbon or Turkish twist. An incomplete weld causes the core sections to come apart during forging. It can be corrected by rewelding the affected area or prevented by sound welds.

Weld Shearing

Weld shearing, like delamination, involves separation of the layers, but it is more prone to happen while the steel is being twisted, which places a severe amount of strain upon the material. Pure nickel is especially prone to this. It is correctable by taking another welding heat after the bar is twisted.

These are the most commonly encountered difficulties in pattern welding. There are other problems that can arise, but they are quite rare, and for the most part, easily corrected by the experienced bladesmith.

DAMASCUS PATTERNS

There are almost limitless patterns that can be achieved in pattern-welding. They range from simple and elegant to complex and gaudy. Some of the patterns take almost no time, while others demand almost endless toil in front of a forge and at the anvil.

To bring out its natural beauty, every pattern must be done well with no inclusions, cold shuts, or other impurities. There is no substitute for craftsmanship and careful attention to detail. Do not rush things; instead, take things as they come, and you should be able to make a considerable array of patterns.

The patterns are broken down into two major groups: surface manipulation and material manipulation. Both result in some gorgeous patterning. Surface manipulation is simpler than material manipulation. However, the patterns that result from this technique tend to be shallow and are easily erased by overzealous grinding or forging. But some of the patterns are very appealing.

Material manipulation can be broken down into two different sub-categories. These are basic manipulation and composite manipulation.

Basic manipulation is where only one piece is patterned, such as a maiden's hair or a ladder pattern. This type of pattern is relatively simple, but the pattern runs more or less throughout the thickness of the bar, so there is little danger of erasing it.

Composite manipulation is when two or more pieces of patterned material are assembled into a single piece. Examples include the Turkish and double-chevron patterns. As with basic manipulation, the patterns run deep throughout the piece, but they tend to be more difficult. They require a considerable amount of preparation and planning, an intimate knowledge of forge welding, and a basic understanding of how to make a pattern. Not for the beginning smith, these patterns can offer a challenge to most advanced smiths' abilities. It is not unusual for some of these patterns to take 20 or more hours to make, but their beauty makes it worth the extra time and effort.

Since this is an advanced study in the art of pattern welding, I won't go into surface manipulation unless it is called for in a particular pattern. Rather, I'll concentrate on material manipulation and its effects.

Blade Design and Its Effect on Patterns

Some of the patterns mentioned below show their patterns better in symmetrical, double-edged blades. There can be a marked difference in appearance between a pattern's execution, such as a ladder, in a single- and double-edged blade.

Double edges reflect a mirror pattern on both sides of the blade, while a single-edged blade only shows the lamination on a single plane. For a good example, look at the ricasso and then the blade bevels of a pattern-welded knife and you can see a difference in the exposed watering.

Some patterns show up better on a single edge, such as a maiden's hair. A mirror pattern on a maiden's hair gives you a star twist. So you must match the blade style with the pattern.

A good way to approximate how a pattern will look is to form your laminations with two different colored modeling clays. Draw out the clay and fold it over a couple of times to get the layer count up, much as you do with the steels. Then, form the clay the same way that you plan to work the steel. Use a wire to cut the bevels. This allows you to see what the pattern should look like and saves you a lot of time, material, and frustration.

Basic Material Manipulation

This category comprises the simplest patterns, including the classic ladder pattern. The ladder pattern can be the basis of several variations, one of which I developed. I call it hugs and kisses after the X and O patterns that run down the center of the blade.

Hugs and Kisses

This pattern is best suited for a symmetrical, fullered, double-edged blade. You need a center fuller to bring out this particular style of watering.

Laminate a billet of 11 to 15 layers of any laminatable material. Draw the piece out, cut into thirds, and shim between the pieces with a 1/8-inch tool steel. The shimming causes a space of plain carbon steel that forms the X in the pattern. The laminates help to form the O that will be seen. Reweld and draw out again. When this is completed, cut into thirds and shim as above. Continue until you have a billet of 200 to 400 layers.

After completing the lamination, form the bar in preparation for patterning. To do this, draw out the bar as if you were making a ladder-patterned blade, which, in essence, you are.

The depth and spacing of the cuts are critical and must be done correctly. Space the cuts approximately 1/4 to 3/8 inch apart and cut down into the center of the first shimmed weld as shown on the facing page. Also, make certain that the grooves are offset from side to side because if aligned, the pattern doesn't work.

Next, flatten the bar and take a finishing welding heat to make certain that any weld shearing or delamination is welded closed.

In making the blade, do a rough forge to shape since you do not want to disturb the pattern. Also, lightly forge in the fuller to grind away some material and reveal the pattern in the fuller.

Edge packing improves the pattern and makes a better blade. Don't do a heavy packing, just a more controlled forging of the edge bevels. Next, profile the blade to shape but do not grind the edge bevels since you still have to form the fuller.

SHIMMING A BILLET

Sandwich the tool-steel shims between
the pattern-welded material as shown.

GROOVE PLACEMENT FOR HUGS AND KISSES

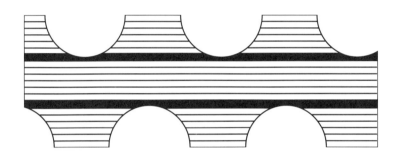

Alternate grooves on both sides of the billet and cut the groove
into the shim so that the pattern will be properly formed.

Grind the fuller into the blade, following the forged groove as a guide. The depth should run into the first carbon-steel shim, as did the ladder grooves. This forms the remainder of the Xs and Os at the same time. If the fuller is too deep or not deep enough, the pattern won't work. Follow the groove by grinding the edge bevels. Use the smallest possible grinding wheel to cut through the most layers and reveal the best pattern.

After grinding the blade, heat-treat and temper. Be careful that the blade doesn't warp during the process. If you are really worried about this, heat-treat prior to grinding. If you do it in this order, you must be watchful during the grinding that you don't overheat the steel and mistakenly anneal the blade.

Etch and mount the blade as you desire. This pattern can generate a good deal of interest if properly made.

Composite Manipulation

Composite manipulation is perhaps the most time-consuming method of making a pattern-welded blade. This extra time is required because the blade is composed of multiple pieces of prepatterned material. This prepatterning can be twisted, folded, upset, or whatever else the smith sees fit to do to make a blade. Mostly, the pieces are twisted in different rates or directions.

Turkish or Persian Ribbon

The most common composite pattern is the Turkish or Persian ribbon pattern. It is formed by welding three or more twisted bars together. The basic process can be modified into several more patterns.

Lucifer's Lace

This is another pattern that I have developed in my research (mostly curiosity) at the forge. Like the ribbon pattern, it is formed of several twisted pieces. But the pieces of Lucifer's lace are not welded side to side;

The hugs-and-kisses pattern was developed by the author. This blade was made from 1095 and pure nickel sheet. Photo by Stephen Jacobson

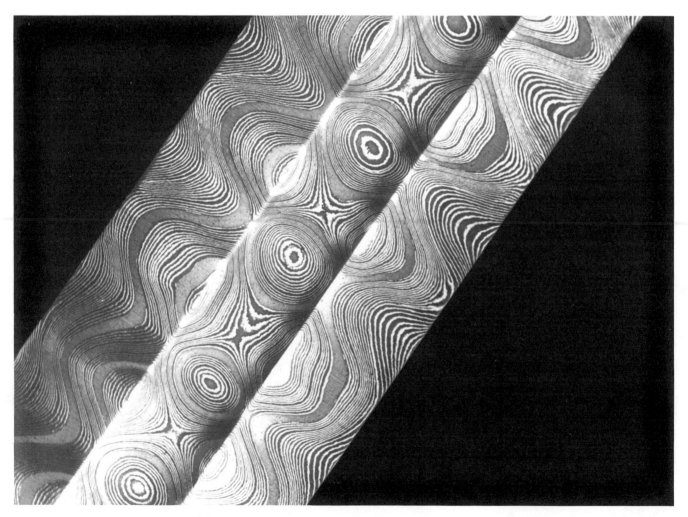

CLOCKWISE/COUNTERCLOCKWISE STACKING

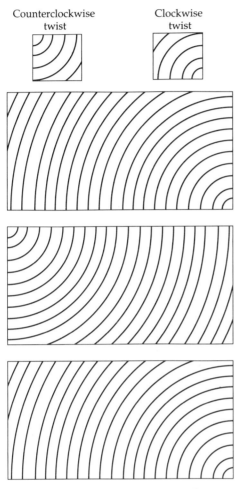

With the bars twisted and forged flat, sandwich the counterclockwise twist between the clockwise twists as shown.

they are sandwiched top, middle, and bottom.

To make this pattern, you need three identical bars of laminated material. Each bar should have 125 to 150 layers so when all three pieces are welded together, the layers aren't fine enough to hinder the watering effect. After all, if you are going to make a pattern-welded blade, you should be able to see the pattern. I have had great results using pure nickel and 1095 as the laminates. It accentuates the watering.

As for the size of the pieces, 1/2- to 5/8-inch square stock is about right for a 1- to 1 1/8-inch-wide, 3/16 to 1/4-inch-thick blade. For larger blades, begin with a larger square stock. Make certain that the bars are the same size.

After squaring the pieces, forge them round to prevent any excessive weld shearing during the twisting. Twist the bars as tight as you can without shearing them in two. The amount and evenness of the twists are important. The twist has to be as even and as tight as possible. Twist two of the bars clockwise and the other counterclockwise. Next, flatten each bar to a thickness of approximately 1/8 to 5/32 inch. Again, the three pieces should be as close to the same size as possible.

After flattening, clean the surfaces to be welded. Laminate the bar with the counterclockwise twist between the two clockwise bars, as shown on the previous page.

Weld the pieces together and true up the bar. You now have a single piece of composite material with twists running in opposite directions. If you were to forge this into a blade at this point, the pattern would be a different but not very interesting one.

After welding the pieces together, lay out a tight ladder pattern. The grooves should be as tight as possible for this pattern to succeed. I have used rungs spaced 1/4 to 3/8 inch apart at a depth of one-third of a billet wide. You can go deeper, but I wouldn't advise it. After all, you need some additional thickness to work with once the billet is flattened.

Make the grooves as uniform as possible in terms of spacing, width, and depth. Remembe, control is the key to successful patterning. With the grooves cut, proceed to flatten the billet as if it were a ladder-patterned piece. Now you are ready to forge the billet into a blade. Flattening this pattern, as with a ladder-pattern, raises the interior laminations to the surface of the bar, thereby bending the bar and exposing a section of the opposite twisted center core. This effect gives the appealing appearance of an opposite rung.

You can improve this pattern by forging to shape, which is relatively easy compared to some others. However, it's the degree of craftsmanship rather than difficulty that makes a pattern what it is.

This design can serve as the basis for further experimentation. You should feel free to make variations and changes as you see fit. After all, this is a learning experience.

Letter Welding

The techniques of making letters and words in steel have been shrouded in secrecy for centuries. I don't know why, because it is not that difficult to figure out once you have an understanding of how things are put together. But even after figuring it all out, it still entails quite a lot of work. There are lots of small, thin pieces to weld together, and the welds have to be perfect for this to work.

There are two ways by which you can form letters. One way uses a small square drill rod and key stock as the material. The letters are laid out similarly to using graph paper. To form a letter H, take the square drill rod and form the letter as shown on the facing page. Next, take the same size of mild-steel key stock and fill in the spaces so the piece forms either a rectangle or a square section as illustrated.

Take four pieces of tool-steel flat stock and box in the formed letter. This prevents the key stock and square drill rod from splaying, moving, or otherwise losing position. Wire or tack-weld the assembly together and weld together. Make certain that you heat the billet thoroughly and that the welding heat penetrates all the way through each piece.

This technique has some drawbacks. It requires numerous welds, and each one must be perfect. When welding, each piece must be rotated 90 degrees (rolled one-quarter turn) after every one or two blows to seal the bar and weld the interior. I suggest working at a higher heat than normal because of the amount of mild steel and the number of welds involved. Work your way down the bar until the bar is welded. This bar can be cut as is or forged down to a smaller size. You should have an

The author made this Lucifer's lace pattern-welded blade from 1095 and pure nickel sheet. Photo by Stephen Eisenberg

FORMING A LETTER WITH SQUARE DRILL ROD

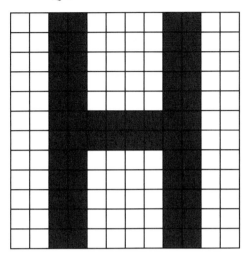

Use the square drill rod and key stock to form letters as shown.

High-carbon tool-steel square drill rod

Low-carbon key stock

"H" formed in the center of the bar.

An easier way to form letters is to use rectangular and square stock in combination. While it is easier than using only the square stock, some letters are uncooperative to being made this way. But the smaller number of individual pieces makes welding easier.

To form an "L," use a rectangular tool steel as shown on the next page. Next, place pieces of rectangular and square mild steel around the letter to form a square. After forming the square and letter, box the entire assembly in tool-steel flat stock as described earlier. Do not be afraid to alter the bar stock if you need a nonstandard size. It doesn't involve that much work, and most of it goes rather quickly.

Welding this assembly is basically the same as welding the grafted letters previously mentioned. It requires the same care and attention to temperature, and again, you should work at a slightly higher temperature. After completing the welding, draw out the piece to whatever size you wish, as long as you keep the section squared and don't twist the bar.

Use the same forging techniques for whatever style you select. Once the letters are formed, they can be welded together to form words.

NOTE: The letters will only be visible when the center axis is cut through. You cannot see the letters unless you are looking end-on, as they are formed inside the bars.

As for working these bars once they are welded together, this is a matter of personal choice. I have welded the letters into words, cut off sections (slices), and worked these into the pattern. This can be done in several ways, mostly by stacking or lining them up so they run down the center of the blade.

Twisting the assembly causes a slight deformity in the patterns, but as long as the letters form the center of the axis, the twist will not deform the letter to the point of its being unreadable.

You have a considerable latitude in making letters and how you can use them in the patterns. There are numerous surviving swords from

MAKING AN "L"

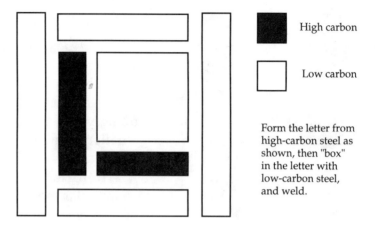

High carbon

Low carbon

Form the letter from high-carbon steel as shown, then "box" in the letter with low-carbon steel, and weld.

more than 1,000 years ago that had phrases such as "in toto" or "Dominea" worked into the blades. The knowledge existed back then to do this work, and the ability to re-create the art of letter welding is within the grasp of anyone who will devote the labor, knowledge, and self-discipline required.

Wire Damascus

Wire Damascus is another popular type of blade construction similar to welded cable. As a matter of fact, you can use cable as a basis for this material, but it doesn't make a first-class blade. I don't want you to misunderstand and think that welded cable doesn't make a decent blade. When compared to a nonlaminated carbon-steel blade, it is superior both in toughness and cutting ability. Yet, it is not as good as it could be. I twist my own cable from drill rod.

Drill rod is usually M-2 tool steel that makes a fine blade in a nonlaminate, and I think it makes an even better blade welded together. It is available in a vast range of sizes from a few thousandths of an inch on up. The smaller the rod, the finer the pattern; but more of the rod is needed to make a given diameter. Also, there is less space between individual rods with a smaller diameter.

With a larger-diameter rod, you need fewer rods, but the patterns are coarser and more space is needed between the pieces. What this space translates into is diameter reduction when the strands are finally welded together. A good compromise is to use a mixture of large- and small-drill rods with the smaller rods placed in the space between the larger ones as illustrated below.

This gives you a different pattern, and you still have a good deal of material left (the volume remains the same; only the dimensions of the bar change) after the welding is completed.

NOTE: If you want a more vibrant pattern, add some thin pure nickel strands in the bundle. These appear as little flecks that give appeal and variety to the watering.

Regardless of the rod diameters, the welding process remains the same as for a basic cable blade. But there is one peculiarity about rod diameters that you must know. The smaller the rods, the faster they come up to heat. If improperly handled, they could easily burn before the larger strands are at a welding heat. For this reason, I would not place any smaller rods on the outside of the bundle. Rather, place them inside where there is little chance that they will overheat before the entire assembly reaches the proper temperature.

If you use any shape other than round, keeping the bundle together once it is formed is a real pain. Wire the round shape in place with several turns of heavy wire in two or three places along the length of the piece. Make certain that you leave the ends free to weld. Next, place one end in the forge and prepare to weld it. Preheat, flux, and heat up to a welding temperature, making certain that the bundle is well soaked.

Weld the end carefully so that the rods do not splay or separate. With a medium-weight (3-pound) hammer, strike light, rapid blows while rotating the bundle on the anvil surface until it is welded securely. When this is completed, reverse the bar to do the opposite end of the bundle. Heat the bundle to a full cherry red, lightly flux, and twist the bundle to tighten the rods and give a more interesting pattern. The tighter you twist, the more wires cross the edge, giving better cutting ability. The direction of the twist isn't as important as the number—unless you are going to use the piece as a laminate with other welded-rod billets, in which case the direction should be taken into consideration.

After the twisting, start the welding process. Work in sections while

LARGE AND SMALL DRILL ROD POSTION

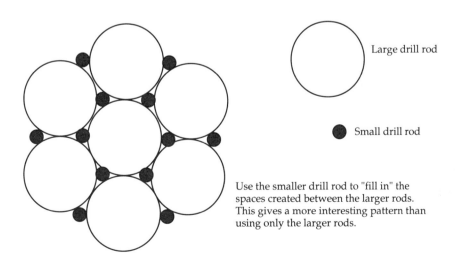

Large drill rod

Small drill rod

Use the smaller drill rod to "fill in" the spaces created between the larger rods. This gives a more interesting pattern than using only the larger rods.

rotating the bundle until the section welds. If you are experienced with steel cable, this should not be difficult. If this is your first attempt, practice this technique on cable until you are comfortable with it.

Overlap the weld areas to make certain that all of the rods are welded. Do two weldings to make certain of that fact. After completing the welding, retwist the bar to further enhance the pattern. Twist the bar in the same direction as the first twist or you will straighten the pattern.

The amount of twisting that the piece can take is dependent upon its size. A long, slender piece withstands more twisting than a shorter, thicker one. There is no hard-and-fast rule about how tightly to twist this material.

Add one more welding heat to seal up any shearing, cold shuts, or other unwelded sections that may have occurred during the twisting process. Next, flatten the round bar into a rectangular shape and form into a blade or laminate into another billet.

When finished and etched, wire Damascus exhibits the same basic watering as a cable blade. The pattern is produced by the decarburization of the welded surfaces of the joined rods. M-2 makes a fantastic blade when used in this fashion. And while the pattern strongly resembles welded cable, there is a difference that can be easily seen by the educated eye of a smith. Besides, it will outcut almost any all-cable knife made.

Gordian Knot

This is another complicated composite pattern based on twisted materials. It utilizes 4 or more twisted pieces, each with 100 to 200 layers.

As for materials, any combination that produces a somewhat vibrant watering is best (such as L-6 or A 203 D/E), although you can use almost anything. While you can use fewer laminations, I prefer a larger number.

Laminate and twist the bars, two clockwise and two counterclockwise. Forge the pieces square and clean, and true the surfaces either on a grinder or with a file. These surfaces must be as true and as straight as possible and corners must be sharp. If you have any gaps, these can become filled with slag, scale, or other impurities, causing problems later in the process.

Place the pieces together as illustrated above. You have to make certain that each piece has an opposite twisted piece next to it for this pattern to work. Wire or tack-weld the assembly together and then weld

This Gordian-knot-pattern fighter was made by Steve Godfrey. Photo by Jim Weyer

ROD POSITIONING

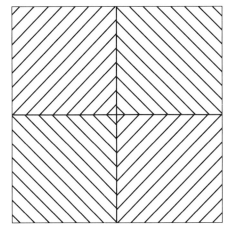

Position the rods as shown so that each rod has two opposite twisted bars next to it.

Clockwise twist bar

Counterclockwise twist bar

the pieces. During the welding, rotate the stack 90 degrees (one-quarter turn) with each blow of the hammer. You can weld all four rods into a single piece with little difficulty. Continue to weld until the entire piece is solid.

After welding the rods, forge the bar round and twist. The direction of the twist isn't as important as the evenness. The twist should be as even as possible and not too tight (two to three twists per inch should do it). Take another welding heat to seal any shears and then flatten the bar.

This particular pattern, a favorite of mine, shows some beautiful watering and gets a lot of attention at knife shows.

Hardening Damascus Steel

Heat-treating a pattern-welded blade is basically the same as for most high-carbon steels. Simply heat to the right temperature and then quench in the appropriate medium. This usually means using either oil or brine.

The oil-hardening steels generally are the easiest to deal with because they aren't shocked as much in the quench. Water-hardening steels can be a little touchy and are prone to cracking in the quench.

The best way to harden Damascus steel is to treat the blade like the high-carbon alloy that you used in the billet. Hence, if you used an oil-hardening steel, use an oil quench.

Most oil-hardening steels harden well in a light tempering oil formula. If they don't, you have a carbon-migration problem, and you may have to use a hot brine to get the blade to harden to a usable degree.

If you are using a water-hardening steel and it does not harden in brine, then I doubt it will ever harden. The carbon migration might be so severe that the steel cannot be hardened. If this is the case, you have a piece of decorative Damascus for a letter opener.

I do not temper most blades. I simply stress relieve at approximately 325 degrees F. If you want to temper, you do not need as heavy a temper as usual because of the softer laminations in the billet. If you have a carbon-migration problem, you may need to draw a temper for the blade to function properly. The migration may be so extensive that the low-carbon laminations have absorbed enough carbon to form carbides and harden on their own.

If you are using all-tool steel for your laminates, heat-treat as a homogeneous tool-steel blade and temper as required. I suggest the same basic temper as for a regular blade as well.

Finishing Damascus Steel

After the blade is forged, ground, polished, and ready for a hard assembly, you are ready to etch it to reveal the pattern.

There are numerous ways to etch steel, but the basics remain the same. The blades must be free of scratches, smoothly polished, and perfectly clean of all oils, greases, waxes, or other impurities. Degrease prior to etching and do not touch the surface to be etched with anything.

Etchants

These can be acidic or base, as long as they have a corrosive effect on metal. Some of the more aggressive etchants, such as nitric or hydrochloric acids, work quickly (in a matter of seconds), while others, such as ferric chloride, take up to 30 minutes to get a good etch.

You find that the slower etches usually give the best results on most materials. Usually the more subtle patterning, such as 1018/1095, benefits from a gentler etch. Any materials that contain nickel, chrome, or any other acid-resistant element respond well to the stronger acids, but the slower etchants also reveal the pattern quite well.

Acids tend to leave a rough appearance on the surface of the steel. The gentler ferric chloride lends a smoother quilted look to the blade. To use ferric chloride, simply purchase printed-circuit etchant at electronics supply stores. This 3-percent solution can be used as is, but it can be aggressive, so it should be cut by one-half to one-quarter with water before using.

This etch takes some time, and the blade should set for at least 20 minutes to get a solid bite on the steel. Check the blade periodically to see how the process is progressing. If the blade needs more etch, simply leave it in for a while longer. It is difficult to overetch a blade with ferric chloride, but it can be done. I once left a blade in for more than 3 hours— it had a hellacious topography, but you sure could see the pattern!

After completing the etchant, clean it off the blade and neutralize the blade to stop any further action. Clean off the neutralizer and then dry and heavily oil the blade to prevent corrosion. When first etched, flash rust and discoloration can appear in minutes if the blade isn't treated.

To make the pattern even more vibrant, I polish the blade's high spots with a soft muslin buff and green chrome oxide. I then clean off the buffing compound with a quality, paste metal polish to further enhance the blade's appearance.

Some of the more artistic bladesmiths use a selective etch on a pattern-welded blade, much like etching a design on a carbon steel. This reveals a pattern on the etched surfaces only, which can be rather attractive when properly done.

Putting the final finish on a Damascus blade is one of the finer aspects of bladesmithing. An improperly etched blade, even a top-quality one, does not show the quality of the pattern to its fullest. But a good etch on a mediocre pattern only improves its looks.

VIKING BROADSWORDS

The broadsword was the standard-issue weapon for most of Europe during the Dark Ages, roughly 500 to 1000 A.D. The Vikings, who roamed the seas from the eighth to the tenth centuries, produced some of the finest metal swords history has ever seen. Their patterns, workmanship, embellishments, and other refinements remained unequaled for centuries.

There are a lot of different theories about why Viking swords sported pattern-welded blades. One of the more credible theories is that the limited supply of steel made it necessary to add lower-grade iron to stretch the steel supply. This allowed them to have more swords. I favor this explanation.

Another theory argues that pattern-welding was the only way to make a sword at the time, given the poor grade (by today's standards) of available materials. There are some literary references that back up this line of thinking. Numerous passages in Viking sagas describe swords shattering or breaking or having their edges fall off in battle. You can interpret these incidents in a number of ways. One is that the materials were very poor. Another is that the smiths who made the swords weren't that good.

Then there are the other legends—of swords lasting for generations, cleaving other blades, cutting through enemy bodies like butter. These heroic tales are just as common as the tragic ones, so legends aren't very authoritative as to the exact quality of the common soldiers' weapons.

The other source of information about Viking broadswords, apart from contemporary sagas, is the swords that survived from that period. In recent years, I have done considerable research on this weapon, trying to duplicate the patterns and the blades themselves with marked success.

While I have figured out the basic construction methods, I have yet to decipher whether or not I am doing it the same way that bladesmiths did it in the old days. The only way to tell for certain is to section some old blades and analyze the sections. Regrettably, I have yet to find someone who would let me do this on an original blade, so I am forced to speculate, based on what materials, tools, and knowledge were known to exist then. In this, I have had considerable aid from Mr. Jan Ake Lundstrom from Dals Langed, Sweden, who has access to numerous examples of Viking blades. And, since he is also a smith, this fine fellow has a basic understanding as to how these blades might have been made.

Since I am more concerned with blade construction than with mounts, I concentrate on how the broadswords were made, with just enough information on mounts and other furniture to enable you to reproduce a more-or-less authentic piece.

Sutton Hoo Discovery

The Sutton Hoo archeological find in Suffolk, England, yielded a treasure trove of artifacts and information about culture during the Dark Ages. The site, believed to have been buried about 670 A.D. in honor of an Anglo-Saxon king, contained a great deal of arms and armor.

The sword contained in the burial belonged to an extremely wealthy man (after all, this was a royal burial site), not a common soldier. The pattern-welded blade is a work of incredible beauty, and I believe it deserves a special mention apart from the more common blades used during that period.

The Sutton Hoo sword comprised at least 9 separate pieces, twisted, welded, and worked together. The craftsman who forged this blade spent endless hours in its construction, and the effort shows even though the blade is now primarily rust and scale. It is a masterpiece by any definition of the word, and I pay my respects to its creator, from one bladesmith to another, though we lived more than 1,300 years apart.

Common Blade Construction

The more common blades exhibited several different construction techniques, mostly based on the twisted patterns, but flat lamination was also known and used.

The type of material used for the twists varied, as did the degree of twist. The twisted material was used principally for the center core, with steel or carburized iron wrapped around the core to form the cutting edges. This is not exactly cutting-edge technology for swords, but back then, who knows? The twisted material generally was rectangular (flat bar) or square bar stock. I have seen no evidence that round stock was used, and I rather doubt it because it takes too long to form by hand.

This metal was stacked and welded together to form a rod or bar. The number of laminated layers ranged from 7 to 64 or more, depending on the sword. The resulting bar was then forged and welded further, or it was welded onto another similar bar and used for the center of the blade.

The more elaborate swords had 3 or more core pieces, each twisted about the center axis, similar to the Turkish twist or Persian ribbon Damascus. The sections of the finer swords were twisted, and the untwisted sections were left unworked. These bars were welded to other similar bars so that the twisted and untwisted sections corresponded as shown below.

This whole assembly was welded to the edge steel. I do not know if this was done when the center core was welded or afterward. It could have been done either way, but my experience tells me that the edging was welded after the cores.

Regardless of the welding sequence, the resulting blade displayed a more-or-less twisted star pattern down the center core. This particular pattern was very common.

Composite Blade Construction

The more complex designs, which I refer to as composite patterns, were made from two or more patterned steel bars. These bars were first welded to a softer iron core and then to an edge steel. These required a lot of skill and labor, resulting in a devastatingly beautiful pattern.

The mirror-image pattern so often encountered in the higher-quality blades was accomplished by twisting a laminated bar and then cutting the bar lengthwise. These pieces were then welded together, and the resulting composite used to make the sword. The more common

This close-up of a broadsword shows simple Viking construction techniques. The author used 1095 and wrought iron with a superfine, pattern-welded edge steel. Photo by Stephen Jacobson

construction method is illustrated below.

In addition to the twisted sections described above, it is not unusual to come across a blade from this era with a snake running down its center. This wavy line was formed in the pattern and welded between the twist patterns.

I don't know the exact construction techniques used by the makers of these original blades, but I can tell you two ways they could have been made. The first entails placing a laminated section on edge and giving it an accordion fold, as shown on the next page. Then grind or cut off the tops of the fold until the bar is straight. This method, though effective, is wasteful. The size of the bar to start must be very thick, and the amount of material removed is considerable. It is unlikely, with the scarcity of materials at the time, that contemporary bladesmiths used this method.

The second technique is much like a ladder-pattern bar placed on edge so the edge laminations are visible on the blade surface. This seems to me to the most likely method of making this section of the pattern. It takes considerably less material and time.

Regardless of the specific technique used, the finished section was

COMPLEX CORE CONSTRUCTION

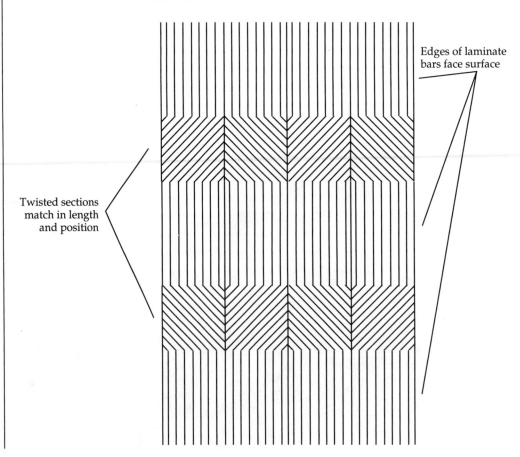

Edges of laminate bars face surface

Twisted sections match in length and position

then welded between the twisted sections, and the whole assembly was welded to the edging.

Making a period composite blade is a complex and somewhat difficult task. Just preparing the sections to be welded requires extensive labor. Then there is the assembly welding, the forging, and all the other work to consider. So you can see why the finer swords were reserved for the rich and powerful, while the simpler blades were used by less affluent minor nobles.

What did the ordinary warrior/soldier carry? The most likely choice was probably either an axe or spear. The soldiers who did carry swords usually had simple patterned pieces or ones forged from carburized iron. My research shows that the life of the common foot soldier was far from comfortable. They were fortunate to have a helm and shield, much less a well-made sword.

The complex swords found at Sutton Hoo were some of the finest blades made during the Dark Ages. And while the Franks and, to some extent, the Poles were making pattern-welded blades, the Vikings were the masters. A ruler in Germany even issued a royal edict prohibiting the importation of Danish blades because German smiths resented not being able to compete with their quality (trade embargoes aren't anything new).

Now that you are aware of the basics of Viking swords, we can learn how to re-create some of the blades of old.

REPRODUCING CLASSIC SWORDS

Traditionally, these swords were made from a mild-steel/iron laminate with a lot of impurities in it. The Bessemer process wasn't even thought of 1,500 years ago, so the smith had to smelt his own iron from ore.

The ores used are interesting in themselves. Most of them were bog iron,

COMPOSITE SWORD CONSTRUCTION

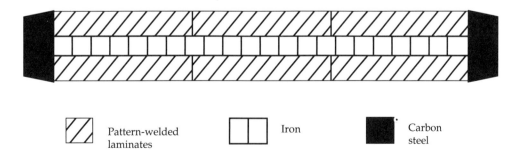

Pattern-welded laminates   Iron   Carbon steel

The pattern-welded laminate is first welded
to the iron core and then welded to the steel edging.
This makes a beautiful, highly durable blade
when properly accomplished.

ACCORDIAN FOLD/LADDER PROCESS

Ladder-pattern bar placed on edge gives
a slight wave pattern on the blade cores.

Accordian-fold edge view. Fold billet
into a series of tight curves.

Cut off top of folds on both sides.

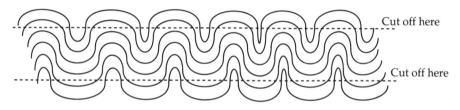

Cut off here

Cut off here

Resulting bar exhibits pattern shown.

but some were smelted from iron deposits or river sand. But no matter what the source, the smith still had to make the iron. Today, we can readily obtain high-quality steels in various alloys. But what alloys should we use?

Almost any alloy will work, but since we are trying to re-create a period piece, then we should try to get at least close to the original materials. I am not saying that you should smelt your own iron. If you want to, feel free; if not, then use a simpler high-carbon alloy, laminated with either wrought iron or mild steel. The pattern is not very vibrant, but it is more or less close to what they were using.

Of course, if you would like a more brilliant pattern, you can use 203 D/E and 1095 for the laminations. While not traditional, these do show better watering. With the laminate material chosen, design is next.

Design

I suggest that you start with the simpler double-cored twist since these are more common than just about any other style. Laminate enough material to make both cores. This can be done in one or two pieces. I prefer the one-piece method because it gives a better pattern, and both core pieces should be more or less identical since they are cut from a single rod. To make a one-piece blade, you need to end up with 14 to 16 cubic inches of laminated material. While this sounds like a lot, it really isn't. It is only a piece 1-inch square and 14 to 16 inches long.

The number of layers on the originals ranged from 7 to 64 (usually), but you can use more. But remember, the higher the layer count, the finer the pattern. The originals didn't have refined patterns. Draw the piece out to a 3/8- to 1/2-inch square. After this is completed, forge the piece round and twist. You should have enough to form two rods 32 inches long, which form the core twists.

If you are forging both rods in one piece, you may want to cut the piece at this time since it is easier to work a shorter length. As for the amount of twist, the tighter the better because the blade will still be drawn out a bit after the pieces are welded together. A tighter twist doesn't straighten out as badly as a looser one will.

You have a choice as to how you wish to twist the pieces. You can twist the entire length or sections, either clockwise or counterclockwise. You can twist one bar in each direction or both in the same direction. As long as the pieces correspond, it really doesn't matter how you constructed them, only how they look.

Weld Preparation

After twisting, forge the rods square and prepare to weld the two together. It is very important that the welding is solid. If not, the whole blade is compromised. An improper weld may separate later during forging, ruining the blade.

Some of the old swords I examined appear not to have been forged square prior to welding. While this may be true for some blades, I can't believe it was done on all blades. It is considerably easier to weld an even surface than an uneven, twisted one. You can try both methods and see for yourself. I suggest that you work on a forged square piece until you get a little experience with this type of construction, and then try your hand at welding unsquared twisted pieces.

Also, there is a slight difference in patterns between squared and unsquared core pieces. The squared pieces have a straight and very defined delineation of the pattern between the welded pieces, while the unsquared, twisted, welded core has a more-or-less flowing border between the two. Either is appropriate for this period.

Start welding at one end and work back toward the other. Overlap the areas to be welded, making certain that the entire length is sound. This takes at least an hour, if not more. After completing the welding, you are ready to forge the core into the general shape of the blade.

The amount of forging needed depends on the design of the sword. Most of the classic blades had a spatulate tip (more rounded than pointed), and this shape must be formed in the core. Be careful that there is no weld shearing during this step. If the pieces do come apart, weld again immediately before forging any further. With the center cores welded and formed, prepare to weld the edges on.

For the edge material itself, I suggest a medium-carbon steel, such as 1060, that is tough and durable enough to withstand the rigors of use. I use either a small rectangular- or square-section rod to make the edges.

Of course, you can always use a pattern-welded bar, but this wouldn't be as appropriate as plain steel. But a ladder-patterned design would create an awesome effect when combined with the twisted center cores.

As for the edge welding, there are two ways to do this, in one piece wrapped around the blade or in two pieces welded together at the tip. The one-piece style is more common and easier to handle. All the weld surface of the core must be as smooth and clean as possible so the welds are solid. This weld is difficult, requiring skill, patience, and time.

To set up and position the edging, forge the edge to shape and form it around the core as shown on the facing page. Next, clean up the inside of the edge material (where it makes contact with the core) and assemble the whole for final welding.

Holding the pieces together and in position is no small task. The edging tends to shift and move as the welding progresses, and you must prevent this from happening. So the entire assembly should be either wrapped with a generous amount of heavy wire or banded with mild steel that is hot-forged onto the blade. Remove these bands as you move from the tip on back. The *actual* welding is next.

Welding

With the weld surfaces ground clean, the edging formed, and the whole blade securely assembled, you are ready to weld.

It is best to start at the tip of the blade for two reasons. It is easier to weld this way, and if the material stretches, the ends lengthen toward the back of the blade where it is no problem to trim off the excess. If you weld from the ricasso forward and the material lengthens, the tip of the edging pulls away from the tip of the core, creating a very difficult situation to correct properly.

Weld with a slow, deep heat. You do not want to burn the edge before the core comes up. Doing the tip presents a real challenge because the weld surfaces are rounded, making the angle of attack a little precarious.

Work quickly and carefully to make certain that the weld takes and that the edge doesn't shift off the core.

I place the blade tip up on the floor and work that way until the tip is welded. Strike the first blow straight down on the end of the tip. This is the most important weld section. If this weld doesn't take, reweld until it does. The tip must be securely welded in position before any further welding can proceed. Weld the entire tip section while the blade is vertical. If the blade bends a bit, straighten it and then continue until the tip is completely welded. After the tip, continue down the blade, overlapping the weld areas to make sure that the welds are perfect and no cold shuts are present.

You must keep three things in mind as you are working:

1. Make certain that the entire bar is at a deep welding heat (well soaked) and that the edge isn't burned.

2. Don't let the edge shift off the core.

3. The cores must stay straight.

FORMING THE EDGE

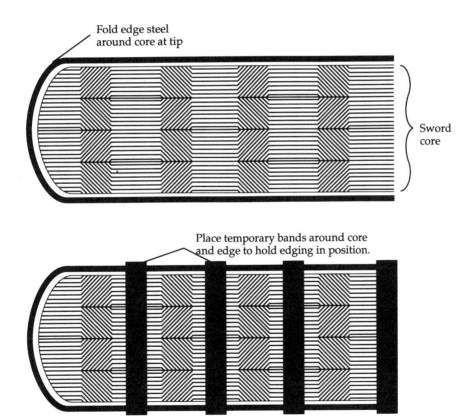

When edging is formed to shape and fitted to the core, hold edge and core in position by using 1/8" thick by 1/2" wide mild steel bands forged hot onto the assembly.

Weld tip first and then work back towards tang, removing the bandings as the work progresses.

263

Making this blade takes a lot of time and work, but honestly, it is worth it. When you make your first successful blade in this style, you'll appreciate what the smiths of old had to go through to make one.

Go back over the blade with another welding course just to be certain that the welding is solid. The next step is general forging.

Forging the Tang

Draw out the tang as you would any other blade. The length of the tang depends on the length of the grip, the thickness of the guard, and the type of the pommel being used. But it should be long enough to extend all the way through the guard, grip, and pommel. The tangs of these swords were somewhat massive. Their weight and length should be taken into consideration as they are being forged.

Grip lengths should be long enough to afford a comfortable grip. About 5 inches should be long enough for most people. Added to this 5 inches is the pommel thickness, which should not exceed 1 1/2 inches, along with a generous 3/4 inch for the guard. This makes for a tang length of 7 to 8 inches overall.

Forging the Blade

The most common blade had a single, wide fuller (about one-third of the blade's width) running from under the guard to within an inch of the tip on either side of the blade. The blade should be fullered after drawing out the tang and before forging in the edge bevels. The fuller can be forged with the appropriate top-and-bottom tool or a single fuller die. The top-and-bottom tool does a much better job.

Once the fuller is forged, forge the edge bevels. As you are working, pay close attention to the condition of the blade. Watch for shearing or delamination. If either occurs, correct it at once. Work the edge bevels slowly, keeping the blade straight. After forging the blade, straighten and stress-relieve before profiling to the final shape.

If you are going to grind before heat treating, be careful not to overgrind the blade. These swords are prone to warping—so prone, in fact, that I consider profiling to finished shape before heat treating as the only option.

Heat Treating and Tempering

The heat treating and tempering of these swords are similar to that of any other sword. This means that you must watch for warping and twisting. Straighten after the first (hardening) quench while the blade is still hot because straightening with a torch causes a difference in the etching. Make certain that you are wearing heat-resistant gloves while you do this. After any straightening, temper as soon as possible.

I suggest that you triple-temper these swords to ensure that there are no hard spots. Temper a bit on the soft side because the blades seem to turn out better when tempered softer than normal.

Grinding

Grinding is simple. Most of the surviving blades that I have examined were either hollow or flat ground. Grind and polish the fuller before grinding in the edge bevels. Pay careful attention so the blade doesn't overheat.

After finishing the grinding, fit the grip core before doing the etching, so that if you have to burn on a grip, you do not mar the finished etch.

Etching

Etching can be a problem because of the blade's length and width. I suggest using diluted ferric chloride, as with any other pattern-welded blade, and a section of PVC pipe (capped on one end), long enough to submerge the blade and wide enough to allow at least a 1/4-inch gap between the edge and the side of the pipe. Insert the blade vertically i to the etchant for best results.

Clean the blade of any remaining oils, grease, or other substances that may cling to its surface and cause an uneven etch. Use either acetone or trisodium phosphate (TSP). If you use TSP, make certain that you wear eye protection and latex (rubber) gloves to protect your skin. This stuff can take the hide right off you in no time flat.

Once the blade is cleaned, etch until the pattern is at the proper depth. This can take from 10 to 45 minutes, depending upon the materials used, the strength of the etchant, and the temperature. A slow etch is better than a quick one.

Assemble the blade and finish as desired.

Hilting

The pommels on the antique swords varied. They could be forged, ground, or cast. Most of them were massive, to help offset the weight of the blades.

The guards were more-or-less short and usually slightly curved, although straight ones were not uncommon.

Usually the mountings (guard and pommel) were forged iron, left undecorated. On the better-quality swords, fittings could be cast bronze or carved iron inlaid with gold, silver, latten, tin, or whatever the smith and/or owner wanted. Some extant examples have amber, garnet, and other semiprecious and precious stones set into the mounts, as well as solid gold or silver grips and hiltings.

(The possible combinations are far too numerous to catalog here. If you are interested in doing further research on hilt decorations, consult the bibliography in the back of this book for recommended reading material.)

The most common grips were smooth leather, but they could be plain wood, leather, horn, walrus ivory, or studded with amber or precious metals. It seems that just about any combination would be proper for this sword.

Sheaths

Sheaths were usually simple leather in a single-seam wrap, but the finer blades had lined, tooled, and/or carved sheaths, with metal fittings to protect the mouth and tip. The sheaths were often decorated in an interlaced pattern common to the period, and the more elaborate ones sported stones and other ornamentations.

Making a reproduction sword such as this is a great undertaking, but it is by no means impossible. And its execution demands your finest work.

Forging a Damascus blade is a testament to the skill and patience of a smith, and the ability is within the grasp of any serious bladesmith. Granted, some of the patterns are difficult to make, requiring a good deal of time and effort, but the beauty and the elegance of a well-made patterned blade are indescribable. Look deep into the pattern, and you will see what I mean.

Damascus Viking-style sword, made by the author, is set with lapis and mounted in sterling silver. Photo by Stephen Jacobson

VIKING SWORD HILTS

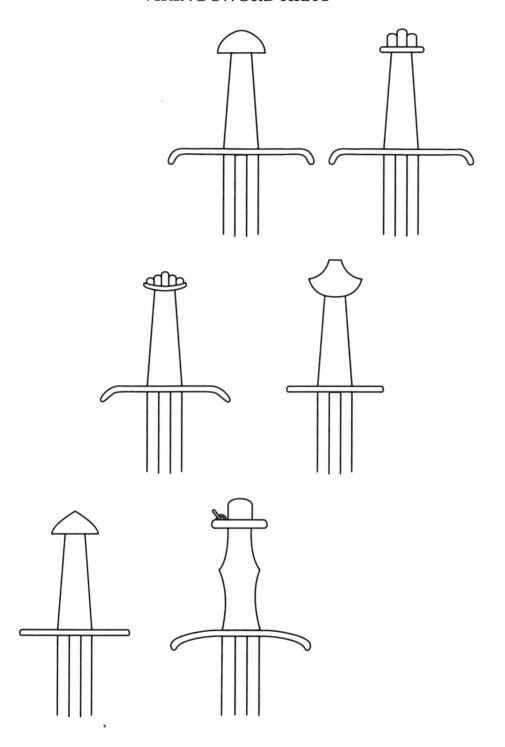

This Damascus steel Viking sword with silver mounts was also made by the author. Photo by Stephen Jacobson

COMPOUNDS AND FORMULAS

There are numerous works available from the last century that cover bladesmithing in general. A lot of the information in them is still useful, especially that about various hardening compounds. The names of most of the compounds are the more colorful local names, such as dragon's blood or horn silver. These names are probably a mystery to most people, so I have included a glossary to help re-create some of the older formulas.

Old Name	Chemical Composition
Acid of potassium sulfate	Potassium bisulfate
Acid of sugar	Oxalic acid
Alcali volatil	Ammonium hydroxide
Alcohol sulphurous	Carbon disulfide
Alumina	Aluminum hydroxide
Ammonia	Ammonium hydroxide
Antimony black	Antimony trisulfide
Antimony bloom	Antimony trioxide
Antimony glance	Antimony trisulfide
Antimony red	Antimony oxysulfide
Antimony vermilion	Antimony oxysulfide
Aqua fortis	Nitric acid
Aqua regia	Nitric and hydrochloric acids
Baking soda	Sodium bicarbonate
Bitter salts	Magnesium sulfate
Bichromate of potash	Potassium dichromate
Black oxide of manganese	Manganese dioxide
Blue copperas	Copper sulfate
Blue salts	Nickel sulfate
Blue stone	Copper sulfate
Blue vitriol	Copper sulfate

Old Name	Chemical Composition
Bone ashes	Impure calcium carbonate
Bone black	Animal charcoal
Borax	Sodium borate
Brimstone	Sulphur
Butter of antimony	Antimony trichloride
Butter of tin	Stannic chloride hydrated
Butter of zinc	Zinc chloride
Calomel	Mercurous chloride
Caustic soda	Sodium hydroxide
Chile nitre	Sodium nitrate
Chile saltpeter	Sodium nitrate
Chromic acid	Chromium trioxide
Copperas	Ferrous sulfate
Corrosive sublimate	Mercuric chloride
Corundum	Aluminum oxide
Cream of tartar	Potassium bitartrate
Dragon's blood	Cannet root
Ferro prussiate	Potassium ferricyanide
Flores martis	Anhydrous ferric chloride
Flowers of sulphur	Sulphur
Gallic acid	3, 4, 5 trihydroxybenzoic acid
Grain alcohol	Ethyl alcohol
Green vitriol	Ferrous sulfate
Hard oil	Boiled linseed oil
Horn silver	Silver nitrate
Iron perchloride	Ferric chloride
Iron pernitrate	Ferric nitrate
Iron protochloride	Ferrous chloride
Iron persulphate	Ferric sulfate
Iron sulfate	Ferrous sulfate
Ivory black	Burnt ground ivory
Jeweler's etchants	3 g. silver nitrate/3 g. nitric acid
	3 g. mercurous nitrate
	100 cc. distilled water
Killed spirits	Zinc chloride
Lime	Calcium oxide
Liver of sulphur	Potassium sulfide
Lunar caustic	Silver nitrate
Muriate of mercury	Mercuric chloride
Muratic acid	Hydrochloric acid
Nitre	Potassium nitrate
Nordhausen acid	Fuming sulfuric acid
Oil of mars	Deliquescent anhydrous Ferric chloride

Old Name	Chemical Composition
Oil of vitriol	Sulfuric acid
Orthophosphoric acid	Phosphoric acid
Oxymuriate of mercury	Mercuric chloride
Oxymuriate of potassium	Potassium chlorate
Peach ash	Potassium carbonate
Pearl ash	Potassium carbonate
Plumbago	Graphite
Potash	Potassium carbonate
Prussic acid	Hydrocyanic acid
Purple crystals	Potassium permanganate
Quicksilver	Mercury
Red prussiate of potash	Potassium ferrocyanide
Sal ammoniac	Ammonium chloride
Salt of hartshorn	Ammonium carbonate
Salt of lemon	5% sol. potassium acid oxalate
Salt of sorrel	5% sol. potassium acid oxalate
Salt of tartar	Potassium carbonate
Salt of vitriol	Zinc sulfate
Salt of wormwood	Potassium carbonate
Saltpeter	Potassium nitrate
Sal volatile	Ammonium carbonate
Slaked lime	Calcium hydroxide
Soda	Sodium carbonate
Spencer's acid	3g. silver nitrate
	3g. nitric acid
	3g. mercurous nitrate
	100 cc. distilled water
Spirits of hartshorn	Ammonia water
Spirits of salt	Hydrochloric acid
Spirits of nitrous	Ether or ethyl nitrate
Spirits of wine	Ethyl alcohol
Sugar of lead	Lead acetate
Sulfuric ether	Ethyl ether
Sweet spirits of nitre	Ethyl nitrate spirit
Tetrachloromethane	Carbon tetrachloride
Tincture ferric chloride	Ferric chloride/ethyl alcohol
Tincture of steel	Ferric chloride/ethyl alcohol
Tin salt	Stannous chloride
Verdigris	Copper acetate
Vitriol	Sulfuric acid
Water glass	Potassium silicate
Yellow prussiate of potash	Potassium ferrocyanide

As you can see, these old names can be quite confusing, especially since several names often refer to the same compounds in one formula.

TEMPERING OILS

Some people may be apprehensive about using oil as a quenching medium. These oils do burn some when the metal is quenched, but you can deal with the flash fire by covering the tank or simply blowing the fire out. Nevertheless, as with any fire, reasonable care and caution should be exercised at all times. One foolish, thoughtless act could be costly.

As a safety measure, keep a CO_2 or a powder-type fire extinguisher. Never attempt to put out an oil fire with water because it will spread. Also common sand or cat litter is a great aid in cleaning up spills because it absorbs the oil off the floor.

Petroleum-Based Tempering Oil Formulas

Petroleum-based oils are best to use. The ingredients are easy to get, inexpensive, and easy to formulate. They also can be made lighter or heavier to suit the quenching speed of the alloys you are heat-treating.

Light-Oil Formula #1
1 part diesel fuel
2 parts automatic transmission fluid
1 part motor oil

Light-Oil Formula #2
1 part automatic transmission fluid
1 part diesel fuel
2 parts motor oil

The light-oil formulas are rather fast in quenching speed and should be used for water-hardening steels.

Quenching a water-hardening steel in light oil instead of water prevents cracking, warping, and excessive stresses from building up in the steel, along with other problems. It does not affect the cutting abilities of the blades.

Heavy-Oil Formula #1
1 part diesel fuel
3 parts motor oil

Heavy-Oil Formula #2
6 parts diesel fuel
8 parts motor oil

2 parts automatic transmission fluid
1 part melted paraffin mixed with the motor oil

The above two heavy-oil formulas are recommended for most of the carbon-steel alloys that you are likely to use. Feel free to experiment with other mixtures and compositions to find out what works best for you. As you can see, the mixtures are simple, easy to mix, and use easy-to-obtain ingredients.

Etching Solutions

Etchants—as with all corrosive materials, liquid or solid—must be handled correctly to ensure that no accidents occur.

A word of caution: *you are mixing acids and water.* Remember to add the *acid* to the *water, not* the water to the acid. Wear a full face shield *and* safety glasses. And, in case of a spill, keep nearby a large open container of baking soda to neutralize the acids and plenty of water, and always wear an apron and rubber gloves.

Etching Solution #1
8 fl. oz. reagent-grade nitric acid
8 fl. oz. distilled water

Etching Solution #2
4 fl. oz. sulfuric acid
4 fl. oz. hydrochloric acid
8 fl. oz. distilled water

Etching Solution #3
4 oz. ferric chloride
16 fl. oz. distilled water

Etching Solution #4 (aqua regia)
8 fl. oz. reagent-grade nitric acid
8 fl. oz. hydrochloric acid
16 fl. oz. distilled water

Solution number 3 is probably best for most of your needs. All of these solutions should be stored in heavy glass containers, with a slightly loose stopper in a cool, well-ventilated place where they will not be knocked over.

Warming these solutions makes them work faster. Remember to use proper safety precautions and to do all your etching outside in a well-ventilated area.

The Master Bladesmith

Welding Fluxes

The basis of flux compounds is anhydrous borax, which is easy to make. Take a package of Borateem laundry soap, place it in a crucible, and melt it down. It bubbles up white and cooks into a dark, glasslike substance. Let it cool and grind it up into a reasonably fine powder. You can then either use it as is or add one or more of the following:

Clean white silica sand
Iron filings (low-carbon steel, not tool steel)
Sal ammoniac

I prefer to use borax with a touch of sal ammoniac. I believe the weld suffers if you add anything else into the flux. Experiment to see what works best for you.

THE ELEMENTS AND THEIR ABBREVIATIONS

Name	Symbol	Atomic Number
Actinium	Ac	89
Aluminum	Al	13
Americium	Am	95
Antimony	Sb	51
Argon	Ar	18
Arsenic	As	33
Astatine	At	85
Barium	Ba	56
Beryllium	Be	4
Bismuth	Bi	83
Boron	B	5
Bromine	Br	35
Cadmium	Cd	48
Calcium	Ca	20
Carbon*	C	6
Cerium	Ce	58
Cesium	Cs	55
Chlorine	Cl	17
Chromium*	Cr	24
Cobalt*	Co	27
Columbium	Cb	41
Copper	Cu	29
Curium	Cm	96
Dysprosium	Dy	66
Erbium	Er	68
Europium	Eu	63
Fluorine	F	9
Francium	Fr	87

Name	Symbol	Atomic Number
Gadolinium	Gd	64
Gallium	Ga	31
Germanium	Ge	32
Gold	Au	79
Hafnium	Hf	72
Helium	He	2
Holmiun	Ho	67
Hydrogen	H	1
Illinium	Il	6
Indium	In	49
Iodine	I	53
Iridium	Ir	77
Iron*	Fe	26
Krypton	Kr	36
Lanthanum	La	57
Lead*	Pb	82
Lithium	Li	3
Lutetium	Lu	71
Magnesium	Mg	12
Manganese*	Mn	25
Mercury	Hg	80
Molybdenum*	Mo	42
Neodymium	Nd	60
Neon	Ne	10
Neptunium	Np	93
Nickel*	Ni	28
Nitrogen	N	7
Osmium	Os	76
Oxygen	O	8
Palladium	Pd	46
Phosphorus	P	15
Platinum	Pt	78
Plutonium	Pu	94
Polonium	Po	84
Potassium	K	19
Praseodymium	Pr	59
Protoactinium	Pa	91
Radium	Ra	88
Radon	Rn	86
Rhenium	Re	75
Rhodium	Rh	45
Rubidium	Rb	37
Ruthenium	Ru	44
Samarium	Sm	62

Name	Symbol	Atomic Number
Scandium	Sc	21
Selenium	Se	34
Silicon*	Si	14
Silver	Ag	47
Sodium	Na	11
Strontium	Sr	38
Sulfur*	S	16
Tantalum	Ta	73
Technetium	Tc	43
Tellurium	Te	52
Terbium	Tb	65
Thallium	Tl	81
Thorium	Th	90
Thulium	Tm	69
Tin	Sn	50
Titanium	Ti	22
Tungsten*	W	74
Uranium	U	92
Vanadium*	V	23
Xenon	Xe	54
Ytterbium	Yb	70
Yttrium	Y	39
Zinc	Zn	30
Zirconium	Zr	40

* Denotes elements that are commonly alloyed in tool steels.

WEIGHTS
AND MEASURES

I have used these tables for so many years I have most of them memorized! I am certain that you will use them often.

DECIMAL SIZES OF NUMBERED TWIST DRILLS

No.	Size	No.	Size	No.	Size	No.	Size
1	0.228	21	0.159	41	0.096	61	0.039
2	0.221	22	0.157	42	0.093	62	0.038
3	0.213	23	0.154	43	0.089	63	0.037
4	0.209	24	0.152	44	0.086	64	0.036
5	0.205	25	0.149	45	0.082	65	0.035
6	0.204	26	0.147	46	0.081	66	0.033
7	0.201	27	0.144	47	0.078	67	0.032
8	0.199	28	0.140	48	0.076	68	0.031
9	0.196	29	0.136	49	0.073	69	0.029
10	0.193	30	0.128	50	0.070	70	0.028
11	0.191	31	0.120	51	0.067	71	0.026
12	0.189	32	0.116	52	0.063	72	0.025
13	0.185	33	0.113	53	0.059	73	0.024
14	0.182	34	0.111	54	0.055	74	0.022
15	0.180	35	0.110	55	0.052	75	0.021
16	0.177	36	0.106	56	0.046	76	0.020
17	0.173	37	0.104	57	0.043	77	0.018
18	0.169	38	0.101	58	0.042	78	0.016
19	0.166	39	0.099	59	0.041	79	0.014
20	0.161	40	0.098	60	0.040	80	0.013

DECIMAL SIZES OF LETTERED DRILLS

Letter	Size	Letter	Size
A	0.234	N	0.302
B	0.238	O	0.316
C	0.242	P	0.323
D	0.246	Q	0.332
E	0.250	R	0.339
F	0.257	S	0.348
G	0.261	T	0.358
H	0.266	U	0.368
I	0.272	V	0.377
J	0.277	W	0.386
K	0.281	X	0.397
L	0.290	Y	0.404
M	0.295	Z	0.413

TAP AND DIE THREAD SIZES

National Fine (NF) S.A.E. Thread Sizes

O.D. Tap	Threads	Size Drill
1/4	28	No. 3
5/16	24	I
3/8	24	Q
7/16	20	25/64
1/2	20	29/64

National Course (N.C.) U.S.S. Thread Sizes

O.D. Tap	Threads	Size Drill
1/4	20	No. 7
5/16	18	F
3/8	16	5/16
7/16	14	U
1/2	13	27/64

FRACTIONS/DECIMALS/MILLIMETERS

Fraction	Decimal	Millimeter
1/64	.0156	0.396
1/32	.0312	0.793
3/64	.0468	1.190
1/16	.0625	1.587
5/64	.0781	1.984
3/32	.0937	2.381

Fraction	Decimal	Millimeter
7/64	.1093	2.778
1/8	.1250	3.175
9/64	.1406	3.571
5/32	.1562	3.968
3/16	.1875	4.762
13/64	.2031	5.159
7/32	.2187	5.556
15/64	.2343	5.953
1/4	.2500	6.350
17/64	.2656	6.746
9/32	.2812	7.143
19/64	.2958	7.540
5/16	.3125	7.937
21/64	.3281	8.334
11/32	.3437	8.731
23/64	.3593	9.128
3/8	.3750	9.525
25/64	.3906	9.921
13/32	.4062	10.318
27/64	.4218	10.715
7/16	.4375	11.112
29/64	.4531	11.509
15/32	.4687	11.906
31/64	.4843	12.303
1/2	.5000	12.700

COMPARISON OF STANDARD METAL GAUGES
(The below thicknesses are in 1/1000 of an inch.)

Gauge No.	Brown & Sharpe (American Wire)	British Imperial Standard	Millimeter
1	0.289	0.300	7.346 mm
2	0.257	0.276	6.543 mm
3	0.229	0.252	5.829 mm
4	0.204	0.232	5.189 mm
5	0.181	0.212	4.618 mm
6	0.162	0.192	4.111 mm
7	0.144	0.176	3.670 mm
8	0.128	0.160	3.264 mm
9	0.114	0.145	2.906 mm
10	0.101	0.128	2.588 mm

COMPARISON OF STANDARD METAL GAUGES (CONT'D.)

Gauge No.	Brown & Sharpe (American Wire)	British Imperial Standard	Millimeter
11	0.090	0.116	2.304 mm
12	0.080	0.104	2.052 mm
13	0.071	0.092	1.829 mm
14	0.064	0.080	1.629 mm
15	0.057	0.072	1.450 mm
16	0.050	0.064	1.290 mm
17	0.045	0.056	1.151 mm
18	0.040	0.048	1.024 mm
19	0.035	0.040	0.912 mm
20	0.031	0.036	0.813 mm
21	0.028	0.032	0.724 mm
22	0.025	0.028	0.643 mm
23	0.022	0.024	0.574 mm
24	0.020	0.022	0.511 mm
25	0.017	0.020	0.445 mm
26	0.015	0.018	
27	0.014	0.016	
28	0.012	0.014	
29	0.011	0.013	
30	0.010	0.012	

TROY WEIGHT
(Used to measure precious metals.)

24 grains = 1 pennyweight
20 pennyweight (480 grains) = 1 ounce
12 ounces (5,760 grains) = 1 pound

AVOIRDUPOIS WEIGHT
(Common weight measurement for the
United States and a few other countries.)

27.343 grains = 1 dram
16 drams (417 grains) = 1 ounce
16 ounces (6,679 grains) = 1 pound
2,000 pounds = 1 short ton
2,240 pounds = 1 long ton

APOTHECARY'S WEIGHT

20 grains = 1 scruple
3 scruples = 1 dram
8 drams = 1 ounce
12 ounces = 1 pound

WEIGHTS OF CARBON-STEEL BARS

The below weights are in pounds per foot of length. This should be taken as an estimate of a carbon steel (nonstainless) bar.

Size	Rounds	Squares	Hex.	Oct.
1/4"	0.167	0.213	0.184	0.176
5/16"	0.261	0.332	0.288	0.275
3/8"	0.376	0.478	0.414	0.396
7/16"	0.511	0.651	0.564	0.539
1/2"	0.668	0.850	0.737	0.704
9/16"	0.845	1.076	0.932	0.891
5/8"	1.040	1.328	1.150	1.100
11/16"	1.260	1.607	1.393	1.331
3/4"	1.500	1.913	1.658	1.581
13/16"	1.760	2.245	1.944	1.859
7/8"	2.040	2.603	2.256	2.157
15/16"	2.350	2.988	2.588	2.476
1"	2.670	3.400	2.944	2.817
1 1/16"	3.010	3.838	3.324	3.180
1 1/8"	3.380	4.303	3.727	3.565
1 3/16"	3.770	4.795	4.152	3.972
1 1/4"	4.170	5.314	4.601	4.401
1 5/16"	4.600	5.857	5.072	4.852
1 3/8"	5.050	6.428	5.567	5.352
1 7/16"	5.517	7.026	6.085	5.820
1 1/2"	6.010	7.650	6.625	6.338
1 9/16"	6.519	8.301	7.189	6.887
1 5/8"	7.050	8.978	7.775	7.438
1 11/16"	7.604	9.682	8.385	8.021
1 3/4"	8.180	10.414	9.018	8.626
1 13/16"	8.773	1.170	9.673	9.253
1 7/8"	9.390	12.000	10.355	9.902

WEIGHTS OF CARBON STEEL BARS

Size	Rounds	Squares	Hex.	Oct.
1 15/16″	10.024	12.763	11.053	10.574
2″	10.700	13.600	11.780	11.267
2 1/16″	11.360	14.463	12.528	11.982

WEIGHTS OF FLAT CARBON BAR STOCK (RETANGLES)
(The below weights are in pounds per foot of length.)

Thickness	Width	Weight per Foot
1/8″	1/2″	0.213
1/8″	3/4″	0.319
1/8″	1″	0.425
1/8″	1 1/4″	0.531
1/8″	1 1/2″	0.638
1/8″	1 3/4″	0.774
1/8″	2″	0.850
1/8″	2 1/4″	0.956
1/8″	2 1/2″	1.063
1/8″	2 3/4″	1.169
3/16″	1/2″	0.319
3/16″	3/4″	0.478
3/16″	1″	0.425
3/16″	1 1/4″	0.531
3/16″	1 1/2″	0.956
3/16″	1 3/4″	1.116
3/16″	2″	1.275
3/16″	2 1/4″	1.434
3/16″	2 1/2″	1.594
3/16″	2 3/4″	1.753
1/4″	1/2″	0.425
1/4″	3/4″	0.638
1/4″	1″	0.850
1/4″	1 1/4″	1.063
1/4″	1 1/2″	1.275
1/4″	1 3/4″	1.488
1/4″	2″	1.700
1/4″	2 1/4″	1.913
1/4″	2 1/2″	2.125

Thickness	Width	Weight per Foot
1/4"	2 3/4"	2.338
5/16"	1/2"	0.531
5/16"	3/4"	0.797
5/16"	1"	1.063
5/16"	1 1/4"	1.328
5/16"	1 1/2"	1.275
5/16"	1 3/4"	1.859
5/16"	2"	2.125
5/16"	2 1/4"	2.391
5/16"	2 1/2"	2.656
5/16"	2 3/4"	2.922
3/8"	1/2"	0.638
3/8"	3/4"	0.956
3/8"	1"	1.275
3/8"	1 1/4"	1.594
3/8"	1 1/2"	1.913
3/8"	1 3/4"	2.231
3/8"	2"	2.550
3/8"	2 1/4"	2.869
3/8"	2 1/2"	3.188
3/8"	2 3/4"	3.506

NONMETRIC TO METRIC

1 inch = 2.54 centimeters (cm) (25.4 millimeters)
1 square inch = 6.451 square centimeters
1 cubic inch = 16.387 cubic centimeters
1 foot = 30.48 centimeters
1 square foot = 929.03 square centimeters
1 cubic foot = 28,317 cubic centimeters
1 yard (3 feet) = 91.44 centimeters (0.9144 meters)
1 square yard = 0.8361 square meter
1 cubic yard = 0.7646 cubic meter
1 mile (5,280 feet or 1,760 yards) = 1,609.3 meters

METRIC TO NONMETRIC

1 millimeter (mm) = 0.039 inch
1 centimeter (cm) (10 mm) = 0.393 inch
1 square centimeter = 0.1549 square inch
1 cubic centimeter (cc) = 0.061 cubic inch

1 meter (m) = 39.37 inches, 3.280 feet or 1.093 yards
1 square meter = 10.763 square feet, 1.196 square yards
1 cubic meter = 35.314 cubic feet, 1.307 square yards
1 kilometer (km) (1,000 m) = 1,093.61 yards, 0.621 mile

AVOIRDUPOIS TO METRIC

1 ounce (oz.) = 28.349 grams (gm)
1 pound (lb.) (16 oz.) = 453.6 gm
1 ton (2,000 lbs.) = 907.19 kilograms (kg)
1 pound per inch = 178.6 grams per centimeter
1 pound per foot = 1.488 kilograms per meter

METRIC TO AVOIRDUPOIS

1 gram = 0.0022 pound
1 kilogram = 2.204 pounds
1 gram per centimeter= 0.0056 pound per inch
1 kilogram per meter = 0.671 pound per foot
1 metric ton (1,000 kilograms) = 2,204 pounds or 1.102 average ton

BIBLIOGRAPHY

Andrews, Jack. *Edge of the Anvil*. Emmaus, PA: Rodale Press, 1977.

Ashdown, Charles Henry. *European Arms and Armour*. New York: Brussel and Brussel, 1967.

Boye, David. *Step-by-Step Knifemaking*. Emmaus, PA: Rodale Press, 1977.

Hrisoulas, Jim. *The Complete Bladesmith*. Boulder, CO: Paladin Press, 1987.

Kallenberg, Lawrence. *Modeling in Wax for Jewelry and Sculpture*. Radnor, PA: Chilton Book Co., 1981.

Lungwitz, A. and Adams, Charles. *The Complete Guide to Blacksmithing*. New York: Bonanza Books, 1981.

Mayes, Jim. *How to Make Your Own Knives*. New York: Everest House Publishers, 1978.

Meilach, Dona Z. *Decorative and Sculptural Ironwork*. New York: Crown Publishers, 1977.

Neumann, George C. *Swords and Blades of the American Revolution*. Harrisburg, PA: Stackpole Books, 1973.

Oakeshott, R. Ewart. *The Archaeology of Weapons*. London: F. A. Praeger, 1960.
———*European Weapons and Armour*. North Hollywood, CA: Beinfeld Publishing, 1980.

————*The Sword in the Age of Chivalry*. London: Arms and Armour Press, 1981.

Pack, Greta, *Jewelry Making by the Lost Wax Process*. New York: Van Nostrand Reinholdt, 1975.

Rawson, P. S. *The Indian Sword*. New York: Arco Publishing, 1968.

Smith, Cyril S. *A History of Metallography*. Chicago: University of Chicago, 1960.

Stone, George Cameron. *A Glossary of the Construction, Decoration, and Use of Arms and Armor in All Countries and in All Times*. New York: Jack Brussel, 1961.

United States Steel, *The Making, Shaping, and Treating of Steel*. Pittsburgh, PA: United States Steel, 1957.

Untracht, Oppi. *Metal Techniques for Craftsmen*. Garden City, New York: Doubleday and Company, 1975.

Wallace, John. *Scottish Swords and Dirks*. Harrisburg, PA: Stackpole Books, 1970.

Weygers, Alexander G. *The Modern Blacksmith*. New York: Van Nostrand Reinholdt, 1974.